DOING BUSINESS
WITH
THE
JAPANESE

SUNY SERIES IN SPEECH COMMUNICATION
DUDLEY D. CAHN, EDITOR

DOING
BUSINESS
WITH THE
JAPANESE

A Guide to Successful Communication,
Management, and Diplomacy

ALAN GOLDMAN

STATE UNIVERSITY OF NEW YORK PRESS

Published by
State University of New York Press, Albany

© 1994 State University of New York

For information, address State University of New York
Press, State University Plaza, Albany, N.Y., 12246

Production by Diane Ganeles
Marketing by Nancy Farrell

Library of Congress Cataloging-in-Publication Data

Goldman, Alan.
    Doing business with the Japanese : a guide to successful
communication, management, and diplomacy / Alan Goldman.
        p.   cm. — (SUNY series in speech communication)
    Includes bibliographical references and index.
    ISBN 0-7914-1945-2 (acid-free paper). — ISBN 0-7914-1946-0 (pbk.
: acid-free paper)
    1. Management—Social aspects—Japan.   2. Corporate culture-
-Japan.   3. Management—United States.   4. Intercultural
communication—United States.   5. Cross-cultural orientation—United
States.   I. Series.
HD70.J3G65   1994
658.8'48'0973—dc20   93-26777
                                                                CIP

10 9 8 7 6 5 4 3 2

Contents

PART IV: UNVEILING JAPANESE CULTURE AND COMMUNICATION

Menu of Fast Messages and Predeparture Training Exercises

TITLE	TYPE OF MESSAGE
"First Meetings Between Japanese and U.S. Associates"	Bicultural
"Business Negotiations"	Bicultural
"Verbosity vs. Verbal Economy"	Bicultural
"Japanese Give Vague Answers"	Media Briefing
"The American Salesman and Japanese Customer"	Cultural Dialogue
"Japanese Advertising and Marketing Make Strategic Use of English Language"	Media Briefing
"Silence vs. Talk in Japanese-U.S. Organizations"	Bicultural
"Women and Corporate Communication"	Bicultural
"The Insiders' Paradise"	Media Briefing
"Corporate Communication: Quiet vs. Obvious Status"	Bicultural
"Japanese Dissect American Language and Culture, Americans Fail to Reciprocate"	Media Briefing
"Overworked Japanese Salarymen Briefed on Play and Domesticity"	Media Briefing
"Media Misinformation on U.S.-Japanese Relations"	Media Briefing

Preface: Fast Messages, Slow Messages: Breaking Through the Veil of U.S. Japanese Misperceptions

BICULTURAL

"FIRST MEETINGS BETWEEN JAPANESE AND U.S. ASSOCIATES"

The importance of first meetings cannot be overstated—especially in intercultural business encounters. Only the most seasoned and experienced of Japanese and U.S. business associates manage to avoid a myriad of clashes as "cultural strangers," fumbling to understand each other's expectations.

The U.S.-Japanese relationship can only be understood within the political and media context of this remarkable global village. Through the media we instantly shuffle from the streets of New York to Tokyo, Covington to Kyoto, Los Angeles to Nagoya. Fast messages of Japanese culture fill up our television monitors, magazines, newspapers, and conversations. Movies like *Gung Ho,* and

Mr. Baseball place Japanese and Americans side-by-side in an automobile factory and on baseball fields. On both sides of the Pacific, millions of Americans and Japanese try to find the "real" culture and communicative style of everyday people, managers, coaches, line workers, athletes, fans, negotiators and investors. Can we coexist and create bridges across the great societies of the East and West?

I wonder whether U.S. business and political leaders, and corporations, considering or engaged in affiliations and joint ventures with Japanese, have a working knowledge of how Japanese communicate? Are we getting real portrayals of true-to-life Japanese consumers and CEOs, or are we dwelling in a world of images, myths, visual bytes, and sensationalism? After living in Japan and working for a variety of Japanese corporations as a cross-cultural communication trainer, I found that both Japanese and Americans are dwelling more in media myths than in realities. Despite a neverending onslaught of international journalism forever explaining the ways of the Japanese, very few U.S. expatriates have a clue when they first arrive at Narita airport. Without sufficient predeparture training, formidable diplomats turn into overnight buffoons. Why? Their intercultural repertoire for communicating, managing, speaking, interacting with non-Americans, is terribly lacking. And although there are some overlooked similarities between our cultures, the inability to cope with differences is overwhelming.

On the political scene, we hear the speeches of Miyazawa, Nakasone, Gephardt, Clinton, Bush, and the leaders of the corporate giants. Overall, an atmosphere and composite begins to form . . . we hear talk of friendship, of Japan and U.S. "bashing," flattery, ethnocentrism, and a thousand and one stereotypes. It is a whirling blitzkrieg of messages shot through the channels of the media, run through the philanthropic and clandestine agendas of untold spin doctors. Through it all, we the public, the workers, managers, professors, politicians, and expatriates, are struggling to form some semblance of an accurate impression of U.S.-Japanese relations. And for those of us more focused upon business dealings between our countries, there are a myriad of impressions, dilemmas, and questions surrounding: What are Japanese like? How do they negotiate? Can we coexist in a joint venture or subsidiary? What should I do to prepare our company for expatriations in Japan? And what about those Japanese *keiretsus?*

It is within this international framework of the media that the text of this book weaves its messages. Some of the information contained falls under the heading of "fast messages." Throughout the book you will find smaller capsules of information that you can quickly sift through: media briefings, cultural dialogues, case studies, biculturals, and intercultural encounters. Some of these capsules of information are hand-picked sound bytes from the media, such as the quotations presented via the media briefings. Other fast messages immerse you in typical slices of U.S.-Japanese communication and culture, unveiling aspects of business and social interaction.

In addition, the chapters supply the "slower messages" of U.S.-Japanese communication and culture. Although we live in an electronic world of "fast messages," it is necessary to grasp that people and cultures are "slow messages"; that is, there is no instantaneous way for decoding or deciphering the communication style of Japanese and Americans. It takes time, patience, and reflection to investigate the cultural roots and lineages that underlie and paint the tones and nuances of U.S. and Japanese styles of management, public speaking, nonverbal behavior, negotiating, leadership, and business and corporate practices.

In this book I attempt to look at the old and the new, the slow and the fast, the big picture and the minutia that make or break U.S.-Japanese business and managerial relationships. An accurate picture of Japanese is not easy to come by. For one, American management must be willing to slow down, recognize that even the most seemingly objectionable of Japanese negotiating, trade and corporate practices may have long, broad roots in the soil of Japanese culture. Frustration with Japanese table negotiators cannot be easily "remedied" or recast within the mold of the more adversarial, confrontative U.S. business communicator. But those extra minutes and hours of investigation can be extremely cost effective and humanitarian in helping to avoid unnecessary conflicts, international incidents, media bashings, failed joint ventures, and grossly inaccurate perceptions.

I have tried to prepare this book in a way that will invite you into the complexity of the intercultural challenge of U.S.-Japanese communication. On the surface, the information should be easily understood; but below the surface, I trust that there is much to think about. There are no magical solutions, nor is there any way to bypass the need for intercultural adaptation, compromise, adjustment, and open-mindedness in dealing with the Japanese.

To the expatriates I am addressing, I trust that this book can accompany you and your family and lead in some peaceful, conflict-reducing directions. As you will discover in this book and through your contact with Japanese, we do have significantly contrasting cultural and communicative codes, and the conflict avoiding Japanese are difficult for adversarial, ideological Americans to read.

As a corporate trainer, I lived and breathed the everyday life of Japan and did not live a sheltered or Americanized existence. I try to bring my most personal discoveries to you through the cultural dialogues, case studies, and writings, and hope that it will be of service in deciphering your relationships with Japanese.

Finally, as a professor, author, and researcher within the field of intercultural and organizational communication, I fully believe that communication is the hub, matrix, center, and soul of human relationships, both business and social. I wish you the best in your dealings with Japanese.

"BUSINESS NEGOTIATIONS"

Respect for both U.S. and Japanese approaches to negotiation, leadership and the decision-making process is not always present when representatives meet face-to-face at negotiating tables.

Respect begins with a careful scrutinizing and understanding of seeming incompatible negotiating prototypes. Foremost to Japanese and U.S. negotiating teams is the necessity of "negotiating the negotiation process itself!"

Delegated more authority, U.S. negotiators have a wider range of options available to them at the table, while Japanese must return to their organizations to engage in intraorganizational consensus building.

Introduction: The Intercultural Challenge: U.S.-Japanese Communication

BICULTURAL

"VERBOSITY vs. VERBAL ECONOMY"

The talkative, eloquent communicator—so prized in the West—is held in suspicion by many Japanese business associates. Even extended exposure to the "talk, talk, talk" of the Western world cannot suddenly change the Japanese lineage or Japanese expectations—it is a history that exalts fewer words and more meaningful silences.

In this global village of the late twentieth century, Americans and Japanese work side-by-side, within unprecedented corporate laboratories. American factory line workers are suddenly faced with alien work area arrangements, U.S. top managers arrive in Tokyo to find that they do not have a private office, and negotiators reach dead ends after trying to muscle in on Japanese tentativeness. It is a world of corporate strangers where culture shock is a fact of life for newly arrived U.S. expatriates in Japan. And on U.S. soil, Japanese and American corporate partners similarly struggle with cultural differences affecting human resource management, motivation, productivity, and quality.

Ask Any Expatriate

Ask any recently arrived expatriate in Japan, or question a repatriate and family who returned prematurely from a Japanese assignment; it is a tough road adapting to Japanese social and business standards. Likewise, Japanese transferred to the U.S. frequently sing the blues when away from the Tokyo, Nagoya or Osaka corporate spotlight, and familiar business and social networks—as homesickness, helplessness, and cultural conflicts fill our joint ventures, on both sides of the Pacific.

International business and global competitiveness cannot be separated from the deep roots of the world's cultures. Up and coming young U.S. managers swiftly discover that their tool kit for motivating employees is not readily transferable to Japanese workers. Without briefings and insight into the physical, social and ego needs of a Japanese workforce, how can a U.S. transplant communicate for productivity or generate respect? Moreover, the urgency of cracking Japanese codes for initiating workplace conversations, conducting business meetings, complimenting or lavishing praise, participating in introductions, or conversing at an afterhours restaurant table, all appear overwhelming.

The Inevitable Cultural Shocks

It is a constant intercultural challenge to read the behaviors and expectations of Japanese hosts. Numerous questions surface surrounding everyday social and business survival: How do you conduct yourself at a negotiating table? What are the appropriate channels for communicating with Japanese affiliates? Do Japanese distrust the eloquent speaker? Why are Japanese so silent at times? How do top ranking Japanese officials tend to perceive high ranking U.S. women managers? Are there clues to communicating more effectively with Japanese in a variety of corporate and social venues?

In the midst of a bewildering, staggering array of missed cues, unintentional insults, and breaches of social and corporate etiquette,

American expatriates falter. They return home prematurely. Their wives and husbands cannot go the distance of a five to seven year Osaka assignment. Conflicts abound with Japanese hosts and the U.S. home office. It is difficult to communicate effectively the complex experiences of cultural shocks, or the mundane exercises of daily conversations. Even among English speaking Japanese hosts, there is a great abyss separating the *gaijin* (foreigners or outsiders) from the native. Without a working knowledge of the culture and how Japanese communicate, it is a mission impossible.

This Book Says, "Culture Should Not Be Overlooked"

This book attempts to supply answers to the questions typically asked by Americans engaged in joint ventures, corporate, political, educational and trade relationships with Japanese. The underlying impetus for writing this book is an outgrowth of my time spent living in Japan and working for a variety of Tokyo based corporations where I was responsible for developing intercultural communication training programs for Japanese-Western business. I was astounded by the lack of understanding of Japanese culture and communication styles by visiting U.S. and U.K. business partners. In response, *I challenge my international and globally concerned readers to answer the following, basic question: Why not be better prepared when doing business with Japanese?* Surely it is a troublesome route when entire U.S. corporations, as well as individual expatriates, do not seriously examine Japanese culture and behavior before crossing Japanese national or corporate borders. Culture should not be overlooked, as it permeates every strand of business and management. Successful U.S.-Japanese affiliations and joint ventures carefully monitor cultural differences, anticipate conflicts, expand their repertoire to include adaptations to their partner's communicative practices, and strive to understand historical, social and political origins of business practices.

Volatile Media Climate Misleads Expatriates

In addition, the media climate between the U.S. and Japan is currently volatile. Frequent bashings, sensationalistic reporting, blatant ethnocentrism and stereotyping in movie making and television programming, all tend to further mislead the inexperienced business sojourner and expatriate. As "cultural strangers," fresh U.S. and Japanese corporate partners can be susceptible to Japan and U.S. journalistic "bashings" that mirror fears of the trade deficit, pending protectionist legislation, and the ugly resurgence of waves of ultra-nationalism. Much as the "yellow peril" rhetoric resurfaces in new and disguised formats within the Western media, news of the "Western barbarians" fill the television monitors and bookstores of Japan. Widely read Japanese authors speak of the enemy as being a "U.S., Jewish lead conspiracy" that roughly brings to mind the sickening verbage of the pre and World War II era.

Cultural Ignorance and the Media

A cultural ignorance is only intensified, magnified by the irrational, emotional, and ratings-oriented misinformation of the media. As media plays a hand in "setting the agenda" for the corporate and political spheres and people on-the-street, it is no wonder that it is hard to separate the images from the realities. Prone to fill their precious, terribly expensive television and newspaper space with the most sensationalistic, cultural clashes and insults, we tend to hear more bad than good.

U.S.-Japanese Media Moments, 1980s–1990s

A brief glance at U.S.-Japanese "media moments" of the 1980s and 1990s shows this media inclination. First lady Nancy Reagan lashed out at the sacred Sumo wrestlers, unwittingly bashing their physical appearance, dress and ritual in the course of skeptically anticipating their White House visit. Yasuhiro Nakasone spoke of the poor state of the U.S. educational system, blaming its disintegration on the lower abilities of American minorities. And former President Bush arrived at Hirohito's funeral decked out in a festive red party tie. Several years later, you may recall how Bush lost his composure (and one-thousand points of light) in Tokyo, showering his (intercultural) motion sickness in front of the world's news cameras. And there is no forgetting the public destruction of U.S. made products in Japan and the mass cremations of Japanese automobiles and electronic products at Japan bashing rallies around the U.S.

During the late 1980s, Ishihara and Morita surfaced with a grossly atypical, U.S. bashing book entitled, *The Japan Who Can Say "No."* The book really stirred up the media, as well as Washington insiders. It is well known that Japanese are incredibly dedicated group players, as well as fierce competitors when dealing with outsiders. But typical Japanese style competition is not verbally direct, insulting, and confrontational; it is usually conducted in a more implicit, indirect, ambiguous fashion, away from the public eye of the camera. So when word of the explosive language and arguments of the Ishihara and Morita book hit Washington, D.C., the text was soon translated into English and hit the streets in the form of a "bootleg edition." The book, originally intended for Japanese only, ignited readers in the U.S. and soon led to an "official" Western edition, translated into English.

Closely following on the heels of the "the book," Bush, Iacocca, and the U.S. "automobile CEO convoy" arrived in Japan during January 1992. They were there to engage in some old time, good ol' boy thrashing of a Japan who just refused to open those selfish doors to American cars or autoparts. Verbal provocations, primetime arguments, and jurisprudence styled briefs were levied against the best of Japan. No matter how "guilty" Japan may be in the eyes of Americans who want to turn around the deficit, attempts at public humiliation and inciting loss of face may not be the most strategic approaches to communicating the message. But then again, the air was thick.

Most recently, look at the furor over the U.S. rediscovery of Japanese *keiretsus*, the post-war "cleaned up" reincarnation of the old Japanese *zaibatsus*. The Structural Impediments Initiative (SII), geared toward removing barriers to free trade and imbalances, has wound up plastering the *keiretsus* on the front pages. Are they cartels, grossly inhibiting free trade and fair competition, or are they families of interrelated companies consistent with the age old Japanese passion for collectivism? If we are to believe the headlines, the answer is simply that *keiretsus* are cartels. Unfortunately, the image of the *keiretsu* in the West, is somewhat out of tune with the reality of these industrial groupings. Suffice to say that tele-news and news-magazine formats do not lend themselves toward more in-depth, cultural analysis of *keiretsus*. The result is a bashing of *keiretsus* analagous to Nancy's smashing of the Sumo, or Nakasone's analysis of America's competitiveness and educational ills.

The Central Role and Challenge
of Strategic Communication

Whether looking at the broad agenda of the media, the formation of U.S.-Japanese corporate alliances and joint ventures, or at individual U.S. expatriates in Japanese based companies, strategic communication is central to our relationship. If this U.S.-Japanese relationship is what former Secretary of State Baker believes it to be—"the most important alliance in the world"—then improving cultural understanding and facilitating effective communication should be high on our national list of international priorities.

Why term this challenge one of "strategic communication?" I use the term *strategic* to convey that business, corporate and political communication with Japanese should be intentional, carefully considered, and the result of a growing intercultural sophistication and preparation. Too much is at stake to engage in random, trial and error diplomacy. Political delegations, entire corporations, and individual expatriate candidates can be strategically prepared for communication with Japanese.

In this book I offer a variety of communication, management and diplomacy strategies born of a multidisciplinary analysis that is directly applicable to the marketplace. Rather than struggling for cues to decipher how to communicate with Japanese at *meishi* (business card exchange) or negotiating tables, public speaking occasions or social encounters, I provide both cultural and business contexts for Japanese behavior, as well as specific menus for **strategically** adapting to Japanese expectations.

About this Book

Although I primarily refer to "U.S. expatriates in Japan," I have prepared this book for an eclectic audience of Americans, British, (and other Westerners) who want to better understand Japanese culture, business, management, and communicative practices, and are entertaining prospects for doing business with Japanese. It should also be of direct use to Western travellers going to Japan, diplomats, educators, and persons having direct dealings with Japanese in the U.S. Moreover, I believe that Japanese will find it interesting to view themselves from the U.S. side of the Pacific, and investigate how difficult it is for Western affiliates to adapt to Japanese ways.

I view the book as "intercultural food," as a multifaceted message that can hopefully penetrate some of the false images, stereotypes, ignorance, and myths perpetuated by the mass media and "bashing" factions, East and West. It is also conceived as a predeparture training volume and a basis for expatriate training programs.

In addition to a full menu of "chapters" on facets of U.S.-Japanese communication, culture, business and management, I also present a series of brief exercises and fast messages pertaining to an eclectic assortment of intercultural issues. The BICULTURALS provide contrasts of U.S. and Japanese communication styles; CULTURAL DIALOGUES are dramatic scripts between Americans and Japanese, usually geared toward business and social interaction, problem solving, culture shock and adaptation; CASE STUDIES develop expertise in U.S.-Japanese conflict management; and MEDIA BRIEFINGS are quotations from various Western and Japanese newspapers, magazines, and books, chosen for their relevancy to this book in either developing issues covered in chapters or in expanding the reference base. The exercises and fast messages are inserted throughout the book and inject some of the elements of the corporate training room and the international media climate. Following every CULTURAL DIALOGUE and CASE STUDY you will find an analysis, discussing the central principles raised and how the information can be useful in your ongoing U.S.-Japanese relations.

I became deeply involved in intercultural training and consulting work, and corresponding writing and research, only after numerous experiences within the Japanese corporate world. It was there that I discovered the avid interest of Japanese top management in learning about U.S. social and business culture and communication practices, and conversely learned of the lack of U.S. corporate interest in cracking Japanese codes. After writing three books on the subject matter of U.S.-Japanese intercultural communication in business and management, which were published in Japan, I thought it high time that I address my indigenous audience.

A Bridge Between Scholarship and the Marketplace

After returning from Japan, I was surprised by the lack of U.S. corporate interest in intercultural training and consulting for doing business with Japanese. I wondered why U.S. management was continuing to turn away from the cultural Tower of Babel that had to be faced. In addition, I found that there was an insufficient bridge between scholarship and the marketplace. Within the academic world, many of the *best* minds were wasting time, spending efforts publishing obscure articles to small audiences of like minded professors. Some of the scholars seriously lacked experience dealing with Japanese, and still fail to realize that much of their research is tragically flawed. It is hard to convince some colleagues that they are conducting research into Japanese communication in a "tourist fashion." How naive is it to pull into Japan for several weeks and conduct a study, with Japanese "strangers" as subjects. Even the most foolish and virgin of U.S. expatriate managers rapidly learns that strangers usually speak the language of *tatemae,* or surface communication. Unfortunately, many of our Western researchers are unable to distinguish between the communication of *tatemae* and *honne* (communication of true intentions). They conduct *tatemae* research, exhibiting that they, themselves, are cultural strangers.

Most important of all, there is a deep gulf between savvy, experienced, marketplace "experts," and the more obscure U.S.-Japanese research of communication, business, management, anthropology, psychology, linguistics, and sociology academicians. On the one hand, the majority of the more "popular stuff" tends to speak to the necessity of breaking through the cultural and communicative barriers in doing business with Japanese; but much of this writing is superficial, fluffy, lacking in understanding of in-depth cultural issues, and at best, primers or "quick briefings." And the most profound and prolific of the writers on Japan have either not directly addressed the interrelationships between business, communication and culture, or are too difficult for lay readers to grasp.

Brilliant critics and researchers on Japanese culture, such as Takie Sugiyama Lebra,[1] Che Nakane,[2] and Dean Barnlund,[3] stack up a bit more on the academic side of the fence, a little out of the reach of the business and managerial practitioner, the expatriate or the lay person curious about Japan.

In writing this book, I hope to fill this void. The book explores a very fine line between the world of research and the realities of the everyday international and intercultural workplace. At times the information is more on the research side of the fence, at other points it reaches more to practitioners. The book hopefully achieves a suitable blend that speaks to the needs of Americans who must improve their skills with Japanese associates. And perhaps it will also interest academics in its marriage of theory and practice.

Accepting the Intercultural Challenge

Ironically, in a society that sings the praises of "multiculturalism," there is a blindness and ignorance attached to *overly generic* approaches to crossing cultural borders. *In order to effectively communicate, manage, engage in joint ventures and diplomacy, or work side-by-side with Japanese, you must specifically study Japanese culture.* Likewise, when doing business with South Koreans, French Canadians, Dutch or Israelis, an analysis of *each* culture holds insights into their respective business protocols and toward the development of strategic communications.

Pivotal in this challenge is the necessity of overcoming the plethora of stereotypes that plague the marketplace. Praise should be lavished on those media who tend to engage in responsible, interculturally sensitive and accurate reporting: *The Wall Street Journal, The Asian Wall Street Journal, The Japan Times, The Asahi Shimbun's Japan Access Newsletter, The Japan Economic Institute's JEI Report,* the *Los Angeles Times, The Washington Post,* and several Japanese based television and radio news broadcasts. Movies such as *Gung Ho, Mr. Baseball,* and others directed at U.S.-Japanese relations must be scrutinized and discussed, separating images from realities.

Japanese as Individuals

Finally, it is essential to also separate truth from fiction when dealing with individual Japanese. *There is more individuality among Japanese than we have been led to believe.* Life in Japan shows the expatriate that many Japanese hold unique views, are critical of their corporations, question their lives, and search deeply for meaning and explanations for Japanese culture, obligation and duty. Complex systems of obligations ("on") bind most Japanese in long-term reciprocal networks of relationships. And although there are strict rules governing public communication (*tatemae*), Japanese visions and emotional turmoils, and the inner self (*kokoro*), are as deep and varied as any American's. It is a highly refined, sophisticated and publicly restricting code of communication and etiquette that veils many of the innermost thoughts of Japanese managers, workers, wives, salarymen and women.

In a word, Japanese are classically "stoic," as public conventions guide behavior, and conflict is complexly sidestepped. But once you establish longer term, close knit friendships, the *haragei* (gut communication) and *honne* may find their way to the surface. The transition from "outsider" to "insider" status with Japanese business affiliates is best conceived of as an ongoing, longterm communication and relationship *campaign*. Once you cross the threshold into the realm of Japanese *honne* and the *kokoro,* you will want to be prepared to accurately read Japanese verbal and nonverbal communication. Do not miss a Japanese confession or friendship; they are among the most valuable social and business assets in this world.

"JAPANESE GIVE VAGUE ANSWERS"

The surefire way to cause the other person to lose face is to give him a flat "no." Therefore, the best way to keep the person at arm's length is to keep him or her hanging by giving vague answers, such as "maybe" or "perhaps."

(from Michihiro Matsumoto, *The Unspoken Way, Haragei: Silence in Japanese Business and Society,* Tokyo: Kodansha, 1988, 108.)

PART I

East Meets West

CHAPTER 1

Culture Shock: East Meets West

CULTURAL DIALOGUE

"THE AMERICAN SALESMAN AND JAPANESE CUSTOMER"

MR. VALDEZ: I was very upset by Mr. Nakeshita's behavior!

MR. ROBERTS: I have always known him to be a gentleman. What went wrong?

MR. VALDEZ: Well, you know I wanted to sell him our line of golf balls. And he just wanted to make "small talk."

MR. ROBERTS: At the first meeting?

MR. VALDEZ: Yes. I started telling him all about the balls, but he only wanted to talk about the weather and Japanese and American holidays. So weird! Rude!

MR. ROBERTS: No business took place?

MR. VALDEZ: Yeah, I got "the business." I think he didn't like me. He was so damn evasive. He smiled, made chit-chat, and was never direct. He insulted me!

MR. ROBERTS: I finally see what you're talking about. Look, Valdez, YOU were the one who insulted HIM!

MR. VALDEZ: Are you crazy?

MR. ROBERTS: No. You must *first* get respect and build a relation-
                ship. You hardly ever sell a Japanese anything at a
                first meeting.

Analysis: Valdez will have to think quite carefully about the confrontation he thought he had with Nakeshita. Inasmuch as Valdez
is the one who is trying to sell Nakeshita, it seems reasonable that
Valdez be briefed on Japanese expectations.

Valdez wanted to get down to business immediately, talk up a
sale, and skip over all the small talk. He became extremely impatient with Nakeshita's seemingly evasive, indirect, "beating around
the bush" behavior.

As U.S. politicians are slowly learning, you can't just show up in
Japan for a single visit and expect to obtain instantaneous Japanese investment. Hundreds of research sources, repatriates and astute international business players constantly tell of the slower
paced Japanese approach to doing business. The first few visits with
potential Japanese investors or buyers are best spent building up a
personalized relationship, with only gradual reference to the business agenda. In essence, Valdez was communicating too rapidly for
Nakeshita. He needed to slow down, listen, and recognize that the
"small talk" is strategic!

As distances diminish in the information age, unprecedented
business, corporate, political, and educational ventures unite the
United States and Japan in what former secretary of state James
Baker recently termed "the world's most crucial alliance." This
meeting of the East and West is extremely volatile, however, as radically different national cultures, histories and lineages easily lead
to conflict, ultra-nationalism, ethnocentrism, and other separatist
and collision courses. It is within this well publicized climate of escalating joint ventures and rising protectionist sentiments that the
U.S. business traveler, public leader and corporate expatriate enters into relations with Japanese.

Culture Shock: The Plight of the U.S. Expatriate Stranger within Japanese Business Culture

Perhaps the single most formidable challenge facing U.S. expatriates in the 1990s is "culture shock." When dealing with Japanese nationals in U.S. or Japanese based subsidiaries, on sojourns to negotiating tables in Nagoya, or in the early days of a five year assignment in Tokyo, the undermining surprises of operating within a foreign environment cannot be overestimated.

In corporate, military, peace corps, and consulting and training circles, the term *culture shock* emerged as a simple, descriptive sound byte, describing a complex phenomenon.[1] The multifaceted challenge of culture shock can be examined from the perspective of the virgin U.S. expatriate in Japan. In the opening minutes of *meishi* (business card exchange), the most sophisticated of Western corporates enter an alien business ritual.[2] As unprepared *gaijin* (foreigners), Americans feel the feelings, think the thoughts, of the "stranger."[3] During the course of a first business day or week, the overall onslaught of culture shock is made up of numerous tremors. All taken-for-granted Western business and social practices are suddenly under scrutiny. Cultural blunders abound. Introductions are unsure and awkward. The manner in which Japanese utilize the English language and use honorifics, appears evasive and ambiguous. How Japanese conceive of business meetings and negotiations is substantively and procedurally confusing. The eloquence exercised so boldly and successfully in U.S. venues does not get a positive, direct response out of a Japanese audience. And your status in the organization is foggy, as it is difficult to read the motivation, perception, individual or group mind of the Japanese hosts.

Understanding how to conduct a conversation, respond at an interview, speak to superiors and subordinates, take and yield turns at negotiating tables, make small talk, decode Japanese systems of seniority and promotion, or establish trust and empathy—all appear to be "red flag" situations. There are few road maps, cultural compasses, ground rules for how to cross the perplexing, pronounced cultural borders. Despite all the talk about Japanese becoming more Westernized, it initially appears as if Japanese hosts are deeply entwined in many extremely Japanese bound rules and codes of business and social etiquette.

This jungle of cultural norms is foremost on your mind. You wonder why you were not adequately briefed or trained for this demanding transition. Why weren't Japanese experts, cross-cultural

consultants and trainers, repatriates, or competent human resource specialists busy preparing you? Your new expatriate status,
or place as a visiting negotiator in Tokyo, seems in serious jeopardy.
Somehow the home office probably had little insight into the cultural perils involved in this transnational assignment.

Face-to-face, language problems further plague expatriates.
The initial shock of hearing Japanese spoken all around you wears
on. The dissonance builds as you are at a loss to determine whether
conversations will be held in Japanese or English. Will translators
always be available? Will the Japanese hosts supply translators?
And even among English speaking Japanese, you discover a peculiar, difficult to decipher version of the English language. After
questioning repatriates and Japanese you find out that this is what
locals call "Janglish," or a "Japanized" version of English. Searching
for definitive answers to questions, your Japanese associates seem
so vague and unclear. It is the most tentative version of English
you've ever heard. And in the meeting rooms, negotiations appear
incredibly inept, ritualistic. You try to speak your mind but this insults the hosts. Perhaps the free exchange of ideas at a public negotiating table is taboo? Yet it is hard to imagine a people who
would not debate, argue, confront one another—is this possible?
How shocking is this business world where the individual must sup-
press personal convictions and unequivocally subscribe to *wa* (group
harmony). Can you exist in a corporate culture that does not encourage or put the spotlight on a home run hitter? Does everything
have to be teamwork and contingent upon allowing everyone to keep
face (*kao*)?

The shock of Japanese business culture continues as you are
ushered into your "group office space." No individual office is provided. There are no partitions, walls or doors for insuring privacy.
Everyone is in view. There are few secrets. Bad days cannot be conducted from behind the thick, secure privacy of U.S. closed corporate doors; on the best and worst of days you are thrown out into the
Grand Central Station of desks; endless rows of identical desks. The
shock of "lack of privacy" hits home; you already wonder whether
you can fulfill this assignment—stay the course in Japan . . . complete the mission. Before you even get a change to experience that
"honeymoon" feeling of being in a foreign country, you feel alienated
and dream of returning to the land of the Yankees and Dodgers.

Surely someone at the home office realizes how difficult it is to
have to constantly interact with coworkers, subordinates and superiors. You do not have your own office! How can this be? You have

lost the screening system you took for granted at home. This culture, of the people and by the people, literally means that you *will* function in a collectivist setting.

The Other Side of Cultural Shock: Japanese Hosts on American Guests

After spending millions of dollars annually on conversational English and intercultural communication training, *Japanese are extremely surprised to find out how little Western expatriates know of Japanese business and national culture, corporate and social etiquette.*

At negotiating tables, Japanese marvel at the perceived audacity, outspokenness, short tempers, and impatience of U.S. representatives. They find it incomprehensible that a single American negotiator could conceivably land in Narita Airport and not have some awareness of Japanese *nemawashi* (informal consensus building) or *ringi* (formal decision-making process). To attempt to defy the slow, methodical, largely non-negotiable Japanese approach to decision-making, is the source of culture shock. Japanese are astounded by the farther reaches of American individualism, as expatriate negotiators "demand" that decisions be reached immediately. Japanese feel the force of further tremors when the expatriates fail to recognize the Japanese chain-of-command, leading to statements made out of turn, to the wrong person, and regarding inappropriate items.

Japanese hosts are shocked by the full brunt of the Western ego, and are ill-equipped to deal with a culture that sanctions rampant careerism, job-hopping and the revolving door of managers in top U.S. corporations. Japanese complain of the waves of insults that flood their companies when *gaijin* populate their business world. Lower ranking subordinates pressure Japanese superiors to speak, not knowing that status determines who initiates and/or dominates conversations in the workplace. There is the overwhelming burden of the American "talk culture." Americans are always talk, talk, talking, chattering away in a sea of needless verbiage. Japanese cannot easily digest the American insensitivity to silence. Worst of all, in the midst of so many cultural insults, no apologies come forth. Japanese contend that the barbarian Westerners are frightfully ethnocentric, blind to the intricacies of Japanese culture, and unwilling to learn. Japanese corporates find it easy to substantiate the "Ugly American" image perpetuated by journalists and films, pointing to the latest gaffes by tall, stupid expatriates.

Ethnocentrism or Adaptation?

Implicit in the experience of *culture shock* is the problem of what can or should be done about it. Life in a global village of joint ventures mandates that Americans and Japanese continuously communicate across their national and cultural borders. The channels for international communication are steadily expanding, as U.S. businesses utilize fax, teleconferencing, overnight deliveries, electronic mail, international telephone systems, video telephoning, letter writing, memos, training videos, and various media formats for information exchange. But behind all of the channels of transmission sit individual Americans and Japanese. Whether an expatriate, a business visitor, or engaged in correspondence through a home office, U.S. business players are expected to communicate with Japanese daily.

Close business ties with Japan clearly point toward the urgent necessity of improving intercultural understanding to the ends of facilitating improved communication. The high incidence of cultural and communication conflict must be examined and reduced. American managers need help in learning how to communicate effectively with Japanese associates in the workplace, through fax, telephone, and other media.

The U.S.-Japanese relationship surely calls for adaptation and mutual study of the other's business and national culture. For there is no task, expertise or specialty that can readily escape from the difficulties of crossing cultural borders and anticipating culture shock. Facilitating smoother intercultural communication is a generic, primary challenge—a calling shared throughout the business world. It requires that U.S. corporations and expatriates carefully decode Japanese protocol, studying Japanese business and social expectations. Everyday marketplace communication should not be taken for granted, nor can Americans continue to blindly assume that the Japanese or international world operates on the floorplans of U.S. culture. Japanese business culture is a labyrinth that can be systematically and strategically deciphered. Even in Western based ventures, all facets of Japanese workplace communication require investigation: introductions, business meetings, conversations between coworkers, superiors and subordinates, public speaking and

"JAPANESE ADVERTISING AND MARKETING MAKES STRATEGIC USE OF ENGLISH LANGUAGE"

. . . . Advertisements are typically full of English words and Japanese expressions which are made up by using English words. Trade names especially carry English or English-sounding names. Sometimes such names are direct imitations of similar-sounding western trade names. . . . For example, a man named Ishibashi, which means "stone bridge" in English, started a tyre (tire) manufacturing company, and used the trade name "Bridgestone" by reversing his name and imitating the American trade name "Firestone." A trade name may be made by adding an English word to a Japanese word so that the whole trade name sounds like an English word. Sometime ago, there was a Japanese-made car called *Datto,* which roughly translated means "rapidly running rabbit." Later, when a new model was launched it was named "Datsun." The word "sun" here was derived from the English word "son," because the new car belonged to the next generation. Thus, "Datsun" means the "son" of *Datto.*

(from Michio Kitahara, *Children of the Sun: The Japanese and the Outside World,* Sandgate, Folkestone, Kent, England: Paul Norbury Publications, 1989, 121).

oral reports, negotiating, decision-making, interviewing, verbal and nonverbal communication, organizational charts, seniority and promotions, and a plethora of issues falling under the headings of business culture and business communication—Japanese style.

Similarly, U.S. companies and players must prepare for everyday, social communication in Japan. Work does not take place in isolation. Partaking in afterhours socializing, dinners, drinks, parties, holidays, travel, and other situations is an important flip side of the business culture. Once again, the expatriate must be extremely

"SILENCE vs. TALK IN JAPANESE-U.S. ORGANIZATIONS"

The notion that the excellent communicator is an eloquent speaker and has the "gift of gab" is a thoroughly Western perspective. This culturally derived view of the "good communicator" should be rethought in the light of the extraordinary Eastern/Japanese reverence for silence and distrust of "talkers."

careful not to assume that Western social etiquette is in effect within Japan. Many culture shocks await the unsuspecting expatriate regarding: tipping, taxis, use of utensils, paying bills, appropriate conversation at restaurant tables, differences between formal and informal communication, Japanese style toilets and bathing, honesty, trust, nudity, entertainment, and so forth.

There are those who disagree with cultural adaptation, however. They are antagonists who do not agree with the maxim, "when in Rome, do as the Romans do." Essentially, the strict isolationist, nationalist or ethnocentric may not actually be "culturally blind," but rather *chooses* to turn his/her back on other cultures. They believe, to varying degrees, that Americans should act American and be under no pressure to have to adapt to Japanese or any other national culture. And even among the ranks of U.S. expatriates, you will find those who want to *consciously* continue to act, think and behave like Americans, even when engaged in Japanese companies and social life in Japan. Likewise, there are Japanese ethnocentrics who believe that Japanese culture and ways just cannot be understood by foreigners. This *nihonjinron* posture (Japan can only be understood by Japanese) is still common, and presents a series of roadblocks to the intercultural challenge of adaptation.

From the perspective taken in this book, there is no simple way of dismissing ethnocentrism and its manifestations by merely taking a liberal, integrationist or convergenist stance. It must be understood and appreciated as the "other side" of adaptation. There are historical, philosophical and political reasons why both Japanese and Americans continue to perpetuate a separatist mentality. Some nationalists are motivated by the desire to preserve the national culture, the history and traditions, the old ways. They do not like the idea of Japanese culture being overrun with Americana. And some Americans deeply believe that American ways should not be tampered with. How we socialize, do business, and enter global markets is the standard of the entire world. Why succumb to alien protocol? to Japanese?

While the ethnocentric and nationalistic sentiments may have their place, U.S. expatriates in Japan are virtually doomed unless they, at least on the surface, learn how to operate in a *bicultural* fashion. If the speaking of Japanese language is not mandatory, the study of Japanese communication style and cultural influences in business and social life are prerequisites for doing business with Japanese. For as much as Japanese have hired me to teach them how to be "actors" in the "theater" of American business and society, so can U.S. expatriates greatly profit from this increased repertoire. It is this belief in the soundness and viability of cultural adaptation, learning the cultural and communicative behaviors and expectations of Japanese, that underlies the mission and scope of this book.

Breaking Through Ethnocentrism and Separatism

A high degree of ethnocentrism or separatism is contrary to the bicultural goals of joint ventures, or multicultural goals of multinational organizations. Yet because ethnocentrism and separatism represent threats to intercultural adaptation, it merits brief analysis.

Within the U.S. there are various segregationist and separatist movements juxtaposed to the integrationist, multiculturalist factions. This is particularly pronounced in the U.S. workforce, as Anglos, Afro-Americans, Hispanics, East Asians, Native Americans, and others are working side-by-side. Some separatists, for example, want rebuilding of the inner city infrastructures, to the end of generating Afro-American businesses. A few go to the extreme of calling outsiders "devils." But within the large corporations, there is little choice but to adapt to cultural diversity, learn how cultural codes and backgrounds affect workproduct and habits, and strive for a communication able to bridge the differences and build upon similarities.

For Japanese corporations opening up U.S. based branches, diversity represents a serious problem, as they are even less skilled and experienced than Americans in this arena. In an effort to sidestep multicultural, interracial, and interethnic "problems," Japanese have been careful to situate in non-urban, more rural locales, predominantly populated by Anglos (and if possible, away from the influence of the unions).

Although the forces of ethnocentrism and separatism are in part *responses* to the threats of culture shock and "infiltration," their numerous manifestations can be traced in Japanese history. Unlike Americans, Japanese have spent extended periods of time, separated from the outside world. Intent upon keeping "Japan for the Japanese," and expelling all foreign culture and influence, the two hundred year seclusion declared by the Shogunate Order of 1639, kept most *gaijin*, outside. In contrast to the early Japanese "bashing" of Portuguese, Dutch, Spanish, Korean, and Chinese, and a movement toward a "purification" of Japanese culture, colonial America was a land of diversity. Both on the frontier, and in the early factories of the late nineteenth century, American business and workers came from all of Europe and around the globe.

After centuries spent idolizing, mimicking, borrowing, adapting language, culture, and socialization processes from the Chinese, Japan repeatedly attempted to offset and reverse the perception of Japan held by China, as the lowliest and most barbaric nation of East Asia. Turning for brief periods to the influences of Portugal, Spain, and Holland, the exposure led to intensified feelings of ethnocentrism, separatism, and nationalism. The order of 1639 was the ultimate act of ethnocentrism—it was a decree to protect Japanese culture from outside influences—both renouncing their lowly status within the East Asian community and declaring their superiority to the barbarians of the West.

The shogunate and emperor, along with unyielding nationalists, were fierce protectionists and isolationists. A succession of cultural shocks had rocked the people of Japan, as the Western traders brought their Anglo faces, strange languages, large bodies, peculiar artifacts, dangerous weapons, advanced maritime vessels, exotic foods, bizarre clothing, and many startling innovations. To be bombarded and blitzkrieged with the messages, talk, ideas, philosophy, and religion(s) of the huge, bearded strangers, was a great source of fear and concern. The final solution offered by the regime was the seclusion.

The *gaijin* had to be expelled, kept at a distance, not allowed to mingle and mix with the pure, aspiring jewel of the Far East. *Gaijin* bashings and *nihonjinron* nationalism were the common topics of the two hundred year seclusion, serving as a prelude to even more troublesome episodes within the twentieth century. The spokespersons for the land of the rising sun spoke a tough, ethnocentric language of distrust to the militarily and technologically superior Westerners. The objective was to preserve the Japanese status quo against the *gaijin* invasion.

Certain reservations and qualifications were articulated during the two hundred year period. Trade and business was substantially reduced with the Dutch and Chinese, the Chinese in Japan were limited to residency in a small territory within Nagasaki, and the Dutch constrained to the island of Deshima, in the Nagasaki harbor. But ironically, the continued practice of learning the Dutch language, considered at the time to be an international vehicle for communication—also illustrated the less than total commitment to the seclusion.

News of the end of China's seclusion via the Opium War, and the emerging world order of the middle nineteenth century, forced Japanese to reconsider their stance of separatism. Finally, the arrival of the celebrated and infamous Commodore Perry supplied the impetus for the opening of the island nation to the world community. With Perry's display of staggering U.S. technology and his ability to address the Emperor and the highest ranking officials of Japan, groundwork was set for the ensuing Emperor Meiji and the Meiji Period (1868–1912).

During the Meiji Period, Japanese reversed the trends of ethnocentrism and isolationism in favor of adaptation, assimilation, and embracements of U.S. and Western culture. Japanese believed that they had met their technological and military superiors, and were more inclined to absorb the lessons of the U.S. and Europe, than to resist.

In the Meiji Period, the great Japanese educational reformer, maverick and rebel, Yukichi Fukuzawa, made frequent trips to the U.S. and Europe, learning Western educational methods. Through the venue of a private school in Japan, Fukuzawa attempted to bring the adversarial and argumentative communication style to Japan. He believed that for Japanese to succeed in the international community they would have to rethink their Buddhist and Confucianist based practices of silence, group harmony, and their distaste for uttering harsh, face-provoking language. Fukuzawa

BICULTURAL

"WOMEN AND CORPORATE COMMUNICATIONS"

Gender is a volatile intercultural issue in international business. Despite obvious Japanese awareness of the Western women's movement (via the media), many of Japan's organizations are headed by traditionalists who remain extremely uncomfortable in dealing with top U.S. female CEOs, leaders and managers. How to negotiate this difficult problem requires careful consideration of not only current exigencies but cultural lineage as well. Some experienced U.S. repatriates and consultants advise that American female managers, doing business with Japanese in Japan, should be initially accompanied by a high ranking male from the U.S. headquarters.

tried largely in vain to get Japanese to learn oratory, debate, and the art of lawyer-like speaking. Afterall, they had to deal with foreign markets, negotiators, and were considering starting the Japanese equivalent of the British Parliament—now the Japanese Diet. Wouldn't the art of persuasive speaking and argument be a necessary import from the West?

In more recent years, the Japanese trend of reversing the seclusion and absorbing Western culture and ideas has been particularly prevalent in the areas of business and management. World famous Japanese development of total quality management, quality circles and other marketplace breakthroughs have all been reinventions of U.S. management innovations. Borrowing directly from the likes of Armand Feigenbaum (total quality control) and Demming and Juran (quality circles), Japanese regrouped after their devastation during World War II, to rebuild management and manufacturing.

Perhaps the key to Japanese adaptation is the way in which they have placed a personalized, cultural stamp on all absorptions. U.S. management theories were reconstituted with pivotal aspects of Japanese national culture and the practices of everyday life.

And the collectivist group orientation of Japanese culture was enfused as a crucial ingredient in the uniquely Japanese surge toward quality control, improvement, team building and worker-management solidarity.

Implications

The diverse issues raised in this chapter can have direct impact upon Americans doing business with Japanese, or preparing for visits and expatriations. It is vital that U.S. business people realize that cultural preparation is central to breaking through a multitude of otherwise unexpected barriers or *culture shocks*. Key areas of concern in expatriations and business sojourns to Japan include:

1. Identification of typical images of culture shocks experienced by the new U.S. expatriate manager in Japan;

2. How inexperienced U.S. expatriates view Japanese managerial, business and organizational communication and cultural practices, and struggle with contrasts to U.S. practices;

3. How Japanese corporate and business hosts view the guest U.S. expatriates; how Japanese see the typical cultural clashes;

4. Recognition of the dialectic and struggle between cultural adaptation and ethnocentrism;

5. Identification of the importance of intercultural adaptation in business relationships with Japanese;

6. Cognizance of sharply contrasting rules and etiquette regarding appropriate communication in the joint venture workplace, and a readiness to investigate Japanese communication practices and expectations in various business venues;

7. Appreciation of the historical roots of the Japanese "nihonjinron" syndrome, ethnocentrism and separatism, and its impact on current U.S.-Japanese business relations;

8. An ability to *anticipate* culture shocks, infractions, insults and misunderstandings; this represents an alternative to trial and error intercultural diplomacy;

9. Recognition of the need to become increasingly bicultural in the course of expatriations and extended business associations with Japanese companies, markets, customers, and audiences; and

10. A dire need for intercultural communication training in meeting the challenge of operating as a *gaijin* and stranger within Japanese social and corporate culture.

"THE INSIDERS' PARADISE"

The Japanese guard relationships—relationships are power . . . new entrants upset old and comfortable relationships; and so Japanese society presents itself as a thicket of obstacles to new entry. Japan is the insiders' paradise, the stakeholders' dictatorship. God help the newcomer, for the Japanese won't.

(from Jonathan Rauch, *The Outnation: A Search for the Soul of Japan*, Boston, MA: Harvard Business School Press, 1992, 79).

CHAPTER 2

Preparing U.S. Managers for Expatriate Assignments in Japan

BICULTURAL

"CORPORATE COMMUNICATION: QUIET vs. OBVIOUS STATUS"

To flaunt . . . or not to flaunt . . . that is the question. By Japanese standards, many U.S. business leaders are a bit too obvious or flamboyant regarding the outer trappings of success. Clothing, offices, jewelry, and other artifacts are more carefully "censored" from the Japanese side of the Pacific. This seemingly small, but extremely delicate issue, is a source of silent conflict in U.S.-Japanese joint ventures. Shall status be quite subtle and controlled, or shall it be communicated more overtly?

It is curious to note that many young Japanese corporate employees turn down offers to obtain an American Express "Gold Card," as it may indicate a status symbol too "advanced" for their ranking within the corporate hierarchy.

The growing numbers of U.S. firms operating in Japan, U.S. owned subsidiaries and U.S.-Japanese joint ventures presents a complex intercultural challenge to the American business, political, legal, and educational communities. Much care is needed in assessing U.S.-Japanese ventures, or in considering breaking ground as a *gaijin kaisha* (a foreign firm operating in Japan).

Within a complex web of legal, trade, human resource management, economic, and governmental considerations, the challenge of *intercultural communication* is a hub, matrix or center.[1] Somehow, American corporations must cross vast cultural boundaries separating Japanese and U.S. social and business etiquette. No matter what the technical or professional expertise, much of the success or struggle of a U.S. venture with the Japanese is ultimately contingent upon *bridging* cultural differences and communicating in a manner most effective with Japanese hosts.[2]

Thorough briefings and analysis of Japanese business, management, corporate and political practices, both in general and vis-à-vis a specific venture, industry and market, is essential. Also necessary, however, is the oftentimes overlooked and underestimated role of intercultural communication. Without a keen awareness and working knowledge of how to communicate with Japanese in the workplace, specialist and technical knowledge will falter.

Communicating with Japanese is something that cannot be learned overnight, nor can the Western honed eloquence of an outstanding U.S. manager be any assurance of success with Japanese. For the ability to communicate with Japanese for motivation, productivity, individual accomplishment, promotion, layoffs, on-the-job training, negotiating, conflict management, interviewing, and related tasks, is hardly a given. Literally, U.S. expatriate managers must consider a radical cultural transformation, whereby they challenge many of their homegrown assumptions about how they communicate in business and social venues.[3] To continue with an Americanized approach to management and communicating on the job, is a blueprint for cultural clashes with Japanese.[4] Care must be taken to consider a myriad of Japanese corporate and national culture rules and expectations governing behavior during work hours and into the afterhours. It is impossible to attempt to separate Japanese business from the profound influences of Japanese culture.

To operate in the Japanese market, U.S. managers, employees, human resource specialists, negotiators, diplomats, publicists, and other professionals must be able to rethink and relearn their expertise within the context of Japanese protocol. Only Americans who

MEDIA BRIEFING

*"JAPANESE DISSECT AMERICAN LANGUAGE AND
CULTURE, AMERICANS FAIL TO RECIPROCATE"*

... The small number of Americans who have learned Japanese is
especially irksome when viewed from the perspective of the millions
of Japanese who avidly study the English language and American
culture......

(from Alan Goldman, *Intercultural Communication Between Japanese and Americans* [edited, with notes and Japanese language
translations, by Roichi Okabe], Tokyo: Kirihara Shoten, 1989, 35).

are prepared to challenge their conscious and unconscious ethnocentrism, their unwitting allegiance to unconsciously followed dictates of U.S. culture, need apply. The task is formidable and
mandates a genuine curiosity for Japanese business and culture,
and an openness and willingness to adapt.[5]

Intercultural Business and Assessment of Expatriations in Japan

The approach advocated is a "hands on" agenda that encour-
ages U.S. companies to groom American managers for expatriations. It is important to have a significant U.S. presence within
American owned (or joint-venture owned) businesses in Japan,
rather than delegating the management to local, Japanese nationals. While there is a place for significant Japanese representation,
to not strive for U.S. expatriations is to shun a proactive management policy, and in effect to make it a Japanese company.[6]

Preparing a *gaijin* or alien for expatriation in Japan is to position a U.S. outsider within the insider, collectivist, group oriented

Japanese society. Both within the walls of a business corporation and in the corridors of society, the expatriate and family are in for severe culture shocks.

Obviously, preparation by the U.S. parent company begins with the selection of a top quality manager and an adverturesome family. Sending a loser or mediocre manager to Japan is not the modus operandi that creates bridges. I urge you to go way out of your way to select the very, very best manager available. Or if you are the "chosen one," the expatriate preparing for a Japanese assignment, avidly study the Japanese culture.

The demands on the expatriate will be significant, and Japanese want the best. Although this appears to be a reasonable and simplistic request, it is most often the case that U.S. businesses do not easily find willing expatriates, spouses and families who are also among the upper echelons of the company.

The U.S. company should make expatriation as attractive as possible, offer extensive predeparture training for the manager, spouse and family, and pay attention to a multitude of details crucial in a successful transplant. Left for a second or third-rate manager, the expatriation is liable to be doomed. The alarming statistics speak extraordinarily clearly. There is a premature return rate of U.S. expatriates from Japanese assignments in excess of fifty percent![7]

The reasons behind the extremely costly, damaging expatriation failures are many. Third rate managers are not well respected by their own U.S. firms. This information is bound to leak out through the expatriate's frequent communication with the U.S. home office, and via the reluctance of the Americans to take his/her judgment seriously. The already dubious reputation of such Americans takes away from their credibility, even before they tackle the formidable Japanese challenge. A more competent, prestigious American based member of the U.S. company is likely to believe that another manager (perhaps himself) would be perceiving the situation differently and recommending alternative actions—if he were able to eyeball the situation in Japan. The ineffective, low prestige expatriate can also cast a negative light on the ethos of the entire U.S. company, sending a negative message to the Japanese partners. It is not difficult to imagine that this scenario regularly leads to premature returns.

In addition, many American companies do not seriously heed the call or challenge of intercultural communication training.[8] *U.S. human resource departments and top management are not suffi-*

ciently aware of the necessity of predeparture training—nor have they the tools to examine the extensive preparation required. While serving as a cross cultural consultant and trainer for Japanese corporations and living in Tokyo, I found that Japanese companies give concentrated attention to preparing their future expatriates for U.S. assignments. Months, sometimes years of training are required of managers—all given on company time, locations and pocketbooks. Since human resource and personnel departments in Japan are seldom equipped to handle this kind of specialized training, the training is usually contracted to outside, independent, cross-cultural consultants or to language schools.

There is far less activity on the U.S. side of the Pacific, as American companies have been rather sluggish in recognizing predeparture training as part of strategic international management. This typically results in a second rate manager, departing with spouse and family, for a five year Japanese assignment, with sparse or no training in Japanese language, culture, social and business practices, history, etc. The predictable result is cultural shock, havoc, and disaster. Not only is the manager ill-equipped for communicating in the everyday workplace, the spouse and children are simultaneously going through a seemingly endless series of shocks and aftershocks resulting from an abrupt entrance into Japanese society. With little if any preparation for shopping, going to the post office and dry cleaners, ordering coffee or food in a restaurant, riding the subways, driving an automobile, enrolling children in school, getting along with Japanese classmates or other expatriate children, or speaking on the telephone—danger lurks.[9]

The alternative is that of choosing a manager who is a winner on American soil, and a family willing and eager for a Japanese experience. As much training as possible should be supplied *all* members of the family in the areas of Japanese language, culture, customs, work environment, management protocol, organizational structure, human resources, understanding the school system and educational options for expatriate children, social life, integration and participation of the spouse, etc. Training may include extended contact with *repatriates,* spouses and families who have successfully completed and returned from Japanese assignments, and customized consulting *after* arriving in Japan.

Specifically concerning the expatriate manager, as many dimensions of business and national culture should be included in training as possible. Managers can be exposed to numerous role plays, case studies, examples of U.S.-Japanese communication and negotiating conflicts, intricacies of Japanese style management, public speaking, decision making and leadership, nonverbal communication, silence, teamwork, and so forth.[10] Training optimally presents the expatriate with previews of Japanese: grievance systems, letter and memo writing (in English), newspaper and television media, and a cross-section of everyday Japanese business and social life. Expatriates can profit from briefings that promote cultural adaptation, assimilation, and acceptance of Japanese corporate practices—oftentimes experienced as objectionable.[11] A non-ethnocentric, non-judgmental, and non-confrontational predisposition is central, if arguments, and public disagreements are to be avoided.

Expatriate and Home Office Understanding of the Japanese Locals in *Gaijin Kaisha*

If the U.S. expatriate is well chosen, thoroughly prepared and briefed for the assignment, and ample training has been supplied to spouse and family, proper footing is established. It is also vital to examine how the expatriates' roles will change, depending on whether they are participating in a "Fortune 500" style, U.S.-Japanese joint venture, or on the other extreme, are the representatives of a U.S. business recently breaking ground in Tokyo.

For expatriates with joint venture corporate assignments, the road is difficult, but not as treacherous as it can be for the outsider involved in a new *gaijin kaisha*. Whereas the big league, joint venture expatriate is dealing with numerous lifelong Japanese managers, staff and employees, the player in a *gaijin kaisha* is primarily dealing with a work force that is considered within the boundaries of Japan to be renegades, mavericks, misfits, and social miscasts who have most likely been in exile from mainstream Japanese corporate life. These Japanese outcasts may be the products of divorces, poor university performance, scandals, or retirements. They are usually not able to return to mainstream Japanese business life.[12]

In the case of the *general manager* in a *gaijin kaisha*, this official must either hire from this pool of potential Japanese recruits or bring large numbers of workers over from the West. It is usually a good idea to choose a well known and respected general manager, someone tough and savvy and well-prepared for dealing with endless pressures from Japanese constituents. Whoever occupies the seat of general manager, a vast variety of logistical and intercultural problems are inevitable.

Since the hiring of a Japanese work force is a particularly tall order for a recent U.S. expatriate, some foreign businesses starting up in Japan elect to hire a Japanese, who in turn oversees the hiring, interviewing and staffing needs. Other companies elect to hire a U.S. general manager or president, and a well known and respected Japanese senior as the chairman.[13]

When the U.S. company chooses a Japanese general manager many intercultural dilemmas for Western expatriates as well as the U.S. home office can arise. As a Japanese who does not have roots in the foreign company, it is more than likely that he (the Japanese pool is 'male') will maintain a very Japanese style of management, a style quite baffling and contradictory to the American co-workers. For example, if he has a U.S. expatriate superior, he would be unlikely to disagree with the higher status official, nor to report any negatives back to the home office. He would be usually limited regarding oral reports or speechmaking to the media, employees or the home office—as verbal eloquence is not likely.

It is up to the U.S. expatriates, the home office, and the existence of a partially U.S. staffed training and development wing of a human resource department, to try to investigate the "double bind" that such a Japanese manager might be in. Working through the Japanese cultural allegiance (can be viewed by *gaijin* as "cultural entrapment")[14] is a profound task, as the U.S. superiors may, in effect, be asking the Japanese to "betray" his native cultural upbringing, and to operate in a shorter-term, more competitive, combative, publicly confrontational manner. Moreover, even Japanese managers of well established U.S. Fortune 500 firms operating in Japan are caught between the Japanese culture and media, and the concerns and requirements of the U.S. home office.

The remedies to these intercultural challenges come from a well-trained team of expatriates and a highly sensitized group of patriates at the U.S. home office. Frequent visits between the U.S. and Japanese offices, much communication between the U.S. and Japan, and the presence of very competent, bilingual and/or bicultural U.S. and Japanese human resource specialists and cross-cultural consultants are a must.

A better alternative is the placement of a highly interculturally competent U.S. manager, well versed in Japanese and U.S. corporate and national culture, in the position of president or general manager. S/he in turn should place a Japanese chairman (an honorary post) in the top position. Combining talents, the prepared U.S. expatriate and the Japanese chairman can tackle the formation of an excellent U.S. and Japanese staff. With time, it may be possible to groom a Japanese national to take over the general manager's position.

The Japanese chairman can extend beyond the reach of the *gaijin* expatriate, and begin to make ties to the Japanese community and diverse constituencies.

Since the chairman's position is an honorary one, he is ultimately expendable, unlike the fate of a Japanese national occupying the position of the presidency. The availability of Japanese seniors for the chairman's position, the lack of availability of Japanese for the president's slot, and the longer term obligations to a presidential hire, make the arrangement suggested preferable. In essence, a successful U.S. expatriate president can help secure, with the assistance of a Japanese chairman, the rare find—a reputable Japanese general manager for the *gaijin kaisha*.

Expatriations in Corporate U.S.-Japanese Joint Ventures

As indicated in chapter 6, corporate expatriations in Japanese based joint ventures necessitate thorough investigations of Japanese organizational protocol. All the "givens" of the U.S. organizational structure are not necessarily applicable in the Japanese company and may be irrelevant or uninvited.[15]

U.S. expatriates should be familiar with the Japanese organizational chart, organizational ambiguity, hiring, firing, layoffs, unions, individual careers vs. lifetime company loyalty, promotions, status, women in management, achievement vs. seniority, communication in the workplace, negotiations, business meetings, decision making, leadership, grievance systems and other fundamentals.[16] It is within the framework of Japanese strategic management and culture that the expatriate functions.

As the *gaijin* and outsider, the U.S. expatriate's success and longevity is determined by the readiness and willingness to culturally adapt. There is no acceptable justification for the prevalence of new U.S. expatriates who are both ignorant of Japanese organizational structuring and also insist upon imposing U.S. corporate standards on the hosts. Preparation in the areas of Japanese cultural beliefs and business communication standards must include a respect for Japanese protocol in corporate structure, relationships, and development of human resources. Along these lines, it is unac-

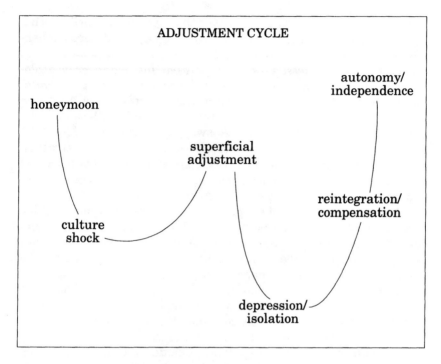

ADJUSTMENT CYCLE

autonomy/
independence

honeymoon

superficial
adjustment

reintegration/
compensation

culture
shock

depression/
isolation

The cycle represented above identifies typical stages of adjustment experienced by U.S. expatriate managers in Japan. Beginning with a honeymoon
phase, the expatriate can be expected to undergo "culture shock." Whereas
at first, the expatriate may want to embrace and experience the "wonders"
of Japanese culture, this may be followed by a series of cultural conflicts,
confrontations, surprises and tremors. A stage of superficial adjustment
may deteriorate into a depression and isolation, as the expatriate becomes
homesick and feels alienated—as an outsider in a foreign environment. If
the expatriate, spouse, family and host are successful, a reintegration may
eventually lead to an independence within Japanese culture and emergence
of a bicultural or broadened, intercultural repertoire. The percentage of
successful U.S. expatriations in Japan is approximately fifty percent, as the
intercultural challenge is formidable.

ceptable, and a source of future crisis, for the expatriate to argue
with his hosts regarding their difficulty respecting an American superior who is younger than Japanese subordinates. Theoretically,
Japanese management is quite capable of grasping the contrasting
systems for advancement, but despite any Western styled, logical

arguments, Japanese generally *prefer* that age and seniority with a specific company—rather than productivity and accomplishments—are the criteria to be used.

It is a difficult lesson for the U.S. expatriate manager or diplomat to learn in Japan: culturally based principles of Japanese management are not readily overturned by the "superiority" of American alternatives. Even the most brilliant logical, verbal ploys and eloquent illustrations are unlikely to sway Japanese hosts. Moreover, to fight organizational protocol is a poor communicative strategy. Your communicative skills are better spent working through and around Japanese management's codes, focusing more upon relationship building than ideological disagreements.[17]

Among a multitude of surprises, the expatriate is likely to discover that some Japanese have superficial or ceremonial titles, and their decision making power may not coincide with their rank. Once again, it is a trait of Western national and corporate culture to be presumptuous enough to expect that such policies are ripe and ready for your personal insights and criticisms. Particularly in equal partnerships or under majority Japanese ownership, the expatriate in Japan only publicly confronts his hosts as a quick recipe for premature return and repatriation.

Through contact with repatriates, budding expatriates learn some of the trench war communication networks operating within the Japanese company. For example, Americans repeatedly report of the inadequacies and impossibilities of Japanese negotiating tables. Rather than fighting city hall, complaining about the deeply ingrained decision making systems of *nemawashi* and *ringi,* it is more fruitful to unravel the "behind the curtain" role of the *newazashi.* Skilled in behind the scene negotiations, the *newazashi* is a player ordained by Japanese management and organizations to bring out a bag of tricks and operate away from the public eye. Oftentimes bringing unexpected reversals of impending decision making, it is important for the expatriate to both acknowledge and plan to utilize the skills and networking powers of the *newazashi.* It is also possible for the experienced or prepared expatriate to communicate the *newazashi* function to the home office, and attempt to arrange for a U.S. counterpart in joint venture negotiations.

In direct relations with Japanese superiors, the U.S. expatriate should be alerted to the subtle cues of management—messages conveyed by repatriates. Many a U.S. manager has seen an innovative proposal crushed within the hand of the bossman. Termed *nigiri tsubushi,* or *"crushing in the hand,"* this nonverbal act symbolizes *and serves as a metaphor for an unreceptive manager who will not*

MEDIA BRIEFING

"OVERWORKED JAPANESE SALARYMEN BRIEFED ON PLAY AND DOMESTICITY"

.....With the country in the full grip of a recession and companies seeking desperately to reduce payrolls and cut back on working hours, Japan's Education Ministry has decided that the moment is ripe to pull men out of the factories and onto the playgrounds . . .
. . . All over the country it is holding a series of experimental seminars . . . Speakers praise the wonders of weekend outings in the Japan Alps, comedians ridicule the demands of corporate life and everyone talks about reversing four decades of state-sponsored workaholism . . . (they) parody the life of the overworked "salaryman." . . .
. . . There is only one hitch, says Teruko Ohno, The Education Ministry official who drew up the program. "Even with overtime hours declining, if worker-bee fathers come home earlier, they find they have no place. They don't know what to do. They are there, I guess, but they are spiritually nonexistent in their houses. This is what we should attack very aggressively."

(from David E. Sanger, "Japanese Men are Urged to Get Out of the Office and into the Playground," *The New York Times*, November 12, 1993, B1, B11).

verbally communicate his lack of interest in, or putting on the shelf (*tanaage*) of, a proposal. Cultural preparation means development of Japanese-like skills of observation and listening. Managerial and corporate messages are rarely expressed in unequivocal language; it is the silent language that contains the brunt of the message.

Summary and Suggestions

Expatriations in Japan are among the most difficult of missions. A broad based program of predeparture training is best addressed to the individual manager, as well as to the spouse and family. Expatriation training, to ensure long-term effectiveness and prevent premature returns, is most effective when it also incorporates continuing consultations upon arrival in Japan. As *gaijin,* outsiders and guests, American expatriates and families are constantly on notice to adapt to the host Japanese national and corporate culture.

Special attention needs to be given to expatriations within larger joint ventures and/or to *gaijin kaisha* assignments. In both types of expatriations there needs to be a thorough analysis of Japanese style organizational and managerial practices, policy structuring and human resource development.

Finally, expatriate managers who develop a genuine passion and curiosity for Japanese culture, history, art, entertainment and lifestyle are at a tremendous advantage. Early exposure and interpretation of Japanese entertainment, media, art forms, dining, corporate trenches, and everyday life are vehicles for immersing the expatriate in Japanese social and business life. This immersion can also be aided by structured participation in representative role plays, workplace dramas, and case studies of typical U.S.-Japanese managerial and business communication (see the "Fast Messages" in this book).

It is hoped that ample preparation can turn around the troubling and escalating premature return rate of U.S. expatriates and families from Japan. As long as the premature returns continue, the need for predeparture training grows.

"MEDIA MISINFORMATION ON U.S.-JAPANESE RELATIONS"

". . . I came across an article in Monday's *Washington Post* with the questionable headline, "U.S.-Japan Relations Seen Suffering Most Serious Downturn in Decades." Upon reading this article, I realized my usual "optimist's" hat was no longer sufficient.

The pervasive tendency to characterize Japan-U.S. relations as headed toward calamity miscasts our broad based and intensive cooperation. The incendiary nature of some of the coverage of U.S.-Japan relations has the very real danger of becoming a sort of self-fulfilling prophecy. If people are told day after day, story after story, that Japan-U.S. relations are heading down the path of confrontation, people begin to expect and even accept this scenario. We cannot allow this to happen. It is clearly not in the interest of either nation . . .

I seek to snuff out the excessive misinformation many Americans have about Japan . . . I am to dismantle the psychological barrier which threatens to trap the Japan-U.S. relationship behind the fiery walls of emotion and innuendo . . ."

(from Seigi Hinata, "Safeguarding the Japan-U.S. Alliance: Dispelling the Fears in Japan and U.S. Relations," *Vital Speeches*, LVIII, April 1, 1992, 361–2.)

"REFRIGERATORS, GOLF BALLS, AND CAMERAS"

AMERICAN #1: The Japanese always say we should study their markets.

AMERICAN #2: We don't always do such a swell job of it. Have you heard about some of the top ten bloopers of all time?

AMERICAN #1: Such as?

AMERICAN #2: Well . . . how about the American refrigerator company that introduced jet set, ultramodern refrigerators into Japan during the 1950s?

AMERICAN #1: What happened?

AMERICAN #2: They were huge monsters. They didn't fit real well into the small Japanese kitchens. And those motors . . .

AMERICAN #1: Motors?

AMERICAN #2: Yeah. Those motors were so damnnnn loud . . . and they were positioned at floor level . . . so stupid!

AMERICAN #1: Why stupid?

AMERICAN #2: Think! The Japanese often sleep on the floor level, and the sleeping area may be very near the humming, grumbling motor of the neanderthal refrigerator motor. What a dreadful and noisy way to sleep!

AMERICAN #1: That's not bad. Got any other bloopers?

AMERICAN #2: Sure. How about the great American film and camera company? Good old Kodak tried to elbow their way back into the Japanese market following the war. They tried to compete with the mighty Fuji Corporation.

AMERICAN #1:   What was Kodak's strategy?

AMERICAN #2:   Tried to offer products at lower prices than Fuji . . .

AMERICAN #1:   Japanese consumers didn't fall for that?

AMERICAN #2:   No way. They thought something was wrong with the product. Then the Americans offered free color posters, and showed them how beautiful the colors came out when the film was developed—the Japanese bought into this strategy.

AMERICAN #1:   How about the golf ball story?

AMERICAN #2:   Yeah. Golf balls! An American company was stupidly marketing golf balls in groups of fours—in "four packs." They didn't sell.

AMERICAN #1:   Why not?

AMERICAN #2:   You should know! The number four is very close to the Japanese word for "death," and you can't readily sell things in groups of four.

AMERICAN #1:   Kinda' like the number thirteen in America?

AMERICAN #2:   Right you are.

AMERICAN #1:   Well, back to work for me. I guess if I'm ever transferred to advertising and marketing divisions, these bloopers will stay on my mind.

AMERICAN #2:   Right. See you later.

Analysis: A knowledge of Japanese culture and communication protocol is strategic to selling in the Japanese market. The refrigerator failure closely parallels stories of the U.S. automobile industry. Many U.S. auto exports were not adapted to the Japanese driving conditions: the steering wheel is on the wrong side of the vehicle (Japanese drive on the left side of the road, like in England, and use right side steering); and the autos, like the refrigerators, are too large for Japanese proxemic or spatial arrangements—U.S. businesspeople must be acutely aware of Japanese use of space, and limitations and expectations regarding the same, and not assume that U.S. standards will apply.

Regarding the consumer strategies employed by Kodak, there was a "trial and error" approach to selling to Japanese consumers leading to a costly and belated success, after repeated failures. A study of Japanese communicative and cultural practices reveals that the "aesthetic" dimension is crucial in everyday social and business interaction, as well as in public, marketplace communication. Rich vivid color posters communicated more effectively than a lower price.

Finally, the "golf ball" fiasco can be avoided by an understanding of cultural superstitions, rules, and expectations. Without briefings on Japanese views surrounding the number four, it is virtually impossible to avoid costly marketing mistakes. This clearly illustrates how all communication strategies are intricately linked to cultural beliefs and practices. A simplistic transfer of U.S. communication techniques in management, advertising or marketing may be inappropriate to Japanese consumers and in direct violation of Japanese codes.

The Central Role of Communication and Culture in U.S.-Japanese Management and Diplomacy

BICULTURAL

"CORPORATE COMMUNICATION AND LABOR RELATIONS: CONFLICT AND GRIEVANCES"

Shall specialists be designated to handle conflicts and grievances within the corporation? And what role will labor unions or attorneys play in this process?

The more specialist prone, adversarial U.S. corporate system favors specialists and utilization of attorneys. Japanese counterparts handle conflict in a more indirect, generalist fashion—as attorneys and unions (with very limited powers) are oftentimes excluded.

In the midst of the Structural Impediments Initiative (SII) growing protectionist sentiment against Japan, and Japan and America "bashing," you occasionally hear talk of *cultural* and *communicative* issues. A few voices on both sides of the Pacific repeatedly try to alert us to the fact that our differences may *not* be primarily due to friction from dollars and yen, trade deficits, unions, managerial turnover, monopolies, dumping practices, and *keiretsus*.[1] What is really gnawing away at the unprecedented relationship between East and West is an inability to effectively understand, negotiate and communicate across a vast cultural gulf or abyss.[2] Every movement of management, politicians, and the press is contingent upon an exchange of information, a communication process that continues to show the symptoms of culture shock. Whether at the negotiating table, in joint ventures in Ohio or Osaka, both Japanese and Americans continually struggle to communicate messages that wind up misinterpreted, distorted, and misconstrued.

Many U.S. and Japanese managers and business leaders are well aware that about sixty percent of their time is spent with the process of communication.[3] Face-to-face interaction in factories and offices, interviewing, oral and written reports, speeches, negotiations, business meetings, memos, faxes, letters, and public relations all require solid verbal and nonverbal skills. It is crucial to note, however, that such managerial communication functions are usually learned according to the dictates, norms, lineage, etiquette, and protocol of a specific culture. In other words, although faced with similar communication tasks, Japanese and Americans approach them differently. The "we" orientation of Japanese managers is located deep in the belly of Japanese national culture, and communication competence and skills are guided by rules favoring the group over the individual.[4] An "I" disposition closely guides the American culture and the communication standards practiced in the marketplace.

The compatibility of the "we" and the "I" orientations is a key to the communication between Japanese and U.S. corporate and business cultures.[5] Can the subordination of the individual to the group coexist with a culture that sanctifies the career and rights of the solo worker over the priorities of a company? Communicating for harmony, group loyalty and the minimizing of differences is the Japanese way. Communicating in a highly individualistic manner, maximizing differences, and celebrating public arguments and confrontation, is the American way.[6] Intercultural communication and managerial experts on both sides of the Pacific are currently engrossed in whether these seemingly incompatible cultures and communicative styles can be successfully blended, fused, or moved in the direction of mutual adaptation.

Virtually any topical issue in U.S.-Japanese relations is contingent upon an interpretation of our respective culturally based viewpoints and how we express ourselves. In the SII negotiations, for example, the Bush administration trade officials consciously decided to phase out all diplomatic strategies regarding protectionist Japanese policies and practices, and the tendency to avoid areas of trade conflict. In addition, in publicly distributed reports, the Bush administration found particular fault with Japanese *keiretsus* and their central role in excluding non-Japanese businesses. Although there are many Americans who stand behind such actions and methods, declaring their disapproval with Japanese trade policies and the need to get tough, I am rather pointing to the cultural undertow and communicative style of U.S. tactics.

A brief examination of Japanese culture reveals that business protocol demands ample use of pleasantries and *tatemae* (surface communication). In this instance, the Bush SII officials are not only confronting the trade practices of Japan, they are simultaneously confronting Japanese communicative etiquette and common sensibilities. While this may be warranted from the perspective of the ultra-U.S. nationalist, the intercultural communication experts wonder whether the publicly confrontative *style* of addressing the problem is strategically wise. There is much research and many war stories indicating that Japanese are terribly adverse and resistant to bullying or face-threatening negotiating tactics or media ploys. Specifically, it is not a question of whether the U.S. team is willing and able to adapt to Japanese communicative expectations, but rather a question of utilitarian and pragmatic strategies. Shouldn't our communication with Japanese be strategically conceived and delivered? If we could yield better results by keeping our confrontation out of the public arena and behind closed doors, might this be a strategic communication alternative?

It is within this strained, publicly combative climate that our CEOs, politicians, critics and media personalities continue to scrutinize U.S.-Japanese relations. Oblivious to the style, manner, and dictates of Japanese culture within the corporate world, Americans are sent to negotiating tables and five year expatriate assignments in Tokyo. There are many pressure points and tensions surrounding joint ventures and it is up to our U.S. representatives to learn how to diffuse and sidestep our differences, and more effectively operate with Japanese culture. It is the vision of this book that this mission can in part be achieved by a more honed and chiseled focus on the cultural and communicative dimensions.

Culture and Communication

Plunging into U.S.-Japanese joint ventures, diplomacy, and expatriations without a careful, systematic consideration of culture and communication is a perilous route. Brief investigation of the "we" orientation of Japanese national culture, for example, offers distressed "SII" U.S. representatives valuable insights into Japanese views of *keiretsu*. From the U.S. cultural lenses of individualism, fair trade, and competition, it is very difficult to comprehend the deep Japanese support for these "families of companies." Japanese national culture and thousands of years of unparalleled collectivism helps to explain why the majority of the Japanese corporate world and the general population avidly supports these elaborate company interrelationships and corporate groupings. To the American manufacturing and corporate sectors who are suffering the brunt of a ferocious Japanese competitiveness, the *keiretsus* are unquestionably Japanese versions of the dreaded and outlawed monopoly or "cartel."

Further investigation uncovers that there are a few vocal critics of *keiretsus*, even among Japanese professionals. Such maverick or rebel voices among the Japanese are rare (at least within the media) and rate close U.S. attention. Japanese lawyer Kanji Ishizumi repeatedly does battle with Japanese *corporate keiretsus,* calling them "huge corporate cliques."[7] Echoing the sentiments of Lee Ioccoca and Senator Gephardt, Ishizumi argues that *"keiretsu and its chummy relationship with government is dangerously out of hand, and that more competition and hostile takeovers would be a healthy challenge to Japan's insular corporate giants."*[8] Likening the extremes of Japanese collectivism as exemplified in the *keiretsu* to "monsters" and "viruses," Ishizumi speaks in a combative language, usually linked to *gaijin,* not Japanese. According to Ishizumi, "you create a hostile environment if you fight a big monster, and in Japan, the biggest monster is the *keiretsu*."[9] The attorney continues to say that *"keiretsu is like a virus which cannot be killed. They only care about taking over market share which ultimately means taking over the world."*[10] Ishizumi proceeds to argue the interrelationships between Japanese press clubs, media and corporate *keiretsus,* contending that the only way to expose the "monsters" and corporate "viruses" is to step outside of the Japanese media, reporting to foreign newspapers. In essence, he claims that there are direct media links to *keiretsus* making any objective reporting within Japan, impossible.

While such information is literally dynamite for U.S. researchers, representatives and negotiators engaged in the SII, it is nevertheless crucial to realize that Ishizumi's rhetoric or mode of expressing himself is quite risky, and epitomizes the antithesis of Japanese business communication demeanor and etiquette. In Ishizumi's thinking, what is "right" and "ideologically worth fighting for," takes priority over social and corporate harmony and the expectation that public discourse will not "rock the boat."

The point is this: topical and pressing issues of business and trade *cannot be neatly or emotionally exorcised from their cultural contexts.* On both sides of the fence, Americans and Japanese must escalate their efforts and willingness to position such issues as the SII and *keiretsus* within cultural frameworks. While Ishizumi's confrontative rhetoric *can* be of some use to U.S. negotiators (and calls attention to the vital importance of constant monitoring of Japanese journalism and media vis-à-vis U.S.-Japanese relations), it should *not* be sensationalized, or blown out of proportion—the usual knee-jerk reaction of the Western press. Make no mistake, the Ishizumi voice is very much in the minority in Japan, and he is hardly a source of a new Japanese idealism or a voice for change. If Ishizumi is to be quoted, it is best to do so, mildly, illustrating that the dissention within Japan illustrates some extreme responses to the farther reaches of Japanese corporate "we-ness."

From another light, it may not be a purely selfish or monstrous financial and market share motive that *simply* motivates Japanese *keiretsus.* To attempt a break-up of the Japanese corporate conglomerates is to "mess" with many indigenous culturally based social and business practices, built upon extremely close interrelationships, reciprocity and mutual obligations and indebtedness ("*on*").

Ironically, much of international business and managerial communication is culturally tied and bound, for unlike Ishizumi, there are precious few Japanese or Americans who *speak* of *keiretsus* or SII negotiations in a manner that contradicts their respective cultures. For every Ishizumi and Ishihara (co-author with Morita, of the combative book on U.S.-Japanese relations, *The Japan Who Can Say "No"*), there are millions of Japanese who avoid publicly confrontative rhetoric like the plague.

A truly *inter*cultural negotiation process only becomes plausible when both Japanese and U.S. advocates and foes of *keiretus,* not only compromise on a topical level, but take the time to unravel the cultural constraints and conditioning operating on both sides of the SII table. Specifically, the powerful groupism of Japanese does not readily allow for the individually outspoken player (the "Ishizumi factor"), and inevitably slows down change and puts a damper on any public showdowns, arguments and immediate solutions (e.g., the slow, tedious, complete decision-making consensus processes of *nemawashi* and *ringi* further "handcuff" the individual Japanese). Conversely, the individualism of American SII representatives drives the Bush team to believe that words, logic, debate, strongly worded reports, ultimatums and deadlines are instrumental tools of communication. But the "dispensing of diplomatic niceties" and public "venting of frustrations" are flagrant, fire-breathing tactics to Japanese associates. Even the "monstrous virus of *keiretsus*" may not warrant a public flogging and bullying, as a kindly public *tatemae* and a private revealing of *honne,* may be far more effective intercultural communication strategies.

"JAPANESE CONSUME U.S. GOODS"

". . . In a recent interview, Michael Armacost, U.S. Ambassador to Japan, stated that "the Japanese market is a lot more open than critics are willing to acknowledge." Ambassador Armacost, in citing the American companies which have done well in Japan added, "It's important that success stores be known because there are plenty of them."

IBM, Procter & Gamble, Schick, Polaroid, Xerox and Pepsi-Cola, to name a few, enjoy an enormous market share in Japan. In fact, from the moment he wakes up to the sound of American music, shaves with his American razor, eats his McDonald's breakfast, goes to work to use his American computer and copier, and caps his day with an American movie and an ice-cold Bud, the average Japanese consumes a wide variety of American goods and services. In fact, in terms of categories of products, Japanese consume more American goods than Americans consume of Japanese goods."

(from Seiji Hinata, Deputy Consul General of Japan in New York, *Vital Speeches*, LVIII, April 1, 1992, 362).

"PRAISING JAPANESE IN PUBLIC WORKPLACES"

AMERICAN: Mr. Sugimoto, I have noticed that you are doing an excellent job on the assembly line. I hope that the other workers notice how it should be done.

JAPANESE: (He is uneasy). Praise is not necessary. I am only doing my job. (He hopes other Japanese workers do not hear.)

AMERICAN: You are the finest, most excellent, dedicated worker we have ever had at the Jones Corporation.

JAPANESE: (He blushes and nods his head several times, and keeps working.)

AMERICAN: Well, are you going to say "thank you," Mr. Sugimoto or just remain silent?

JAPANESE: Excuse me, Mr. Jones . . . may I take leave for five minutes?

AMERICAN: Sure. (He is annoyed and watches Sugimoto exit). I can't believe how rude some Japanese workers are. They seem to be disturbed by praise and don't answer you . . . just silent.

Analysis: Mr. Jones is unfamiliar with Japanese expectations regarding the communication of praise or compliments. Japanese workers may feel ostracized if singled out for praise. Compliments should be directed at entire work groups or if spoken to an individual, expressed in private. Moreover, Jones appears to be unaware that Japanese will usually refrain from publicly stating that they feel insulted. The other Japanese workers may lose respect for Jones as a result of his publicly voicing pleasure with Sugimoto. Conversely, Sugimoto is equally unprepared for Jones' public praise and appears unaware of how American managers publicly communicate compliments.

CHAPTER 4

Setting Up the Channels for U.S.-Japanese Corporate Communication

MEDIA BRIEFING

"JAPAN AS A REACTIVE NATION-STATE"

". . . the future U.S.-Japan relationship will inevitably deteriorate without greater American and Japanese cooperation and understanding . . . We (Japan) tend to be a very pragmatic, utilitarian people guided by trends. We are less influenced by moral or legalistic principles or absolute values than transient and relative values based on time, place and situation. In this sense we tend to react constantly to the surrounding society and what is considered socially acceptable. If you study the history of modern Japanese foreign policy, you will learn that since the arrival of Perry, Japan has been characterized also as a reactive nation-state, to *gaiatsu* or pressure from abroad . . ."

(from Takashi Uyeno, "Japan's Role in the Changing World Order," *Vital Speeches*, LVIII, 24–5.)

Managerial and business communication between U.S. and Japanese business organizations is an exercise in crossing cultural boundaries and adjusting to unfamiliar behavioral codes. No matter how well prepared, miscommunication and culture shock are inevitable. Yet if American management spends sufficient time and effort to examine relevant Japanese cultural and communicative practices, they can reduce uncertainty and communication apprehension, minimize culture shock, and establish increasingly efficient, trusting and profitable corporate affiliations with Japanese companies.

In this chapter I examine eight interrelated categories of communication issues and practices central to effective U.S.-Japanese corporate communication. Addressed to both individual U.S. expatriates and corporate management, I point toward ways of anticipating relationship and organizational problems with Japanese associates and how to create more fluid channels of communication. My analysis is based upon participant observer data collected while living in Tokyo and training Japanese corporates, as well as a synthesis of relevant literature from both sides of the Pacific.

I. Trust

Communication at multinational and multicultural levels is contingent upon trust. Especially with Japanese, the establishing of empathy, intercultural listening skills, and a knowledge of Japanese corporate protocol are important in overcoming cultural differences. Japanese typically value communication for building trust, in their interpersonal social and business interaction. Oftentimes the "getting-down-to-business," task communication is secondary to the more personalized, interpersonal agenda. The principle of Japanese *ningensei,* for example, places highest priority on "human beingness."[1] Any prospects for business ties are thought to be intertwined in getting to know your partner. Exploratory conversations, small talk, and numerous social encounters and meetings all "target" the human side of business visits, joint ventures, and expatriations.

Japanese strive to find the *honne* or "true intentions" of their Western associates as part of the process of establishing trust. Enroute to these discoveries, Japanese may begin a series of friendly gestures, hostings, and gift giving, silently anticipating that you will reciprocate and join in an ongoing relationship. A benevolent spirit frequently guides the Japanese search for a trusting communication, as it is important for Japanese to discover whether they can establish:

ningensei (a personal, human relationship);
wa (group harmony);
honne (communication of true intentions); and
haragei (gut level communication).[2]

II. Establishing a Clear Communication Infrastructure

In setting up the channels for communication, the creation of mutual trust allows expatriates to explore Japanese personalities within the organizational hierarchy. Building upon an early and growing climate of trust, it is essential to pinpoint the key contact people in the Japanese company (or *keiretsu*).[3]

Care should be taken to locate precisely the appropriate person to communicate with for various alliance issues. Phone and fax contacts, who to speak with to set up meetings—including agenda items for upcoming negotiations—should all be researched and identified. Do not assume that the standard protocols practiced in the U.S. home office will prevail in the Japanese company. Be careful not to aim messages too high or low, as such communication attempts may abruptly violate a long established hierarchy and create silent resentment among Japanese. Especially in the case of expatriations in Japan, U.S. managers should assume some of the intercultural challenge, and not anticipate that the Japanese host corporation will be able to anticipate your questions or moves.

In the course of identifying contacts and establishing who to address for specific purposes, it is advisable that you avoid asking too many questions in public forums. *The negotiating table, for example, is not the place to find out the Japanese "rules" or expectations guiding the communication process.*[4]

There is ample time (hopefully) to investigate the protocol for Japanese style negotiators through recourse to readings, cultural training materials, predeparture training programs and/or *private* questioning directed at other U.S. expatriates or repatriates, and Japanese hosts. Asked in an inquisitive, curious fashion, Japanese corporate hosts are usually impressed that Westerners care enough about cultural issues to want to prevent conflicts. Without prior exploring, it may be almost impossible to isolate the appropriate Japanese to address at a negotiating table, or to interpret what is meant by a senior Japanese negotiator's lengthy silences at a joint venture or contractual meeting. It is a valuable piece of information to learn that this senior official is most likely exercising his power and role through silence, and it is usually not an indication of disapproval.[5]

Another aspect of creating a communication infrastructure is to have your overseas subsidiaries (in Japan) serve as the primary channel for communication with Japanese associates. In some cases, a Japanese based subsidiary may be far more experienced with Japanese style communication systems between organizations, lending valuable assistance and insight to some newly arrived expatriates. Note, however, that there are exceptions; some Japanese companies may require direct contact with U.S. headquarters, necessitating that these channels be open, accessible and *known*.

Another strategic dimension of setting up a communication infrastructure may entail use of a go-between or third party. U.S. corporations and expatriate managers can greatly enhance communications and earn the trust of Japanese partners by locating a company, within Japan, who is competent and experienced in Japanese national and corporate culture. In the Harris-Matsushita corporate relationship, the U.S. company deals directly with Matsushita *and* also communicates through SSS Ltd. As a Tokyo based company, SSS has extensive experience as a representative of Lanier Corporation, a company later acquired by Harris. The introduction of Lanier to Matsushita automatically "warmed" the channels of communication, making Matsushita particularly amenable to Harris and thoroughly impressed with their insight displayed in using Lanier.

Another way of enhancing U.S.-Japanese communication channels is through the trust built and courtesy displayed when informing your Japanese partner of relevant activities with other corporate alliances. For example, when General Motors keeps Fujitsu informed of activities with UK-based ICL or Fanuc of Japan, it surely communicates goodwill. The American player can strengthen the alliance with Japanese via timely, ongoing communication updates and briefings of Fujitsu vis-à-vis negotiations, contracts, expatriations and disputes with mutual alliance partners, such as ICL, United Kingdom. Simply, the channels of communication are open, and vital messages are flowing. And more information generates more empathic corporate listening.

III. Frequency of Communication

Instrumental to both building trust and establishing a communicative infrastructure, "frequent communication" warrants attention as a separate category of U.S.-Japanese corporate management and diplomacy. In addition to expediting communication access via faxes, personal CEO phone lines, cellular phones and home lines (if necessary), frequency of communication is strategic.

U.S. partners can gently examine Japanese interest in senior official involvement in meetings, at regular intervals. The objective is to increase the frequency and contact hours of face-to-face communication between similarly ranking top U.S. and Japanese management. *American companies must be careful, however, to always provide the highest ranking U.S. officials, available, as it may be irreversibly detrimental to send junior or middle management representatives to meet with Japanese seniors;* when in doubt, Japanese status, hierarchy, and corporate roles should guide decision-making regarding the appropriateness of U.S. delegates.[6]

Frequency of meetings, face-to-face, saves wasted efforts on both sides of the Pacific. In a G.M.-Isuzu joint venture, if there is a meeting of a four member management team, the G.M. participant and the three Isuzu counterparts may use their frequent communications to stay abreast and informed. Such exchanges can help avoid needless duplication of efforts, doubts, and uncertainties; and they can be an asset in cross-fertilization.

It is especially productive if the face-to-face frequency is shared by CEOs and chairmen of both Japanese and U.S. partners on a regular basis. Too often senior management is totally engrossed in the initial negotiation phase of an alliance but interest and communication tapers off after contractual agreements are reached. Some consulting firms, such as McKinsey and Company, have found that *a lack of active communication on the part of senior management is pivotal in U.S.-Japanese communication conflicts and overall joint venture failures.*

IV. Cross Fertilization

An oftentimes overlooked facet of setting up channels for U.S.-Japanese communication is in the corporate arena of "cross-fertilization." The essential meeting of U.S. and Japanese senior minds can be paralleled within the lower ranks of the affiliate companies and throughout the organization. In subsidiaries, joint ventures, consortiums, mergers, overseas investments and numerous expatriations, *maximizing* contact between American and Japanese workforces is at the heart of cross-fertilization.[7] A plethora of contact situations between Japanese and American corporations are orchestrated, as an increase in worker, staff, and managerial interaction facilitates communication, reduces cross-cultural fears and uncertainties, helps build foundations for individual and company-wide trust and relationships, and reduces conflict.[8]

Models for successful cross-fertilization can be found in such alliances as Westinghouse-Mitsubishi and Xerox-Fuji. Side-by-side on assembly lines, or sharing large, unobstructed white collar office spaces (devoid of Western styled doors, partitions and privacy), Westinghouse-Mitsubishi and Xerox-Fuji workforces are subjects in a formidable, intercultural laboratory.[9] It is within these cross-fertilization workplaces that Japanese and Americans open up the channels of communication for such post-war innovations as total quality control management, quality circles, just-in-time-production, zero defects, management by walking around (MBWA), theory Z, and work teams.[10] And it is also within these fertile intercultural venues that managerial and engineering innovations are diffused and reinvented.

V. Language Skills

There are serious considerations to take into account when choosing interpreters. English-Japanese interpreters are vital to establishing efficient, trusting, profitable channels of communication—and their strategic role must be closely examined. The most fluid speaker of English and Japanese may have little understanding of Japanese or U.S. business, history, society or culture. This variety of interpreter may be considered more *bilingual* than *bicultural*.[11] In some instances, it may be smart to choose the second or fourth best interpreter and bilingual conversationalist, if s/he is thoroughly experienced in dealing with the Japanese corporate world or has already served in similar capacities within Japan.

The central role of language skills should furthermore be placed within the broader context of intercultural communication. For example, perhaps a Japanese national should be chosen over a bilingual American, as the American may not equal the Japanese's knowledge of culture and the marketplace. Whether utilizing an interpreter as a lower level staff position aiding higher ranking expatriates, or as a top management appointment calling for sophisticated intercultural skills, a Japanese with extensive U.S. experience can be a source of strength for U.S. expatriates.

An interesting intercultural challenge that necessitated delicate judgment calls regarding use of interpreters came up in the General Motors joint venture with Fanuc-Japan (GMF). President Eric Mittlestadt was briefed by an unidentified source, outside of the venture, that "language interpreters could be a source of problems." Mittlestadt realized that virtually all of the English-Japanese interpreters used to date were supplied by Fanuc-Japan. The "source" explained to Mittlestadt that a Japanese national interpreter, chosen by the Japanese partner, would most likely silently side with Fanuc, over General Motors. Why should Mittlestadt expect the Japanese interpreter to tell him everything that Fanuc is saying? It would be an improvement to have GM search for their own interpreters—perhaps a Japanese who has spent extensive time in the U.S. as an expatriate.

Too often, U.S. companies are steeped in ethnocentrism, especially when it comes to the English language. They assume that English is the international tongue, and moreover expect that the translation burden falls with the Japanese affiliate. This is not a wise course of action, as it unwittingly underestimates the importance of the interpreter as a serious link or channel in the communication chain. *Viewing the "interpreter issue" as little more than a footnote or insignificant matter places this power dimension squarely on the Japanese side of the table.*

A second alternative is both difficult and obvious; it requires that Mittlestadt learn Japanese language firsthand as a necessary tool in dealing with Japanese.

VI. Organizational Restructurings

In some cases, intercultural communication between Japanese and U.S. companies is seriously hampered by significantly different organizational structures and bureaucracies.[12] With starkly contrasting organizational charts, rules and chains of command, it is confusing and time consuming to establish effective, efficient channels for U.S.-Japanese communication, or reliably specific points of contact. In the Fuji-Xerox joint venture, it was Fuji who stepped forward, offering to restructure its operations and management, fol-

BICULTURAL

"CORPORATE HIRING POLICIES"

This area has been troublesome to expatriates and joint venture associates. Westerners do not readily appreciate the Japanese "koshinjo," the Japanese use of investigative agencies and practices sometimes utilized during the interviewing process. Japanese in contrast feel that many of the U.S. hiring policies are a bit on the naive side. Isn't it common sense that many employers will give a glowing recommendation for poor employees—anxious to help position them elsewhere? Moreover, aren't many resumes partially works of fiction?

Inasmuch as there is more tolerance of turnover in U.S. corporations, perhaps there is less of a need to understand a potential employee before hiring him/her. Among Japanese, longer term commitments, the nurturing of team work, and group oriented corporations make the company selection process extremely sensitive.

lowing an organizational plan roughly approximating that of Xerox. Conversely, many U.S. based Japanese subsidiaries and joint ventures have had U.S. theory X and scientific management styled manufacturing plants restructured into total quality management and just-in-time organizations, following the Japanese parent's lead.[13]

In particularly troublesome areas of interorganizational behavior such as table negotiations, the indigenous communication processes itself, may be restructured. The tedious and elaborate Fuji decision-making process via *nemawashi* and *ringi*,[14] for example, was the subject of continuous frustration and culture shock to Xerox negotiators. In an effort to create cultural and communicative bridges and improve the channels for corporate communication, Fuji set up meetings with Xerox for the express purpose of *streamlining* and expediting the Japanese approach to negotiating—adjusting it to the U.S. partner's expectations and protocol.[15]

VII. Intercultural Communication Training and Consulting

In recent years, Japanese have exhibited a growing interest in intercultural communication training for doing business with Americans. As a preparatory and supportive measure in setting up the channels of U.S.-Japanese corporate communication, intercultural training allows Japanese to experience Americans, or reasonable facsimilies, in a safe, laboratory situation.[16] During my time spent developing and launching intercultural and predeparture training for Japanese corporations in Tokyo, I attempted to simulate numerous business and managerial communication contacts between Japanese and Americans.[17] Spanning such everyday venues as: communication between assembly lines workers and foremen; top management interaction at negotiating tables, and public speaking situations, I encouraged cross-fertilization through training. I believe that the most profound impact I witnessed in training was through trainee involvement in role playing and acting out short dramatic dialogues between Japanese and Americans, face-to-face.[18] By reading scripted lines, and making blatant culturally based mistakes, both Japanese and Americans are able to mentally and emotionally step into the shoes of conflict, and are forced to find creative, intercultural solutions.

In some joint ventures, such as Mitsubishi-Westinghouse, psychological screening is an early measure employed in determining expatriation candidacy and adaptability to life in Japan (can be administered to expatriates, spouses and entire families). If the test was "passed," U.S. expatriates and families proceeded with mandatory enrollment in an intensive thirteen week course offered through the University of Pittsburgh. The rapid immersion in Japanese culture included intensive training in Japanese language, social, and business communication codes.

Through intercultural training intensives, future Westinghouse expatriates discovered how many shocks awaited them within the Japanese workplace. Compliments and praise need to be directed to entire groups of workers, not individuals. In some Japanese companies it is expected that an overcoat and shoes be removed before passing beyond the corporate lobby (e.g., Japan Victor Corporation, Tokyo). Trainees learned of the close worker spatial arrangements in Japanese companies, forewarning them of "group space," and the low priority given territoriality and privacy. And expatriates witnessed that the close physical proxemics between Japanese workers, and the overall team work and immediacy of the channels of communication, lent itself to Japanese working as a very close knit group. Additionally, the Westinghouse trainees must have been quite surprised to find out that the one-person-per-job work ethic is obsolete in Japan. Stripped of any professional protocol for specialization (e.g., in TQM factories), Japanese rather replace careerism with a loyalty to the company and the mastering of as many jobs and skills as possible.[19]

In the most comprehensive sense, intercultural communication trainers and consultants can also be valuable in setting up contacts, assessing joint venture and expatriation candidacies, and in examining the scope and focus of predeparture training programs. All of the communication channels and dimensions examined in this chapter are fair game for the consultant, as they may be a valuable ally in building bridges, not walls.

VIII. Flexibility in U.S.-Japanese Communication

Especially in international and intercultural alliances, things change. *Flexibility* in U.S.-Japanese corporate communication is a strategic virtue. American partners, negotiators or expatriates must be willing to embrace *more uncertainty* when setting up alliances and building business relationships with Japanese.

Why should U.S. corporations accept more uncertainty and ambiguity? Japanese thrive on levels of uncertainty and ambiguity usually avoided by their U.S. counterparts.[20] Firmly, clearly worded contracts, allowing for little future modification or alterations, are more a product of how U.S. companies communicate agreements and conditions for alliances. *Japanese companies typically avoid overly direct, unambiguous wordings of agreements, as their national and corporate culture find the U.S. jurisprudence style too constricting, and a source of future corporate face-challenges and confrontations.*[21] Flexibility demands that you partially suspend the quest for certitude, and be willing to risk the business venture, in part, on the basis of a trusting relationship and Japanese styled *haragei*, or "communication of the gut."[22]

In an ICL-Fujitsu joint venture, for example, the U.K. firm exercised an extreme flexibility in their agreement with the Japanese, realizing that rigid adherence to the printed, verbal, logical contract would have doomed the alliance. Rather than pointing fingers and breaking the *wa* (group harmony) through a direct face-provoking contractual language, U.S. companies can strive to find ways *around* expressing disappointment or talk about failures, in relation to the Japanese affiliate. *Whenever possible, blame can be shared, and the communication of failures diffused among all affiliates.* Along these lines, a more loosely worded contract, depending primarily upon oral understanding, is the more flexible (and risky) approach. As things change, and specifications aren't met, the indefinite verbal contract allows for continued alterations and modifications. The key here is to recognize that the same indigenous principles of *face (kao)* that guide one-on-one communication in Japanese society, also hold true on the macroscopic, corporate plane. Hence the overly explicit contract will be a predictable source of public confrontations and challenges to face. This should be avoided.

Summary

In summary, this chapter provides a broad framework and "fuel for thought" in attempting to enhance effective communication between American and Japanese corporations. The following behaviors have been recommended:

1. Communicate to establish trust and long term relationships.

2. Establish a clear communication infrastructure by locating contact points or people within the Japanese organization.

3. When communicating with Japanese corporates, respect the hierarchal rules regarding appropriate protocol, and who to address messages to.

4. Identify who serves as spokespersons or listeners at Japanese table negotiations.

5. Do not overlook the power and influence of Japanese use of silence at negotiations or in the workplace.

6. Continually inform Japanese associates of relevant activities with other affiliate organizations.

7. Utilize "go-betweens" or "third party organizations" as means for facilitating smooth channels of communication.

8. Strive to achieve frequent communication between Japanese and U.S. affiliates.

9. Attempt to orchestrate regularly scheduled face-to-face communication between CEOs and senior management of both Japanese and U.S. corporations.

10. Increase communication access and channels of immediacy via frequent use of fax, E-mail, Bitnet, teleconferencing, videophoning, and other electronic communications media.

11. Encourage and implement cross-fertilization as part of a bicultural, companywide effort to nurture and maximize intercorporate communication at all levels of the organizational chart.

12. Carefully examine the importance of bilingual interpreters and choose broadly based bicultural experts, over narrower language specialists.

13. U.S. corporations should consider the advantages of choosing their own interpreter, rather than allowing the Japanese affiliate to do so.

14. Consider the prospects and pragmatics for restructuring the internal organization in order to improve U.S.-Japanese communication channels and message flow. Currently antagonistic organizational structures may hinder communication.

15. Examine the "need" for altering indigenous communication practices in order to expedite communication between Japanese and American partners; for example, Japanese may choose to streamline their decision-making process, and U.S. firms may elect to minimize their confrontational public relations strategies.

16. Utilize intercultural communication trainers and consultants as a means of preparing for business, managerial and workplace interaction between Japanese and Americans.

17. Explore the option of having expatriate candidates and families undergo testing or appropriate assessments to attempt to determine whether they appear to be suitable for lengthy assignments in Japan.

18. Utilize intercultural communication training as in-house laboratories for pinpointing potential cultural shocks and conflicts before they occur.

19. Utilize predeparture training in an effort to reduce the high percentage of premature returns of U.S. expatriates and families assigned to Japan. Make ample use of repatriates who had successful expatriations in Japan.

20. Develop a flexible approach to corporate communication with Japanese.

"VERBAL vs. NONVERBAL COMMUNICATION"

U.S. business communicators engage in verbal agility and the sport of a good showdown featuring command of the adversarial word or phrase. Japanese rather fence via nonverbal communication and exercise true intentions or *honne,* and belly communication (*haragei*) through subtleties of body language.

Only with specialized predeparture training and extensive expatriate experience can Japanese and Americans even begin to crack each other's verbal and nonverbal codes.

"CULTURAL SUPERSTITIONS"

HIDEO: Cultural superstitions can really cause problems for international business.

MULRONEY: No question about it. Heard about the Japanese company that built an office building in the U.S. and they included a thirteenth floor?

HIDEO: What's the problem with a thirteenth floor?

MULRONEY: Sorry. Here we go. I thought everyone knew that the number "thirteen" is unlucky, and we usually don't have thirteenth floors in the U.S.

HIDEO: Is that right? What did the Japanese company do when it learned of the problem?

MULRONEY: It hired someone to renumber the buttons on the elevator, all the thirteen floor offices, and every office and floor above the thirteenth floor, and paid for all of the changes in the stationery, etc., for everyone involved.

HIDEO: That was quite considerate and a lot of work and money for one mistake! But did you hear about the Americans who showed up during the hot Tokyo summer for negotiations with leaders of several Japanese corporations? They showed up wearing WHITE SUITS!

MULRONEY: What's the matter with white suits? It's cooler in hot summer weather and looks rather sharp!

HIDEO: Perhaps it is the height of Western fashion but it conveys and symbolizes DEATH in Japan! And those same American negotiators gave the Japanese presents wrapped in white paper!

MULRONEY: I suppose you never said anything to the Americans about these cultural blunders?

HIDEO:	Of course we did not say anything. I'm only telling you because you've lived in Japan so long and we've known each other for ten years . . .
MULRONEY:	And work for the same company . . . But do you know about walking under ladders and black cats?
HIDEO:	What are you speaking about, my friend?
MULRONEY:	Now, Hideo! No conversation regarding American superstitions is complete without some reference to black cats and ladders! If you "allow" a black cat to cross your pathway while you walk, it is considered bad luck!
HIDEO:	Strange. Why is that so?
MULRONEY:	Lord knows. I don't know. It's just that way . . . maybe it goes back to Salem, and the witches and their black cats . . . the old Salem witch trials.
HIDEO:	Witch trials?
MULRONEY:	That's a whole other story . . . How about the ladders? If you walk UNDER a ladder, on the street, that is also considered bad luck!
HIDEO:	I won't ask why?
MULRONEY:	Good, don't ask. Also, what about when you break a mirror?
HIDEO:	What happens to Americans when they break a mirror?
MULRONEY:	Every American knows! Seven years back luck!!!
HIDEO:	Outrageous superstition! How about switching to bad manners and restaurant and eating etiquette?
MULRONEY:	Switch subject matters? Okay. Shoot.
HIDEO:	I was eating with American negotiators recently and we were eating Chinese food in the Ginza. And the Americans used their chopsticks to reach into the common plates . . . you know, the plates in the center of the table that we were all sharing . . .
MULRONEY:	So what's the problem with that?

HIDEO: My dear, Mr. Mulroney! You must turn your chopsticks around and gather the food with the side that you were holding!

MULRONEY: I didn't know. Did you hear about the Americans who insisted upon pouring beer and sake only for themselves? They didn't pour for other Americans or Japanese present at the restaurant table! Great manners.

HIDEO: How about the story of the American negotiators who insisted upon a decision from Japanese negotiators, immediately! They argued and confronted, and didn't even take into account that the Japanese had to conduct a *ringisho!*

MULRONEY: Maybe they were inexperienced and didn't even know about Japanese decision-making?

HIDEO: Possible . . . but it is not always easy to be open minded in international business situations. Do you agree?

MULRONEY: I think we agree on almost everything today, Mr. Ishida!

HIDEO: I have had a pleasant talk with you again, today, Mr. Mulroney.

MULRONEY: Likewise, Hideo. Goodbye. Enough talk about superstitions and cultural differences for one day . . .

Analysis: The "cultural superstitions" dialogue illustrates the broad range of differences and shocks facing expatriates and joint venture managers and employees. While many U.S. business people take *our* superstitions for granted, they are ill-equipped to understand how Japanese are confused by them. Along these lines, it is vital to identify and perhaps even catalog many of the U.S. and Western superstitions that perplex Japanese: black cats, walking under ladders, thirteenth floors, breaking a mirror, etc. Care should be taken to explain these superstitions to Japanese guests or hosts. And likewise, we Americans are often dumbfounded by customs subscribed to by Japanese and must strive to decipher them.

Inasmuch as we *communicate* through such nonverbal messages as *clothing,* it is essential to recognize the messages "sent" by white suits. This Western message of summer, heat, the Great Gatsby, and country clubs in Long Island, New York, is decoded quite differently by Japanese associates. Rather than sending a summer message of "the good life," white suits generally communicate a message of "death" to Japanese. Several other examples offered in this cultural dialogue should serve notice that the social and business marketplace is a regular "mine field" of cultural shocks. Many U.S. expatriates are not briefed in eating etiquette—for example, pouring drinks for associates and not for yourself; and turning the chopsticks around when dipping into a group plate.

Finally, this dialogue creates a bridge between the social and the business world as it ends by focusing upon contrasting negotiating protocols. Americans, for example, are typically frustrated with Japanese *nemawashi* and *ringisho* procedures—slow and tedious, group consensus building processes utilized behind-the-scenes in negotiating. The point is that, much as Japanese and Americans need to constantly learn and adapt to social and cultural superstitions and etiquette, so must they adjust to business communication practices.

PART II

When in Japan

"THE STREETS OF TOKYO"

JACKSON: It's good to be meeting with you again. Can you tell me some more about Japan? I'm leaving next week. What you told me at the bar several weeks ago really opened my eyes to the cultural differences.

MULRONEY: Be happy to tell you all I can. Maybe I'll start with the trains. Be sure you figure on getting your travelin' done in Tokyo before 12 P.M. cause that's when they shut down.

JACKSON: What are the alternatives after midnight, if I'm drinking with some Japanese business associates?

MULRONEY: Smart question. You can take a cab back home. And that could cost big American dollars. Or you can stay in one of the overnight "businessmen hotels." Some of them are little cubicles that you crawl into and they're equipped with clocks, t.v., radio, just no standing room, kind of like a horizontal closet or coffin . . .

JACKSON: Sounds strange. What about the "love hotels?"

MULRONEY: That's a whole different story. Japanese who want to have, shall we say . . . "liaisons" or discrete relationships check into love hotels. There is usually no check-in counter or desk and you choose from a neon, or lobby "menu" of rooms . . . theme rooms . . . like the "jungle room," the "Las Vegas room," etc. And you check in over a speaker-intercom—with wrong names . . . of course.

JACKSON: Of course . . .

MULRONEY: You might also see people walking around with mouth and face masks.

JACKSON: Tokyo pollution?

MULRONEY: Hardly. They ALL have flus and don't want to spread their germs around.

JACKSON: Pretty damn considerate.

MULRONEY: Oh, before I forget. Have packages of tissues with you, little Kleenex-like vest pocket packages . . . they're a necessity . . . some Japanese restaurants and toilets don't have napkins or toilet paper . . . oh, and never blow your nose in a cloth handkerchief at some business meeting or social gathering!

JACKSON: Now that is bizarre! What are you talking about?

MULRONEY: Japanese consider it very barbaric, unclean, to use and reuse cloth handkerchiefs and put it back in your pocket . . . it ain't worth the cultural wierdness . . . believe me . . . only use paper tissues . . . and if you want to get rid of your old newspapers that accumulate after weeks . . . save them for the man who comes around everyweek . . .

JACKSON: The Japanese "recycle man?"

MULRONEY: No. The swap and recycle man. He trades rolls of toilet paper for old newspapers!

JACKSON: Crazy. A smart system!

MULRONEY: So much to tell you. Do you like great European style coffee?

JACKSON: I'm an espresso and caffeine addict!

MULRONEY: Tokyo is right for you. Forget the tea! They are coffee fanatics. Thousands of terrific coffee shops and cafés, and you can get excellent coffee, cold or heated, from cans, available from vending machines . . . everywhere!

JACKSON: This is outstanding!

MULRONEY: Well, I gotta' run, buddy . . .

JACKSON: You're my mentor, Mulroney. My Asian connection. Can't thank you enough.

MULRONEY: Have fun.

JACKSON: Hope to pick your brain again, before I leave. Ciao.

Analysis: The "Streets of Tokyo" dialogue identifies some of the confusing "messages" awaiting the U.S. expatriate in Tokyo. As the American walks the streets of Tokyo, s/he discovers many unfamiliar sights, ranging from the "love hotels," signs identifying the availability of coffin-sized hotel cubicles, thousands of people wearing paper face masks, an avid use of small tissues, the "recycle man" and the smell of strong espresso coffees.

Of immediate importance is a grasping of those "messages" of concern in business venues, as with time, the expatriate can sort through a myriad of social surprises. Be on guard regarding the versatility and importance of common packs of facial tissues. When at business meetings, it is considered dirty and uncouth to blow your nose in a cloth handkerchief; moreover, paper tissues may have to substitute for napkins within little Japanese local restaurants, and in public bathrooms devoid of toilet paper. If you want toilet paper, get ready to swap your old newspapers for toilet rolls, with the "recycle man." Your neighbors will help you identify him. He's a useful fellow.

"TOKYO TISSUES AND GAIJIN HANDKERCHIEFS"

JULES: I blew it.

JAMES: At the meeting with the Japanese investors?

JULES: Yeah.

JAMES: How did you blow it?

JULES: I blew my nose.

JAMES: Be serious. What went wrong at negotiations?

JULES: I blew my nose and insulted them.

JAMES: What are you talking about?

JULES: When I blew my nose at the table . . . you know I got some kind of flu . . . the Japanese looked at me real strange . . .

JAMES: What went wrong? I don't get it.

JULES: Goldberg took me aside after the meeting, you know he's real experienced with Japanese . . . he said that it's considered barbaric to blow your nose into a handkerchief!

JAMES: You couldn't be serious . . .

JULES: I am. In Japan they only use disposable tissues, never a cloth handkerchief . . . considered unclean . . .

JAMES: What if they don't have tissues at a meeting?

JULES: You supply your own. Seems everyone in Japan carries around these little miniature packs of tissues in their coat pockets . . .

JAMES: Did your blowing affect negotiations?

JULES: Well, if I add another ten infractions, keep breaking these Japanese rules . . . their cultural laws . . . it could add up to some kind of disrespect or insult . . .

JAMES: I wonder what Japanese do use handkerchiefs for . . . wiping their glasses. . . . pocket squares?

Analysis: Simple, taken-for-granted acts, like blowing one's nose, can be a source of cultural clashes between U.S. and Japanese business associates. Nose blowing into a cloth handkerchief sends a negative message to Japanese, quite different from the U.S. perception. Also, note that it is rare that Japanese communicate your "violation" to you. Japanese rather stay quiet and at most express these cultural differences in private, social venues or via subtle nonverbal responses.

    Doing business with Japanese requires a general understanding of cultural codes operating, particularly those rules governing nonverbal behavior. Keep in mind that any bodily movement, gestures and facial expressions, or "acts," such as nose blowing, convey nonverbal messages. Specifically, the dilemma can be resolved by using disposable paper tissues. But on a broader plane, the nose blowing incident can serve as a metaphor or prototype for hundreds of similar "infractions." Be on notice!

CHAPTER 5

Strategic Dimensions of Japanese Social Behavior and Everyday Life

"KEIRETSUS ARE MODERN DAY CARTELS"

... Today I own 26% of a Japanese company called Koito Manufacturing, which supplies the lighting systems for Toyota vehicles ... Instead of welcoming my involvement, Koito has fought me at every turn ... A year-and-a-half ago, I had never heard of the *keiretsu*. Today, as a result of my Koito investment, I'm witnessing firsthand the anti-competitive aspects of corporate Japan's secret weapon ... Because of Japan's anti-competitive cartels, American is being forced to compete in the global economy with one arm tied behind its back ... In short, Japan is refusing to compete fairly with the U.S. by exporting an economic structure condoned in Japan, but outlawed under U.S. anti-trust laws ... Japan must abandon its *keiretsu* business practices before it can become a welcome participant in the global economy. Until that happens, these anti-competitive cartels are a wedge threatening to drive the U.S. and Japanese people apart.

(from T. Boone Pickens, "Foreign Investment in Japan," *Vital Speeches*, LVII, January 1, 1991, 171–172).

I intentionally utilize the term "strategic" in titling this chapter on Japanese social behavior. As Western business visitors and expatriates, much of our survival and success is inseparable from an ability to adapt to everyday Japanese social life. Even the pampered Fortune 500 expatriate will have to face the unexpected, when she partakes outside the confines of a lavishly Westernized Tokyo hotel, such as The New Otani. Many expatriates and families find that they are expected to leave the extremely expensive venues of Western accomodations, dining, and shopping and face the culture shock of daily Japanese existence. Other American visitors are guests at Japanese homes, or must interact, sooner or later, in Japanese social life.

There is ultimately no way of antiseptically separating business and social realities in Japan. *In order to do business with Japanese, it is necessary to somewhat happily and skillfully participate in the "social side" of business.* Especially in corporate Japan, the formalities and restrictive codes operating within the walls of the company make afterhours socializing of great importance. Additionally, functioning in Japan obviously requires an ability to mingle, take trains and cabs, order at restaurants, deal with Japanese crowd behavior, and make sense out of the bewildering array of unfamiliar sights, sounds, and messages. Surely there is no avoiding having to take baths and utilize public toilets, stepping into small, out-of-the-way Japanese restaurants, asking for directions in public places, dealing with the rain, knowing etiquette for slippers and shoes, and becoming familiar with a broad spectrum of social rules.

The following depiction of Japanese social behavior and everyday life primarily draws upon both personal experiences in Japan, and upon my interpretations of same, based upon a background as an intercultural communication researcher and consultant. I rely upon my own encounters as an expatriate in Japan as it allows me to most directly address you, and reveal what I learned firsthand, about Japanese culture. I am strongly of the opinion that a mastery of seemingly trivial, everyday social matters are of direct and dire consequence if the expatriate wants to prevail successfully in business communication with Japanese. The social experience and business performance are two sides of the same coin. Expatriate managers and visiting diplomats and negotiators sorely need briefings on Japanese social behavior and everyday life—as it helps place business within a wider, cultural context.

Welcome to Japanese Social Life: Early Days of an Expatriate

You are well aware that Japanese are group oriented. But are you prepared for Japanese hosts who will oversee your every move, make decisions for you, and generally orchestrate your daily activities and social life in Japan?

Bathing: A Microcosm of U.S.-Japanese Relations

As a business visitor, I was first invited to stay at the home of the senior executive of a Japanese company. During the course of my first few days in Japan, I discovered how my individualized approach to decision-making was being ironically challenged. I was first instructed as to the time of day when I would be taking my bath, and the order of bathing in the family. This came as a mild culture shock. I assumed that I would be free to take a bath or shower whenever I *chose*. I found it hard to think otherwise. Further discussion with my old time Japanese friend of the family (whom I had met in the U.S. and was my contact for this business visit), yielded some of the group oriented ground rules.

To begin with, the senior member of the family (also the company head), told me when I would be taking my bath; this was not an "optional" matter. Also, the fact that I was expected to be the first person to take a bath during the early evening was hardly an accident. This was a firm and non-negotiable "command." I was told by my associate that I should not put up any resistance and needed to comply graciously. To rock the boat would only upset my host and reflect badly upon everyone. My gut level response was to argue and debate the merits of this system and the affront to my dignity as an "individual." But I was assured that this would be a cultural conflict. Was it worth creating a civil war over bathing? For such behavior would have obvious consequences for the business relationship with my corporate host.

At first I privately explained to Yoshi that "I could not take a bath at 7:00 P.M., I was not in the mood, and I can't ever remember, since becoming an adult, having been told that 'I had to take a bath'."

Yoshi was concerned. He articulately and emphatically explained that "in both Japanese homes and companies, there is usually a prescribed order and structure for doing things. If I refused to take the bath, I would be stepping out of line, violating the ordered arrangement, and defying the status and hierarchy chart governing guest and host relationships." He went on to say that "who bathes first, who speaks first at a business introduction or meeting, who sits where, etc., was not a matter of choice or up to egalitarian American methods."

I saw this first dilemma as a pure and simple case of my "ideological rights" as a free thinking individual. Yoshi depicted it as a "stupid American notion," that the individual comes before the family, group, or organization. I was stunned when he also called it "American *selfishness!*" Additionally, I realized that defiance constitutes a disrespect for the host, family and Japanese lineage. And Yoshi warned me that Mr. Sato would "never let me know, publicly, that I had offended him, by not following his invitation and directions, and would most likely internalize his displeasure and remember how I responded." It was what Yoshi called a very "minutia item in my rites of passage, but a test of the *gaijin,* nevertheless." Somehow, the mundane issue of taking a bath seemed to be blown out of proportion; it appeared to take on all the dramatic potential of a full blown international incident based on cultural conflict. During those early days I barely knew of the subtle issues of "face" (*kao*) resting upon my compliance. If I did not comply, I would be forcing a face-threatening or face-provoking situation, as Mr. Sato would have to struggle with this problem.

After considering the trying cultural challenges of U.S.-Japanese world diplomacy, all embodied in my first showdown, I reluctantly complied. I forced a smile, was given a pair of slippers and a robe, and proceeded to experience my very first Japanese bath, here in the outskirts of Nagoya, Japan. I looked around the room for a shower option. There wasn't a shower or hose in sight. I faced a deep, small tub, and was about to climb in when I was abruptly stopped by my bicultural friend (he was from Tokyo and was also staying at the house). Yoshi warned me with a tone of urgency that the bathtub was only for soaking—after I was finished lathering and cleaning myself. He quickly went through the ABCs of Japanese bathing, showing me how to utilize the entire room as a site for cleaning. I noticed that the entire room, housing the tub, had wooden boards across the floor, with a drain at the center. I further noticed that the toilet was in a separate room.

Yoshi told me to lather down with the soap and washclothes, while standing or seated upon a little stool, outside the tub. The water supply was secured by dipping plastic bowls into the hot tub, as I needed it, pouring it over my lathered body. Once completely clean, I was then to proceed into the tub.

I was genuinely surprised by this bathing etiquette and noticed every little nuance and detail. There was no hot and cold water faucet. Only a dial controlling the gas or electric heating of the water in the tub. The tub temperature was extremely hot, and when I entered, I screamed my very first "hot water scream" in Japan. This was to be echoed many times over the next year.

I was impressed by the depth of the tub, as it appeared two or three times as deep as the average U.S. bathtub. And, as I later learned, bathing is viewed as more than a quick, abrupt necessity in Japan. It is seen as a daily pleasure of life—to be savored and enjoyed . . . like good food . . . drink . . . and relationships.

A Few Words about the Organizational Implications of Japanese Toilets

Later questioning of Yoshi revealed that the separation of the toilet and bathing functions was hardly coincidental. Throughout Japan, the two are separated as the cleaning and toilet venues are thought better segregated. Reflection upon this resulted in the first of many discoveries regarding sound reasoning behind seemingly strange Japanese conventions. In some cases, there was no denying that Japanese innovations and etiquette was superior to what I was accustomed to. For example, I was amazed at the eloquent Japanese ingenuity in the cycling of water in Western styled toilets (traditional Japanese toilets are floor level—cut into the floor). When you flush the chain, the water first comes out of a fountain or faucet as clear water. After you have a chance to wash your hands, then the water is recycled through the toilet.

It struck me that this minimizing of waste, and maximizing of the water supply, was an insight into Japanese total quality control management. Cornerstones of this U.S.-Japanese managerial hybrid are the reductions of waste, excess, and unevenness.[1] I saw the groundwork for eliminating aspects of waste and excess in the Japanese reinvention of the toilet. I was now on notice that the workings of everyday Japanese social life could yield insights into Japanese business, management, and organizational behavior. For there is no question that Japanese business is pregnant with the indigenous, national culture.

Country Club Bathing with a Corporate Host

Several weeks later my knowledge and comfort with Japanese style bathing was further tested. My corporate host invited me to dine, golf, and bathe with him at his country club. Of course there was no option of turning down this "invitation." The most difficult part of the visit was bathing as the only *gaijin* at a huge country club bath, populated only by extremely curious Japanese males. In typical fashion, we first lathered, cleaned ourselves, and then were free to meander about in what appeared to be an almost Olympic size bath, shared by many men.

Once naked, I discovered a version of "naked culture shock." Although I have certainly examined my nude body, I was not used to thinking of myself as a 6'2" spectacle among smaller, Japanese men. Several men walked up to me at different points during the bathing session. One man opened a conversation about the "size of my body," and how "Japanese bodies and bodily parts were smaller than Americans'." Another man closely analyzed the hair on my chest, finding the hairy American male's chest to be strange and "like a beast." Mr. Sato seemed to discretely enjoy my discomfort, as he carefully decoded my responses, emotional reactions, verbal and nonverbal replies. He offered little, if any explanation, of his behavior, what went on at the bath, and why he was entertained.

Some months later I continued to think this through. I realized that public bathing was a time for Japanese to be candid, unwind, and to probe for the person behind the social mask. In an indirect fashion I believe that my corporate host was looking for aspects of my *"haragei,"*[2] or the "language of the gut" I displayed in an obviously strange, uncomfortable situation. He was well aware of the clash of cultures, but was most interested in how I stood up to social pressure, uncertainty, and the Japanese propensity to "move in" and innocently "violate" my Americanized notions of privacy.

Most of all, the host hoped to gain some subtle insight into what was "in my stomach" (*haragei*) and "who I was," divorced from clothes, status, superficial words and conversations (*tatemae*) and the trappings of business life. With hindsight, I would rate myself

MEDIA BRIEFING

"JAPANESE WOMEN"

In Japan a few women work in the elite, but most still work for it, many of them as office ladies, O.L.s, the ubiquitous, chirpy-cute tea-servers. On TV commercials and in service jobs the Japanese woman is Helium Voice: a baby talking child-mother who speaks in a piping squeak that one would have thought unattainable without a surgeon's help. Many Japanese women instinctively cup the hand over the mouth when smiling, so as not to show teeth: the Japanese veil . . .

(from Jonathan Rauch, *The Outnation: A Search for the Soul of Japan*, Boston, MA: Harvard Business School Press, 1992, 66.)

as scoring a "B" on a "cultural adaptation scale," if there was such a measurement—or if grades were applicable. Although emotionally threatened by some fairly lewd and bizarre statements directed at my nude body, I maintained a levelheadedness and recognized that the club members were just gawking at a foreigner's form. To them, it was child's play, and the venue was such that it was permissible to be playful and childlike in their curiosity. The same gentlemen would have shown very great reserve and constraint in a corporate setting—a lesson I was in the process of learning.

You Gotta' Have "Wa": Baseball and Competition

Mr. Sato seemed to cherish those hours we spent together at the country club. While on the golf course he appeared to take great pride in the fact that he was accompanying a *gaijin* in the presence of his business and social friends. He made several references to the importance of "internationalizing," and why Japanese have to think global, learn English, and not be provincial. He offered that he was one of the first businessmen in Nagoya to require that his middle managers all receive in-house language and intercultural training

"JAPANESE HAVE STEREOTYPED IDEAS ABOUT PHYSICAL CHARACTERISTICS OF WESTERNERS"

. . . The Japanese have certain stereotyped ideas about the physical characteristics of Westerners, and these ideas are shown in their popular culture. When a Westerner is drawn in a cartoon, he or she has a huge, pointed nose and is very large, compared with a Japanese in the same cartoon. When a Western woman is drawn, she is likely to have a huge bust—showing the artist has implicitly accepted the Western idea of an attractive woman through exaggeration. At the same time, these drawings project the Japanese ideal in men and women . . .

(from Michio Kitahara, *Children of the Sun: The Japanese and the Outside World*, Sandate, Fokestone, Kent, England: Paul Norbury Publications, 1989, 118–119.)

for doing business with Westerners. Meanwhile, I was happy to serve as his international link on the golf course, a temporary bridge to the U.S.A.

On the golf course, Mr. Sato's *honne* (true intentions) seemed to be thinly veiled by his friendly conversational style. Below the surface talk (*tatemae*), Sato san was probing for my sense of "competition." I played along. After the near fiasco over bathing, polite *tatemae* wasn't that challenging—or so it appeared.

Mr. Sato was very skilled at *tatemae*, however. He presented hypothetical situations to me, mostly taking place on an international baseball field. I listened to his accounts of the "Randy Bass" phenomenon, and endless talk about the great strength of "Cecil Fielder." What I suspected Sato san was "up to," was my feelings about American baseball players breaking longheld Japanese records for achievement. He was surprised to learn that I considered it unfair for Japanese pitchers to "refuse to pitch" to American sluggers who were threatening the all-time Japanese single season, homerun record.

When it came to sports, Mr. Sato was an ultra-nationalist. He believed that Japanese records should be protected against *gaijin* invasions. Despite efforts to control my thoroughly Western orientation to "debate and argue," I did get somewhat argumentative when we discussed the "noble, Japanese reasons behind the manager's benching of an American ballplayer who threatened a record."

Sato san explained that the Japanese essential of *wa* or "group spirit" was at issue. It could be a source of "injury" to the team and to Japanese national pride, if a foreigner could displace a Japanese homeboy in the record books. Any measures were justified, he argued (with a smile). I just could not tolerate his line of reasoning.

As we walked across the green, Mr. Sato then wanted to know my thoughts about American aggression on the baseball field. He referred to an American batter who recently had attacked a Japanese pitcher, after being hit on the body by a pitched ball. "Wasn't this barbaric" . . . he asked? After responding that "it happens all the time in American baseball," Sato san said that this behavior distressed both sports audiences and Japanese corporate leaders. He told me that "Americans shouldn't fight so much, get all steamed up in public, and lose their composure; this is immature behavior and is not good for joint relations."

I had an interesting reaction, one for which he was unprepared. I offered that it was a sad reflection upon Japanese, as well. Wasn't it time for Japanese to finally realize that Americans *are* more aggressive and face-threatening than Japanese? Why keep rediscovering the wheel? Wasn't it just the nationalistic Japanese press, combined with ethnocentrism, collectively sensationalizing Western-styled behavior on the baseball field or negotiating table?

Mr. Sato did not disagree. He changed the subject to the fact that Japan was not easily understood by non-Japanese (the *nihonjinron syndrome*) and that the *wa* of Japanese baseball and management eluded most Americans. He "wished it wasn't so" and "thought it sad that Americans couldn't adapt a little better while on Japanese soil. Everyone for himself is the death of American business and baseball, don't you think?" . . . he asserted. "How can you American managers ever get team work in your factories and companies if you can't even find *wa* in baseball? Only Davie Johnson, the Mets manager, understands *wa*. You know why? He lived in Japan and was with Japanese baseball!"

We soon ran out of baseball, cultural, management, and nationalism stories. An unbearable silence came over the afternoon. Sato san seemed so comfortable with this silence. My mind worked like a computer, and I was a bit stressed out over the lack of words. I flipped through my inner dialogue and research regarding the Japanese reverence for silence. I desperately tried to calm my emotional upheaval, especially following the "sports conversation." I thought, "maybe this is the calm after the storm."

The Failure of my Japanese Hosts

On the second or third morning of my stay with the Japanese corporate host and family, I was abruptly awakened by Mr. Sato's wife. She gave a faint knock or two on my bedroom door and immediately walked to the foot of the bed at a brisk pace.

She told me that we would be going out to breakfast in about half an hour. I rolled over, semi-conscious, and muttered that "I drank too much last night" and would not be able to join them.

After she left the room, my friend, Yoshi, quickly joined me at the bed and warned me that I "could not turn down the invitation." I was still very much asleep and did not heed him.

Some hours later, after the family returned from breakfast, I was up and about, and was amusing myself. Mrs. Sato then sent a message to me via the go-between, Yoshi (I immediately thought of the parallel "go-betweens" in Japanese organizations). He explained that Mrs. Sato was very ashamed of having been a "poor host," and she wanted to invite me to a special Kobe beef lunch that she would be fixing at home. I, of course, accepted. I was extremely interested in sampling the expensive, world renown Japanese beef.

Further discussions with Yoshi explained some of the intercultural undercurrents of the morning's events. Since I did not go along with the group to breakfast, I had gravely violated the social code. Mr. Sato was now secretly upset with me and "wondered about my ability to be a team player." Yoshi only offered that everyone knew that I was undergoing adjustment problems and probably did not "mean to be so rude." I then thought back to the discussions I had with Sato san, at the golf course. Perhaps he had been using baseball as a metaphor, instructing me to be a team player?

But I was still confused over the reaction of Mrs. Sato. Why the Kobe beef invitation after my rude behavior? Yoshi explained that since I had "responded badly" and adversely affected the *wa* or group harmony, that it was the Japanese way to interpret this as a "failure on the part of the host." Accordingly, Mrs. Sato wanted to save face as a host, and graciously bring me back into the fold by this gesture.

Still in my first few days of expatriation, I was further baffled. Why doesn't she just come out and say what is on her mind? Maybe some apologies were in order? Yoshi offered that there was no "direct" recourse for Mama san. She was being "typically Japanese" by trying to bring about a good group spirit (wa) through indirect means. I found out that it was not the "Japanese way" to call attention to such infractions of social etiquette. Learning by my mistakes, I was particularly nice to Mrs. Sato and the whole family, and repeatedly expressed my appreciation during the Kobe steak dinner. I realized that by not going along with the group plans I had precipitated an "incident."

I was not through with my cultural surprises for the day, however. I was having a little trouble comprehending the loud, slurping sound made by everyone at the table. It sounded pretty crude. They were slurping their soup. A whispered huddle with Yoshi uncovered that this was a way of "showing appreciation" for the soup, and telling the cook that it is "delicious." It was another expression of individual and group approval and team spirit. It was a "collective soup."

MEDIA BRIEFING

"OPINION SURVEYS SOLICIT WHAT WEST THINKS ABOUT JAPAN"

. . . The Japanese government regularly conducts opinion surveys in the West, in order to find out what the West thinks about Japan . . .

(from Michio Kitahara, *Children of the Sun: The Japanese and the Outside World*, Sandgate, Folkestone, Kent, England: Paul Norbury Publications, 1989, 120.)

Although the more important issue, of my not going along to breakfast with the family, did not make much sense from an American perspective, I gradually learned to appreciate the farther social reaches of Japanese use of "team work" in the workplace. Whether in the family or the villages of old, Japanese closely monitor their behavior to achieve a fragile social balance. This balancing act is always in progress, requiring that individual and group motivations be in harmony, oftentimes at the expense of the private, personal agenda.

On Japanese Walls and Doors: Beyond Personal Space

It took several months to begin to fully fathom and digest the cultural blunders and contrasting American and Japanese expectations surrounding Mrs. Sato's invitation to breakfast. Her brief knocking on my bedroom door, and brisk, immediate walk toward my sleeping body, emerged as one of the central and extended cultural metaphors of my expatriation in Japan. It eventually was a source of direct insight into the culture shock I experienced in confronting Japanese organizational proxemics.

Mrs. Sato's knock on the door and subsequent entrance, without any attention paid to my response (i.e., "come in" or "just a moment, please"), was not unusual. It was in fact, typical Japanese behavior. Simply, there is little thought given to the "sanctity" of personal space in the Japanese home or company. Mirroring the social relationships and proxemic behavior of the Japanese home and everyday life, the Japanese company does *not* take its doors and walls seriously. This is further evident in the Japanese use of sliding doors and paper thin, *shoji* screens, as fixtures in the Japanese home. Movable, semi-transparent room dividers are not constructed for the creation of separate, compartmentalized, segregated and personalized space. Group space takes priority over personal territories. Much as Mrs. Sato "barged" in on me (from my virgin, newly expatriated, U.S. perspective), so do numerous Japanese managers "violate" our Western expectations regarding personal offices or privacy. Fully anticipate that Japanese associates will innocently waltz into your space or office (if you are among the very few in Japan with a private office), without a knock, warning, or thought of your expectation of privacy.

The groupism in the Sato family of Nagoya was further reiterated in the spatial arrangements of the Sato owned company. The office workers did not have their own private offices and were all positioned within a large, unobstructed room of identical desks. No walls, doors, or partitions separated them. And Mr. Sato constantly engaged himself in "managing by walking around" (MBWA), unaware that this constant face-to-face communication between managers and coworkers was a recently acknowledged technique of participatory, "theory Y" and "theory Z" styled management.[3] To Mr. Sato, "walking around" was the normal and natural thing to do, and Japanese always shared their work and home space. Why should Sato san even dream of separating himself from his staff?

Predisposed by thousands of years of shared history, and a lineage of family life, and conditioned by crowd behavior and the severe space limitations of the island nation, Japanese are surprised by the Western reliance upon partitions and spatial dividers. *Japanese function well without the territorial imperative mandated by the majority of U.S. national and corporate culture.* As depicted by Edward T. Hall, the Japanese are a "high context culture," sharing much more in common than their "low context" Western counterparts.[4] And foremost in the "sharing" context is the elbow-to-elbow crowd and spatial arrangement.

In sorting through these thoughts I considered whether all or most meetings of cultural strangers, such as Japanese and Americans, were necessarily "low context." In other words, if we are relatively unfamiliar with each other's business and social protocol, or overall cultural history, then it stands to reason that we have little in common. We do not share cultural context. But this is slowly changing. In the information age, a global village populated by numerous U.S.-Japanese joint ventures, we are gradually building a shared culture and history. Until then, we must continue to struggle with deciphering "alien" cultural and communicative standards in daily social and business life.

It is a mission requiring that Americans be willing to strip down the doors, walls, and partitions separating our national, political and corporate cultures. And it is a challenge requiring Japanese to reciprocate, by allowing Americans to more freely experience and participate in their partitionless, group space.

At the Japanese Dinner Table: Social Chat
Regarding U.S. Competitiveness

In the midst of early adaptation struggles, and the continuing tremors of culture shock,[5] I found that the Sato dinner table frequently was the site of lighthearted chat regarding U.S.-Japanese

MEDIA BRIEFING

"JAPANESE INDIVIDUALISM"

. . . The Japanese are no more alike than you and I are. Again and again I met people, including many who spoke no English, with whom I felt more in common than I do with many Americans I meet. I found no fundamental similarity, no template, no recipe for Japaneseness. The closest thing to such a recipe, perhaps, is the general belief that one exists: the belief that somehow *wareware nihonjin*, "we Japanese," are all alike and the willingness to act as though this were true . . . Undeniably you do see fewer outward signs of human diversity in Japanese society than in American society, but that is an artifice, a strategy. The myth of homogeneity isn't substantially true, in any nontrivial way, but it is behaviorally true, insofar as it shapes expectations and pretense. Why do people work so hard to preserve it? In order to cope with the most basic of all social problems: the problem of conflict.

(from Jonathan Rauch, *The Outnation: A Search for the Soul of Japan,* Boston, MA: Harvard Business School Press, 1992, 45–6.)

relations. Although the Satos did have a daughter who had spent time in a U.S. university, they only knew of America through some of her stories, the talk of friends, and the programming of Japanese media. I was their source of information and also served as an American "ear" for their cultural curiosity.

Several of the dinner talks remain etched in my memory, particulary those surrounding the typically negative Japanese predisposition toward American products. Generally speaking, the family, especially Mr. Sato, believed that American products were not very suitable for Japanese consumers, and American management, marketing experts, and other professionals were largely oblivious or ignorant of Japanese homes and everyday life.

On the subject matter of "refrigerators," Mr. Sato expressed some strong opinions, largely "disguised" in a kind of "polite irreverance." On at least two occasions over the course of approximately three weeks, he brought up the "entrance of advanced U.S. refrigerators into the backward Japanese kitchens of the 1950s." Just the very "thought" of this subject matter made him roar with laughter. As I recall, he prefaced the story by explaining in fine detail how Japanese kitchens are very small, but very functional. He pontificated about the careful use of Japanese space throughout homes and companies—as space is always at a premium. Pointing around the combination living and dining room in which we were seated, he explained how Japanese were "clever" in their use of space, and "Japanese ingenuity" made it possible to move furniture about, have dual purpose rooms, and not "waste" space like the Americans.

The refrigerators that the Americans exported to Japan, were in Mr. Sato's words, "dinosaurs" and "monstrosities" that should have "stayed in Texas." I wondered whether I was privy to a real-life example of Japanese ethnocentrism. He continued, saying that "the big, pig refrigerators couldn't even fit into the doorway of the Japanese home, so we had to trash it before it could be used." This talk served as the source of a big, Papa san belly laugh. "When you could get the dinosaur into a kitchen, it would hum and make monster noises, right by our eardrums!" Evidently, the refrigerators were built to U.S. specifications, U.S. engineers did not take into account the dimensions of Japanese homes, and also ignored the fact that many Japanese sleep, floor level, on bedding only a few feet away from the kitchen. The roar of the close-to-the-floor motor scared the Japanese children, and kept entire families awake. Although I did not have any case studies or data surrounding this marketing fiasco, the Sato story was echoed around the streets of Tokyo, a familiar narrative regarding the roots of lack of U.S. competitiveness.

In prejudicial, nationalistic tones, Sato frequently utilized a particularly objectionable phrase, epitomizing his view of America as a "has been." He served up the phrase, "the wounded White Elephant," with great pride. Sato san depicted the U.S. as the great power, who was now mortally, tragically injured. In contrast, he spoke of Japan's "great ability to adapt" and create products that "fit the specific lives of specific people, anywhere in the world." Sato called Japan an "octopus." The octopus gathers information and resources from everywhere, mixes it together, synthesizes data, and produces a highly Japanese styled combination.

Heating and Air Conditioning

Since it was winter, the chill of the wet Japanese weather filled the Sato home. I noticed as we sat around during one of our dinners

MEDIA BRIEFING

"TV—MOST POWERFUL JAPANESE MEDIUM—FEATURES AMERICAN CULTURE AND OPINIONS"

.....TV in Japan, like the rest of the industrialized world today, is undoubtedly the most influential medium of mass communication, and identification with the West, especially American culture, is consistently seen on TV. For example, if a Japanese soap opera involves a romance between a Westerner and a Japanese, the viewers' response is invariably favorable. There is also a clear tendency to get Westerners to appear on TV and offer their comments and opinions on "things Japanese," such as customs, mishaps, accidents, political scandals, educational systems, and almost anything that is a topical issue of debate. . . .

(from Michio Kitahara, *Children of the Sun: The Japanese and the Outside World*, Sandate, Fokestone, Kent, England: Paul Norbury Publications, 1989, 120.)

that there were was no central heating in the house. One night, I diverted the conversation to the subject of the heating "system," wondering whether their heating was the norm. I found out that the archaic, individual heaters (usually gas generated, sometimes electric), were widely used. Yoshi explained that the Japanese heating system was "connected to how Japanese think about things." The Japanese approach is to avoid the excess and waste of heating an entire room, apartment, home or company, and to concentrate more upon where people congregate. Smaller space heaters warmed up segments of rooms, rather than the entire space. And as we sat, floor level, at the beautiful cherrywood table, our feet dangled into a cutout pit or space below, designed to heat our shoeless feet, only covered in socks.

About a year later, I recognized that the same principle of avoiding excess and waste was used by Japanese hotels. When staying in a businessman's hotel in Tokyo, the Maruko Inn, I immediately felt the coolness of my air conditioned room in contrast to the extreme heat in the hallways. The humidity of late July and August was alive and well in the corridors, and I made haste to get back into a stream of cool air, wherever it could be found. I recognized that the economy of this heating and cooling system *was* a reflection of Japanese mind, and Japanese total quality management—in everyday and organizational life. Clearly, it was another manifestation of the double cycling of water in Japanese toilets.

While the lack of air conditioning in the hallways was not the most comfortable policy, the "mind" behind this practice deserved respect. There is method and reason behind the policy makers, innovators and engineers, and it is a logic that seemed to emerge from the depths of Japanese national culture.

Newspapers for Toilet Paper

Looking out the Sato window I spied what appeared to be some version of an American "junkman." He was yelling out in Japanese, "paperman, paperman," or something like that. I wanted to know what he was all about.

He had piles of old newspapers on his truck, and he roamed through the neighborhood, on prescribed days and times, picking up the old papers. And there was much to gather. The Japanese are voracious readers, consuming more newspapers, magazines, *manga*[6] (comic books), and reading material, than any other people on earth (per capita).

Mrs. Sato had her bundles of newspapers and other printed matter all neatly prepared and bound by string. I followed her out the door, helped with some of the bundles, and then there was the "surprise." Apparently, there is a system whereby Japanese exchange their old newspapers for rolls of toilet tissue.

Trained to synthesize ideas, research, and cultural data, I automatically rethought the Japanese propensity for recycling, and avoiding excess and waste. I briefly contemplated how this system of bartering and exchange also shed some insight into the total quality management practices so celebrated in Japan, and publicized in the West. Somehow, Japanese *structure in* relationships between people and make it natural to recycle. There is an instant reward and a pragmatic, tangible reason for complying with the recycling of old newspapers. The light at the end of the Japanese social tunnel was, in this case, the toilet tissue. I questioned whether this widespread and successful Japanese method held implications for the West. Or was I just fishing for connections between everyday life and the greater issues facing corporates and environmentalists?

Japanese Crowd Behavior

I first ventured out into the jungle of downtown Tokyo at the infamous *Shinjuku* Station. After a civilized lunch at a French restaurant, owned by a Japanese chef who had studied in Paris, I was accompanied to *Shinjuku,* via the *"Odaku* line" subway train. Once we arrived at *Shinjuku,* we agreed to proceed in separate directions. Equipped with a color coded, English language description of the Japanese train system, I was suddenly on my own. Yoshi wished me the "best of luck."

In a real sense, this first solo train experience was a "setup." My official role in the Japanese company was that of a cross-cultural communication trainer and consultant for Japanese business people and managers. I was expected to travel daily to on-site locations for corporate training, requiring extensive train travelling, and some taxicab transportation after arriving at the appropriate train station. After having the luxury of native, corporate escorts, I was finally "cut loose," and expected to do what any Japanese child was capable of—ride the subway trains and find my way around the endless maze of Tokyo.

I found the train system to be remarkably clean, efficient, and most of all, crowded. To have a theoretical notion of "crowd behavior" is hardly what Japanese crowd behavior is all about. I was surprised, indignant, shocked and confused by the Japanese crowds. Beyond the staggering numbers of bodies and the crowded conditions of the trains, I was completely unprepared for Japanese rudeness. Mr. Sato never even hinted at this darker side of Japanese social behavior.

Something didn't add up. Everything I had experienced to date indicated extreme degrees of Japanese politeness. Everyone at my corporation and other companies I visited were extraordinarily considerate, with the most refined of manners. Yet within a crowded train and station I was witnessing a barbaric, savage onslaught that surely contradicted everything I thought I knew about Japanese.

I was pushed, shoved, stepped upon, elbowed, and jockeyed out of seats and standing positions on the trains. During the first few weeks of riding trains, I was very agitated when I was repeatedly shoved by a Japanese salaryman one crowded evening. I finally shoved back with all my force, making a spectacle of myself. Luckily, this did not result in an "incident," and somehow blew over. For a moment, I had lost all composure, the crowded conditions and the rudeness of the Japanese masses was all epitomized in the outrageous pushing of this one man. I literally "cracked" and was ready to "fight back."

Several weeks later I interpreted what I was experiencing. In the walls of my company I was "one of the team," a *gaijin* who had been invited into the group. On business time, all insiders were expected to act in only the most civilized way. Any rude behavior was to be reserved for special afterhour drinking holes or prescribed social venues. But when engaged in a crowded train stations, I was in the midst of an endless sea of "strangers." Since we didn't know one another, we were passing ships in the night, it was all right to push and shove.

This was my first personal revelation surrounding what *gaijin* like to depict as the double standards, contradictions, and hypocrisy of Japanese social and business relations. In actuality, two contrasting social and communicative codes govern behavior among "outsiders" and "insiders." Only insiders, persons immediately relevant to your group, family, organization or realm of personal experience warrant the full tilt treatment of Japanese pomp and circumstance, and civility and politeness.

It gets very trying when you are shoved by a fellow worker who does not realize that he is in a neighboring department of your company. Later that day, in the capacity of a co-worker, he would certainly give you all the respect accorded your status and rank, and then later shove you through a plate glass window—if he failed to recognize you.

It is vital to prepare for these seeming "contradictions" and to not expect Japanese social behavior to follow the dictates of Western style logic. Consistent behavior is hardly a given in Japanese culture, as appropriate social action is largely determined by who you are in relation to the actor and a highly situational code of etiquette and ethics.

Still unadjusted to Japanese crowd behavior, I arrived at some of my early corporate training assignments, thoroughly disoriented, hot and angry. My social and cultural ineptness out in the everyday world of Japan was having a negative impact on my professional performance. Not having an option of taking taxicabs for long distances (it can cost hundreds of dollars), I braced myself for adaptation and adjustment to Japanese crowds. I carefully observed the behavior of Japanese locals who appeared to be experts at gaining seats or more comfortable positions within the crowded trains. I calculated how to position myself for entrance and exits. I learned how to create a cocoon of privacy, reading many novels or doing business related work while spending hours on the trains. I became an expert at cushioning the impact of the train warriors. And most of all, I slowly turned the cultural shock around, and shed the skin of the outraged, *gaijin* victim, and took on the silent realm of the curious, Western social anthropologist. I jotted down notes (space permitting) regarding Japanese nonverbal behavior, gestures, facial expression, interaction with strangers, rudeness, and chivalry. And I remembered that this was supposed to be a memorable experience, not an intercultural nightmare.

I began to enjoy the Japanese cuisine offered at the train stations: the bento boxes, sushi sets, confections, and local foodstuffs. And I always found a copy of the English language newspapers, *The Japan Times* and *The Asahi Shimbun*. I noticed that the salarymen

BICULTURAL

"BUSINESS COMMUNICATION: ACHIEVEMENT vs. SENIORITY"

This delicate arena concerns many U.S. and Japanese expatriates and joint venture associates. Centered about "seniority," the Japanese organization is not favorably predisposed to the young U.S. CEO who arrives in Tokyo and outranks Japanese who are his chronological and organizational seniors. Conversely, American and European expatriates are frustrated at the lack of Japanese management's recognition of achievement.

This strategic difference must be worked out on a case-by-case basis by U.S. and Japanese joint venture candidates and partners. A great deal of this responsibility should fall on the shoulders of both Japanese and U.S. human resource departments and managers.

and women are avid readers. They always seemed to have a newspaper, magazine, or *manga* in their hands.

In the early A.M. hours, the salarymen most often read the respectable morning editions of *The Asahi Shimbun,* or *The Yomiuri Shimbun,* the largest circulated paper in the free world. But during the later P.M. hours, the same men, now showing wear and tear, typically turned from the very high quality newsreporting (by anonymous journalists/unnamed to subsume "individual journalists" within the fold of the organization or group) of the *Asahi* or *Yomiuri* to the sexually explicit, sensationalistic *Nikkan Gendai.* I interpreted this as "two sides of the Japanese character," as the A.M. newspaper served the *omote* or "front door" needs of the salaryman; the tabloids, complete with ongoing escapades of individual "sexual organs," hard-core pornographic serials, and photos of the *yakuza* (Japanese mafia), and actresses and corporate leaders entering or emerging from *love hotels*—served the *ura,* or "back door" appetite.

In talks with Japanese, I found out that this broad, dichotomous appetite for all sorts of information is the norm. Japanese have less of a tendency to get "hung up" with having to choose sides, deciding whether one is prone toward the "good life" or a life of pornography and smut. There is a place and a time for both sides of Japanese needs and behaviors.

Specifically, I overcame my train and travelling obstacles, one-by-one. After a few weeks, I was no longer shocked by well dressed Japanese salarymen reading what appeared to be purely pornographic material. I just wondered whether there was any correlation established in Japan between the moonlighting, corporate, pornographic enthusiasts, and an incidence of rape or violence. But a brief examination of statistics revealed a very low rate, compared to the U.S.!

My more pedestrian frustration with Japanese, floor level toilets, was slowly overturned. After some terrible experiences (including dropping my passport, wallet and papers into the toilet water during my first night in Tokyo), I became fairly comfortable getting into the crouching position. It also became increasingly apparent that there was some logic behind the floor level toilet, as users did not make direct skin contact—making it more sanitary.

Other arenas of culture shock were slower in overturning. Usually being in a rush to leave my house, I would oftentimes crash my head on the low Japanese doorways. The impact was at times almost frightening. It added to the overall discomfort en route to another two to three hour train ride. Eventually, and it took many,

MEDIA BRIEFING

"PINK INDUSTRY AND FLOATING WORLD PROVIDE SAFETY VALVE FOR JAPAN INC."

. . . . .Although prostitution is technically illegal in Japan, the "pink industry" as it is known, thrives in all its myriad forms in Kabuki-cho. There are clubs with booths where women fondle the customers and "soaplands," where men get a good scrub and other services . . .
. . . . .Kabukicho is the successor to the famous old pleasure quarters of Tokyo—once known dreamily as the "floating world"—that have been an integral part of life here for hundreds of years. In the eyes of some, it is no less essential today, providing a safety valve for the white-collared minions in the pressure-cooker known as Japan Inc. . . .

(from James Sterngold, "Dark Days for Those Who Live for Night," *The New York Times*, October 22, 1993, A4.)

many months, I learned to minimize my cursing of ethnocentric Japanese architects and builders and automatically ducked to clear the head of a 6'2" frame.

And on the old walkways of Umagowka, enroute to the station, I became increasingly accustomed to terribly narrow streets. I could not at first comprehend how two large trucks could pass one another down the narrowest of streets, with a clearance of three or four inches. I became tolerant of the bicycles riding within a couple of inches of my legs and feet, and could finally hold a conversation with locals, conversing over directions, food, change, and other necessities.

The Social Side of Business Relations

Whether a guest at a corporate host's home, learning how to bathe Japanese style, or experiencing Japanese crowd behavior, social life necessarily impinges upon and impacts business relations.

This is particulary evident when the American expatriate realizes that a significant part of survival depends upon an ability to switch between business and social behavior—Japanese style. This necessity is a strategic part of everyday Japanese business culture, as afterhours relationships are pivital. In actuality, there is a bridge joining Japanese social and business communication, and its discovery is at the heart of expatriations, joint ventures and diplomacy.

After many hours spent at business meetings or in a corporate training room, I became increasingly comfortable with afterhours invitations. It was at the watering holes, the *yakitori* restaurants and cabarets that true business relationships were forged. Drinking with Japanese trainees and associates became an art. I recognized the various tests and rites of passage in operation during a drinking and eating session with Japanese. Business was usually a distant topic of conversation, with travels, sex, lifestyles, language, cultural differences, and ways of having fun, most appropriate (depending upon levels of familiarity and the occasion or setting).

In the course of being "looked over," I found out that my Japanese partners were extremely concerned with how they appeared individually and collectively to Americans and the outside world. There was a constant fascination with how I was adjusting to Japanese culture, what I thought of Japan and Japanese etiquette, how Japanese business practices differed from American protocol, and the subject of personal relationships.

Japanese paid undivided attention to my reactions to Japanese cuisine. Once when "treated" to an eel luncheon, or to pickles and fish for breakfast, I knew enough to disguise my true feelings. My Japanese friends wanted so much to please the expatriate, for him/her to have a highly favorable reaction to everything Japanese, and to participate fully and willingly. I did my very best to preserve their status as gracious hosts, and my place as a very agreeable, appreciative guest. What was "true" or "honest" no longer guided my *public* communication. I was far more concerned with face, harmony, and good feelings.

I found out that Japanese are very, very gracious social hosts. They will not quibble over restaurant bills; they consider it rude to hassle over a bill. Most of the time, I was absolutely not permitted to pay in cabarets or local *yakitori* houses. I poured drinks for my Japanese associates, and they poured for me. A group spirit prevailed, and the fun times were many and memorable.

Yet I grew to recognize that there was a very Japanese way of handling the familiarity that grew out of afterhours socializing with business associates. Although it was a time to try to get behind the status, professional and organizational masks, to reach beyond the surface (*tatemae*) and find the *honne* (true intentions), there were some subtle stipulations to be learned. For example, the "first name basis" that prevails at the bar, was not usually carried over into the business meeting or training session the following morning. This was one of the cultural shocks experienced in my first few weeks in Japan. It was so hard to change gears and communicate in a formal mode, after throwing away the formalities just hours ago.

There is a very clear distinction between socializing and conducting business. Western expatriates all around me were constantly dumbfounded by this sudden turnabout, from a "social" to a "business" stage. The distinction within Japanese corporate culture is more abrupt and radical than with U.S. corporates. But most important, it is the ability of the U.S. expatriate to grasp that the social setting, afterhours, is a primetime venue. Japanese do search for the stuff of which the Westerner is made. It is a longterm excavation for *honne* and *haragei*.

In the most serious sense, the interaction at social situations is the best indicator of the U.S.-Japanese business relationship—not the formal communication during company workhours.

Postscript

Do not underestimate or overlook the crucial role of everyday Japanese life and social relationships as strategic dimensions of business and corporate expatriations. A preparedness and appreciation of Japanese social life is instrumental in understanding the broader cultural dimensions shaping Japanese organizations. U.S. expatriate managers and diplomats should experience Japanese homes, hosts, hospitality, and the fundamentals of day-to-day existence. While numerous cultural shocks are inevitable, it is also advisable to gradually immerse expatriates and families in the etiquette, rules, ironies, and realities of Japanese life. In this way, the expatriate manger or business visitor is less inclined to jump to conclusions, and more apt to position Japanese business practices within the larger whole of Japanese society.

"CORPORATE COMMUNICATION: MELTING THE ICE vs. BREAKING THE ICE"

How rapidly or slowly do Japanese enter into business associations with other Japanese? And likewise for Americans? The more "breaking the ice" pace of U.S. businesses clashes with the slower "melting the ice" campaign approach of Japanese. At stake is the pacing of individual, corporate, organizational and national U.S.-Japanese relationships.

"CULTURAL SENSITIVITY AND JAPAN-U.S. MARKETING: UNDERSTANDING INTERCULTURAL SUPERSTITIONS"

Wiggens Athletic company of August, Georgia, introduced the new line of golf and tennis balls into the Japanese market. Sales were very slow and sluggish. The Wiggens marketing team was an all U.S. and European group largely unfamiliar with Japanese culture. They were very perplexed by the failure of the Wiggens lines of tennis and golf balls as they had been very well received throughout Europe, North, South, and Central America, and other parts of the world. Why wouldn't the balls sell in Japan?

After great losses in the Japanese markets, they hired a U.S. consulting group, Goldman and Associates. Goldman and Associates sifted through mountains of printed communication, such as advertising, marketing promotions, and TV advertising. After an extensive sampling, it was found out that both the tennis balls and golf balls were offered to Japanese customers in groups of four, eight, or twelve balls per package. In the opinion of the consultants, the number four was usually associated with "death." The Wiggens people were dumbfounded. They were in disbelief and couldn't conceive that the fact that their balls were sold in units of four would not allow for penetration of the Japanese market. After several rounds of talks, consultations, and examples of the number "four" in Japanese culture, the Wiggens Group decided to follow Goldman and Associates' suggestions. All packaging was changed to units of threes and hence balls were sold in groups of three, six, and nine. This was combined with a new advertising campaign created by the consulting group, that had a Japanese clown juggling threesomes of golf balls and tennis balls in the air while speaking of their virtues and aesthetic grace.

Although it is always difficult to determine how a single factor or number of factors contributed to a turnaround in marketing and sales, the Wiggens Group was nevertheless elated with the reverse of fortune. Once the new packaging in threesomes was initiated along with the juggling clown, sales rocketed.

From that point on, the Wiggens Group realized that to penetrate Japanese markets, they must know Japanese culture and even Japanese superstitions. The Wiggens Group now is quick to express their experiences with other Japanese corporations as they (the Wiggens group) exalt the virtues of intercultural consulting and understanding the culture of the market you wish to penetrate. The Wiggens Group has introduced many of their Japanese corporate friends to consulting services that familiarize them with U.S. and European markets. Wiggens is convinced intercultural understanding is the key to profits and success, while intercultural ignorance is the source of real life failure and financial blunders.

Analysis: Wiggens Athletic company is a prototype of the "ugly European and American" corporation who learn how to communicate with Japanese consumers largely through costly "trial and error" marketing.

There is no excuse for the "number four blunder" as a basic understanding of Japanese culture is instrumental in communicating with consumers. You do not sell sports products by conjuring up images of death, funeral parlors and grieving families.

Without expertise in Japanese culture, Wiggens wisely turned around their failures by bringing an intercultural consulting group into the picture. The group quickly cleared up the cultural clash, and was able to put into practice the useful maxim "think globally, act locally." Evidently, Wiggens never considered that many invisible elements of local culture enter into international marketing, and must be surfaced and responded to.

Moreover, the outside consultants appear to have revamped the Wiggins approach to advertising in Japan. *It is quite possible that the earlier round of advertisements lacked the indirect aesthetic, "atmospheric" approach preferred by Japanese consumers* (This Japanese approach was utilized in the first round of TV advertising in the U.S. for Nissan's INFINITY luxury automobiles; this ad campaign was far better suited to Japanese sensibilities than Americans', as it depended upon ambiance over "the beef." The ad was a much discussed failure and was followed by more direct, U.S. styled pitches.) Whereas U.S. consumers are used to a more direct sales pitch, heralding the merits of the product, Japanese advertising communicates more "ambiance" than substance, more *tatemae* (surface) than *honne* (truth). The description of the juggling clown fits within the Japanese framework for commercial messages, as it is a "cute" and friendly image, is entertaining, and only indirectly deals with the product.

CHAPTER 6

Management in Japan

"KNOCK, KNOCK"

WATANABE: Jones appeared surprised . . . maybe insulted.

SATO: Why?

WATANABE: I broke the rules of American business behavior.

SATO: What did you do?

WATANABE: I knocked on Jones' door, lightly and quickly . . . and entered his office.

SATO: What was the problem?

WATANABE: He appeared very shocked that I walked into his office without his secretary's approval or announcement.

SATO: Where was his secretary?

WATANABE: She wasn't at her desk.

SATO: Why did you need her permission to enter his office?

WATANABE: It seems as if a closed door and walls are serious items in American corporations—they mean "stay out" unless formally invited in.

SATO:	How did you find out? Did Jones tell you that?
WATANABE:	No. He just acted rather annoyed. I could tell by the tone of his voice, the way he shuffled his papers with abruptness . . . that he was angry.
SATO:	Body language? American body language?
WATANABE:	Perhaps. His face, the tone of his voice, his hands and nasty handling of the papers—all spoke very clearly. Perhaps I'm accustomed to Japanese companies where there's easy access to everyone . . . people are easy to talk with . . . and group oriented . . . I'm confused.
SATO:	Americans just love privacy, closed doors, independence.

Analysis: Watanabe and Sato have uncovered a silent problem in U.S.-Japanese business relations. Japanese and Americans have different approaches to the use of "space" and "privacy." Sato is quite correct in stating that Americans love privacy; U.S. business people are also far more territorial than Japanese. Here we see a clash between contrasting codes of "group space" and "individual space." Watanabe did not realize that he was violating Jones' private space when he entered his office, unannounced. For a majority of Japanese, there is nothing sacred about "private space" within the walls of a company building. Virtually all space is "group space," and there are a minimal number of doors, walls, partitions or other devices serving to separate workers or create private offices.

Along with the "proxemic clash" are additional, unintentional violations by Watanabe. He is unaware that a brief knock on a door with rapid entry, can easily constitute what U.S. associates see as an intrusion. In other words, there are various "regulating mechanisms" for controlling business and office territories. When Watanabe knocked on Jones' door, Jones "naturally" (by U.S. standards) expects Watanabe to wait for a reply before entering. This is not usually required in Japanese organizations or homes.

Finally, Jones appears to either "internalize" his displeasure, or he is beginning to learn Japanese styled restraint. Notice that Jones does not overtly communicate his feelings that he was intruded upon, and Watanabe has to read the more indirect, nonverbal behavior of Jones. Largely because cultural conflicts are not voiced by Japanese, and Americans soon learn of this expectation, it easily shortcircuits direct confrontation, asking of questions, and explorations of insults and expectations.

Whether visiting Japan for a series of formal table negotiations or preparing for an expatriate assignment in Japan, predeparture training should include an awareness of management practices— Japanese style. American managers should not, however, seek out simple "how to" recipes for deciphering Japanese organizational behavior. The most fertile profile and insights on Japanese management are those closely linking organizational behavior to culture— a complex tapestry of philosophy, history, religion, socialization, beliefs, attitudes, values, morals, customs, art, architecture, interior design, and business protocol.

Teamwork

Although the American manager may expect that corporate cultures are unique, it is inevitable that Japanese management practices are inseparable from the rudiments of national culture.[1] The common denominator in both Japanese national culture and corporate cultures is that of teamwork, reciprocity, and interdependence (amae).[2] Although some Japanese managers do favor individual over group work assignments,[3] research indicates that Japanese are among the most collectivist oriented of the Asian world, with Koreans and Chinese being far more individualistic than Japanese.[4]

For thousands of years, Japanese have emphasized teamwork, with Buddhism, Confucianism, the feudal period, and village life all heralding the central force of the group.[5] In the contemporary Japanese organization, allegiance to the corporation is of utmost importance. Individual careers are subsumed by the commitment to a single company. Particularly within the larger Japanese corporations, a fierce, lifelong loyalty tends to prevail. Turnover, career moves, and other symptoms of managements' and workers' less than complete engagement in the company is avoided, discouraged, even shunned. For the advancement of the Japanese organization must come first, and the careful management and nurturing of individuals is conducted within the framework of the welfare of the entire company—the common good being the highest priority.

Accordingly, it is not uncommon for U.S. expatriates to be treated as "visitors" or "temporaries," as Japanese managers become quite calloused about the quick fix, short term, high turnover, turnstyle of American managers. Just when Japanese management becomes accustomed to the style and mannerisms of a particular U.S. negotiator, they arrive one afternoon to find that he has been replaced. It is very difficult for Japanese to begin the whole process, again, engaging in *meishi* and a series of interpersonal situations for discovering the trustworthiness, ability, group commitment and knowledge of another new expatriate.[6] For it is implicitly understood amongst Japanese that U.S. business associates must pass a series of subtle "tests" and "screenings" as a prerequisite for serious involvement (similar "rites of passage" are practiced between Japanese). Turnover means that past efforts are largely wasted and that the *ningensei* process, placing high priority upon a Japanese version of human "bonding" is once again at the top of the agenda—possibly stalling the tasks lurking.[7] In other words, Japanese management is especially concerned with "finding" the true person behind the business mask, a process that is delicate and time consuming.

While the pursuit of individual careers and job hopping between corporations is quite common in the U.S., it is only in recent years that there are a few Japanese who are doing likewise. For the majority of Japanese corporates, teamwork requires stability, and it is natural for them to expect that this practice is paralleled within the United States. Depending upon the building of specific, personalized relationships (*ningensei*), the importance of establishing interdependencies (*amae*) and establishing mutual obligations (*giri*), Japanese efforts are thwarted when facing the revolving door of U.S. management.[8]

Office and Workplace Arrangements: Group Space

Management in Japan is characterized by the use of group space as a major factor in structuring teamwork. Expatriate managers in Japan repeatedly tell stories of the cultural shock they experienced when they discover that they do not have a private office. Closely related to Japanese spatial arrangements or proxemics within the society-at-large, the organization consciously positions managers, staff and line workers within extremely close proximity of one another. I was personally quite distressed to find out that dozens of desks, sometimes as many as fifty to a hundred, are positioned within a single unobstructed room. Japanese appear to get along very well without the aid of walls, doors and partitions.

Collective space, prevalent in Japanese homes and throughout society, puts individuals within inches to feet of one another, visually and audibly accessible. The buzzing of voices, the rapid fire flow of information, and the instantaneous relay of messages are all dividends of group space. The noted anthropologists, Edward and Mildred Hall, have aptly referred to this essential ingredient of Japanese management style as "fast messages and message flow."[9]

Japanese group space is the antithesis of U.S. management's assumptions surrounding the sanctity of private territory. Expatriates and U.S.-Japanese joint venture partners are in for some rough times and conflicts when the individualism vs. collectivism codes collide through radically contrasting spatial arrangements. Faced with a situation that can easily be perceived as demeaning, threatening, and counterproductive, U.S. expatriates do not readily adjust to this radical shift to a doorless world of group space. In theory, the influx of popular writings on Japanese management has mentally made an impression on a majority of American managers—they are surely aware that Japanese are team workers. But to actually experience a complete lack of privacy can be shocking. Unintentional Japanese violations of American privacy are a result of deeply ingrained corporate and national assumptions surrounding the sanctity of group space. American expatriate managers and diplomats who have to suddenly function within a sea of Japanese workers, presents quite the intercultural challenge.

Interestingly enough, Japanese spatial arrangements also permeate the factory workplace. Line workers are generally arranged on "U-shaped lines" allowing for easy visibility to each other. Unprepared U.S. line workers and expatriate foremen experience a similar cultural shock to that of the white collar manager, as they suddenly are forced to give up the privacy and partial anonymity afforded on a "L-shaped line."[10] Positioned in the "L" configuration, U.S. workers can only view the backs or sides of fellow workers and are unprepared for the we-ness of the "U" shaped arrangement.

Waste, Unevenness, and Excess

Japanese management does everything it can to further perpetuate the groupism already present in society. Through development of corporate cultures that minimize individual territory and discourage pursuit of career specializations in favor of group space and generalist workers, Japanese build lifelong organizational networks of solidarity.

Implicit in Japanese teamwork and proxemics is management's commitment to limiting waste, unevenness and excess in production, service and communication. This challenge is characteristic of both Japanese national and corporate culture. Coming out of a very high context culture, Japanese managers usually have far more in common with their fellow workers than do their American and Western counterparts.[11] The affinity for group work and sharing is tangibly seen in office and factory spatial arrangements. By "structuring in" collectivism, Japanese managers make superiors and subordinates immediately accessible to one another. Within large office rooms managers may easily stroll up to workers' desks, and frequently engage in face-to-face communication. Having constant and almost instantaneous access to the workforce, Japanese managers have far less reason for spending time on interoffice memos and other delayed forms of communication, contrary to a majority of Western managers. To the surprise of American expatriates, the majority of the interoffice paper flow may be considered wasteful and excessive, as face-to-face contact situations are generally considered by Japanese managers to be more effective and immediate channels for everyday business exchange. As a result, *Western managers should be on notice that the citadels of privacy, personal office space, and the distance and delays afforded through paperwork are fundamentally at odds with dominant Japanese management schemes.*

Similarly, workers on the "U" shaped line are placed in work stations so close to each other that little time or effort is wasted in making contact. Japanese superiors commonly practice MBWA (management by walking around), making them immediately accessible to subordinates and eliminating delayed, excessive paper work for managerial-worker communication.

A particularly revealing facet of Japanese management's avoidance of unevenness can be also witnessed in manufacturing plants subscribing to total quality management (TQM) and just-in-time (JIT) systems. Few U.S. expatriate managers on assignment in Tokyo are prepared for the complete shutdown of manufacturing work stations due to a problem on a separate, neighboring factory line. In an effort to prevent unevenness, Japanese management does not want a successful and productive work station to outproduce a faltering station. To do so would be an exercise in unevenness; exces-

"WHEN JAPANESE TAKE THEIR SHOES OFF"

Many foreigners explain . . . that the Japanese are wonderfully polite when they have their shoes off. What is meant . . . is that the *Japanese usually have their shoes off when in the presence of persons within the inner circle, on the right side of those all-important lines:* neighbors, classmates, co-workers, relatives, etc . . .
   . . . Doors in Japan are not made to be knocked on. To do so is a violation of proper manners. If there is no bell, the caller should slide open the front door, step into the entrance-way, and call out, *"Gomen kudasai" for "Pardon me"—or even "Hello!"*
   . . . The Japanese do two things while eating that repel and even nauseate most Westerners: They slurp with unstinted enthusiasm while partaking of soup and noodles and they lift their rice-bowls to their lips and literally shovel the rice in . . .

(from Jack Seward, *More about the Japanese*, Tokyo: Yohan Publications Inc., 1988, 176, 184, 188–9.)

sive, wasteful buffer stock piles up in the healthy station, while everything is at a standstill on the distressed line.[12]
   For the American manager in Japan there is little preparation for the putting-into-practice of such teamwork methods. All plant operations support and nurture a groupness that strives for evenness in production, immediacy in communication, the sharing of information and elimination of all excess, wasteful movement between work stations, offices, and diverse sectors of companies. *The minimizing of physical distances between managers and all employees challenges the U.S. reliance upon a sea of interoffice memos and delayed responses between workers.* For Japanese organizations, this modus operandi results in an extremely rapid flow of information.[13] Many U.S. expatriate managers emerging from theory X, scientific management, centralized, authoritative styled companies are ill equipped for the free flow and sharing of information.[14] Expecting a

privileged, separatist, bottlenecking information flow, with messages controlled by top management, expatriates are bewildered, threatened, and lag behind.[15] Only those Western managers thoroughly familiar with TQM, theory Y, and participatory management formats will be able to partially adjust to this just-in-time, instantaneous flow of information and teamwork essential to Japanese companies.[16]

Japanese Generalists

The rapid flow of information within Japanese organizations can be further traced to the prevailing policy of training generalists rather than specialists. Inasmuch as the success of U.S. or Japanese managers is in part contingent upon an ability to communicate effectively with co-workers, this process is significantly aided by having "stepped into the shoes" of various roles within the company. Japanese management puts cooperative teamwork into practice by having employees master as many as five or more different jobs within a company. A wage scale is partially determined by the number of jobs mastered.[17]

Through this process, Japanese companies breed managers who are familiar with a variety of jobs, tasks and specialties within the organization. As generalists, having occupied numerous positions, such managers are better able to "speak the language of the workers."

U.S. expatriate managers not only face broad national differences in cultural etiquette, they must also cope with the fact that they will be strangers to the well-integrated, interwoven, generalist bent of Japanese companies. Especially when placed in a leadership role, American expatriates must strive to be carefully briefed by repatriates, Japanese hosts and human resource managers—regarding the background and experience of workers. In situations where the American expatriate is free to speak English to Japanese, s/he must still understand how to establish common ground for communication.[18] This search for commonalities leads the expatriate manager into the general terrain of business culture as well as to the specific backgrounds, expectations and competencies of the workforce. It is vital to ascertain whether current Japanese middle management have also served in a myriad of other capacities within the company and how this background impacts current communications and objectives.

U.S. expatriates should gingerly handle their careerism, specialization and expertise in the presence of Japanese business hosts. *The fact that an American manager has served in a managerial capacity in* several *"Fortune 500" companies may hardly be a source of status in the eyes of Japanese top management.* Putting an "individual spin" on a Westerner's managerial record may be perceived by Japanese as instability, or the pursuit of a "selfish" career track—a pathway regarded in a far lesser light than longterm allegiance to a single company. Although Japanese are well aware of these characteristics of the U.S. managerial marketplace, it is nevertheless not representative of the kind of traits or vita that senior Japanese usually find personally attractive or promising. In addition, the American prioritizing of specialization is not similarly valued among Japanese corporates, as the generalist is held in far greater esteem. American expatriates may want to consider whether their specialization will serve as a positive message to Japanese hosts or associates. There is a distinct possibility that the specialist, individualist message will conjure up an image of someone with a narrow expertise, lacking company-wide understanding of teamwork, and unsuitable for managing Japanese or active participation in joint ventures.

BICULTURAL

"HOMOGENEITY vs. HETEROGENEITY"

Although there is far more heterogeneity or diversity among Japanese than is ordinarily recognized by U.S. intercultural specialists or recent expatriates, the majority of this diversity is not openly displayed in pubic, formal business venues.

While U.S. businesses struggle to understand so-called Japanese groupness, Japanese are baffled by the cultural, racial and ethnic diversity of the United States. Communicating with U.S. business leaders brings Japanese face-to-face with women, Afro-Americans, Hispanics, Asians and many other sub- and co-cultures.

The Part and the Whole

A central principle of Japanese management, the preference for valuing the "whole" over the "part," may be viewed as a philosophical and cultural assumption. On the Western side of the Pacific, U.S. management (and European management) has been greatly influenced by the analytical, piecemeal, scientific management studies of Frederick Taylor.[19] In contrast, Japanese management's underlying managerial principal is that of paying more attention to the whole than its parts.[20] American management is more familiar with analytical studies of productivity, efficiency, cost-benefit reports, and the infamous time-and-motion studies.[21] Japanese management is less concerned with assessing human resource factors individually and objectively and is more oriented toward unveiling a whole that envelops the details, and the driving forces behind a company-wide work force.

Western expatriate managers may insist upon an analytical breakdown of the points and issues leading to lower productivity, employee turnover, or lack of worker motivation. But in U.S.-Japanese joint ventures, Japanese associates are prone to examine general factors such as teamwork, work atmosphere, an absence of

MEDIA BRIEFING

"JAPANESE MORE RIGHT HEMISPHERE DOMINANT THAN AMERICANS"

.... The Japanese tend to be more "right hemisphere dominant" than Americans . . . That is, they think more synthetically and create wholes from parts. Americans are more comfortable with analysis and create parts from wholes by reducing phenomena to their components . . .

(from Charles Hampden-Turner, *Corporate Culture: From Vicious to Virtuous Circles*, London, England: Random Century House & The Economist Books Limited, 1990, 120.)

group spirit (*wa*), or insufficient interdependency (*amae*) as broad sources of managerial-subordinate conflict—usually articulated in positive language, not to cause any loss of face. This principle of Japanese management is indicative of Japanese distaste for the Western passion for breaking things down into smaller and smaller bits of data.[22] The synthesizing and holistic Japanese organizational behavior philosophy is a serious source of culture shock and frustration for U.S. expatriates who are sometimes denied a forum for their powers of analysis or unprepared for dealing with the "whole" worker.[23] In the Japanese organization, everything and everyone is interlocking and mutually dependent, and even concern with minutia in manufacturing plants, engineering and research and development (in total quality control, for example) is seen as part of a larger whole.

Further reflection upon the part-whole distinction unveils that this is exemplified in U.S. and Japanese approaches toward management and workers. For example, the U.S. reliance upon specialist workers and managers tends to fragment co-workers from one another. Each worker is responsible for their part or job. In contrast, the Japanese manager and factory worker are both generalists, not just single cogs in a wheel.[24] Managers and workers are expected to master as many jobs and specialties as possible, making them increasingly knowledgeable to the company as a whole. Complete involvement in the group and company tears down traditional walls of Western scientific management specialization.[25]

Many unsuspecting American managers are not adequately briefed in the ramifications of this holistic managerial practice. Much as their Western powers of analysis may be less relevant within the Japanese corporation (this is not to dismiss, however, the importance of minutia analysis for both Japanese and American engineers), so is the value of the individual manager dwarfed within the greater "whole" of the company. American expatriates are expected to learn to place their individual motives somewhat secondary to organizational goals; individual sacrifice for the group is appreciated and highly esteemed. The difficult transition for expatriates is moving from a primary focus upon the individual to company-wide accomplishments and objectives.

Dwarfing the Individual

Search Japanese newspapers for the writer of an article; examine whether famous individuals have been commemorated via the names of ships and public places. You will find that with the exception of the Western influence during the Meiji Period up until World War II Japan (approximately 1868–1945), Japanese will not call attention to or usually honor individuals. Glory goes to the newspaper, not to an individually identified writer as authors remain typically anonymous, a policy followed by the widest circulation Japanese daily newspaper, *The Asahi Shimbun.*[26]

Western expatriate managers can profit from consideration of this dimension of Japanese culture. Within business organizations, Japanese managers do not call too much attention to their individual achievements and are expected to subsume their personal merits within the common good of the group. Private agendas are held suspect in Japanese organizations, as the manager most concerned with the whole organization is greatly preferred. Even the simple act of an American expatriate manager in Tokyo praising a worker should be addressed more toward the work group than an individual. Innocent, well-intentioned statements of praise can create intercultural tensions as an individual Japanese worker rarely wants to be publicly singled out for compliments or inadequacies. The solution is to praise the entire work team, or not utter a word. When praise or criticism is absolutely necessary, then U.S. managers should have a firm grip on the proper venue within which to express these sentiments. In most cases, it is Japanese protocol that such statements be made in private rather than public situations.[27]

A seriously challenging consequence of the negative Japanese view of selfishness or private goals (*shishin* and *watakushi*), juxtaposed to the good of the entire group or company (*oyake*), is in the arena of leadership. The sanctity of the group throughout Japanese history (e.g., in rice paddy cultivation and throughout the Tokugawa Shogunate and feudal eras) is still practiced in the Japanese organization of the 1990s. There is little precedent, room or need for strong, individualized, charismatic leaders within Japanese corporations.[28] Once again, the postulates of Western individualism stand in stark contrast to Japanese national tradition. In a nutshell, the American manager who is used to communicating in a forceful, charismatic fashion (perhaps quite appropriate for a U.S., theory X styled organization), will find few Japanese receptive to an individualized form of leadership. In sum, Japanese oftentimes voice the maxim, "the clever hawk hides his claws" as a central insight into Japanese management and diplomacy.

"COERCIVE ETIQUETTE"

Beginning in about the sixth century, the Japanese began to emphasize "behaving in an expected manner," e.g., following rigidly prescribed rules of conduct in which the morality as we know it in the West, e.g., basing our actions and words on certain abstract principles, was merely incidental.

Whereas we devoted ourselves to substance without much heed to form, the Japanese concerned themselves with substance within a form, which consisted of performing a great many acts, large and small, in a precisely specified manner: how to sit, how to eat, how to open doors, how to wrap gifts, how to arrange their bedding so that its head is always pointed in a certain direction . . .

The slightest variation was not merely frowned on. In serious cases, it was classified as a crime. This led to the development of what Inazo Nitobe characterized as *"coercive etiquette . . . our etiquette begins with learning how to hold a fan and ends with the rites for committing suicide."*

(from Jack Seward, *More about the Japanese,* Tokyo: Yohan Publications Inc., 1988, 179–180.)

"SCRUTINIZING RESTAURANT CHECKS"

YOSHI: I found it very strange, what our American hosts did last night . . . in the restaurant.

HIDEO: What did they do?

YOSHI: They insisted upon paying the bill for everyone.

HIDEO: Sounds polite, considerate, and generous . . . what was the problem?

YOSHI: They looked over the bill very, very carefully. The American paying the bill used a little flashlight and looked over every item.

HIDEO: He did not trust the restaurant? the waiter? the owner?

YOSHI: I am not sure. But this is of course not the way we Japanese pay for a check.

HIDEO: Well, our American hosts must be perhaps gently briefed . . . told about this . . . before they spend time in Japan? What do you think?

YOSHI: I am not sure that this is something I would bring up with the Americans. But it could be awkward in Tokyo.

HIDEO: Yes, it could be awkward.

Analysis: Even when hosting Japanese corporate or business guests on American soil, some of the little things are noticed. In "Scrutinizing Restaurant Checks," the Japanese guests are bewildered and surprised by the U.S. host's method of scrutinizing a restaurant bill.

A cataloguing of several thousand "rules" of Japanese social and business behavior could be of use to U.S. hosts and expatriates, as a myriad of basic differences constantly interfere with joint venture associations. In this cultural dialogue, despite being gracious hosts in picking up the tab, the Americans are busy examining whether the check has been tabulated correctly. This offends the Japanese guests—as such behavior is virtually taboo among Japanese corporates and public officials.

Although it is difficult to tell American business people that they are acting "inappropriately," as many people scrutinize restaurant checks (with more than ample reason), the issue is specifically that of a contrasting Japanese expectation.

As indicated by Yoshi and Hideo, they are "concerned" about their U.S. associates' social performance or communication skills when they arrive in Japan. In Japanese culture, there is far more trust between customers and waiters, clients and establishments. It is not uncommon for Japanese business players to have ongoing accounts with a number of restaurants, and to only receive a bill at the end of the month. *It is considered uncivilized and untrusting to review checks in public.* Too much direct attention paid to bills, finances, money, etc., is poor business and poor social etiquette.

"SETTING UP JAPANESE-U.S. BUSINESS COMMUNICATION: GETTING ACQUAINTED"

Intercultural experts report that Japanese tradition and corporate life orients contemporary business people toward seeking out lasting, humane, personable business relationships ... In contrast, U.S. business is more "task oriented" and less "relationship oriented." These cultural differences are particularly evident in the getting acquainted phase.

PART III

Intercultural Communication with Japanese

CHAPTER 7

Talk and Conversations

"JAPANESE UNEASINESS WITH FOREIGNERS"

After an initial acquaintance with the ritualistic politeness of the Japanese, the foreign visitor may be shocked when he enters a store to make a purchase and finds himself coldly ignored. He may wonder what, short of leprosy, could have brought on this dramatic about-face, but he need not think he alone has been selected for this disdainful treatment. It happens to most of us and in many places. Partly it is because the concept of the hard-sell has not, luckily, permeated Japan to the regretable extent it has the U.S., but mostly this apparent indifference should be contributed to inability in English and uneasiness in the presence of foreigners whose eccentric ways are legend.

(from Jack Seward, *More about the Japanese*, Tokyo: Yohan Publications Inc., 1988, 179.)

When American tourists, business people, and expatriates attempt to communicate with Japanese, little should be taken for granted.

Numerous rules and conventions guide even the simplest acts of business communication. Many of these rules are unconsciously followed by both Japanese and Americans and guide the boundaries, expectations and behaviors of what is acceptable or unacceptable behavior.

Japanese are *undercommunicative* and generally more comfortable with less talk.[1] In contrast, Westerners are more verbose and somewhat apprehensive and distrustful of silences in speech.[2]

The implications of "how much talk" are significant in U.S.-Japanese business and social situations. At informal business luncheons, for example, a variety of potential communication conflicts lurk for the unsuspecting U.S. expatriate. *While a Japanese businessman is simply following Japanese "code" when sparsely speaking while eating, this is typically baffling to American visitors.* Still unfamiliar with the unspoken rules underlying business and social communication, the American is likely to question whether the silence is a response to an infraction or unknown insult. The Japanese silence described is hardly a "response" to the American but rather just ordinary Japanese eating etiquette: some vigorous talk before and after lunch may be in order, as is a brief period of utter silence while eating.

Once the Western business person is alerted to the sensitive issues of "when to talk," and "how much talk," this may be further examined in a variety of contexts. *When in the presence of a high ranking Japanese, for instance, the "right" to initiate speech rests with the senior.* This hierarchally based Japanese rule of business and social communication means that Japanese or Americans of lower rank are expected to be prepared for an appropriate silence, if conversation is not initiated by the superior. Moreover, particularly when conversing with a senior, verbal economy is advisable, as it may be a serious code violation to speak too much, ask too many questions, or fail to defer.

Another typical business venue may involve the American, Canadian, British or Australian English speaker who is accustomed to selecting a specific person that they choose to address during a business meeting. When the moderate ranking Japanese does not verbally respond to the Westerner's question or statement, whatsoever, misinterpretations soon follow. Unknown to the U.S. or British negotiator, however, is the fact that the Japanese finds it difficult to break with hierarchal rules requiring that he defer to a pre-assigned spokesperson. The Westerner, from the Japanese point of view, is ignorant of the communicative infraction and has addressed the wrong person in the group.

At the same negotiating table, the American businesswoman may echo the discomfort with silence exhibited at the luncheon table recently described. Frustrated or distraught with seemingly overwhelmingly long pauses, Americans frequently rush to fill the silences with an abundance of unnecessary talk.[3] Whereas Japanese may utilize the silence as another form of communication reserved for contemplation, digestion and consideration of talk and ideas being expressed (usually the prerogative of a Japanese senior executive), this tends to elude newly appointed U.S. expatriates. Similarly, as Japanese hold the floor and exercise lengthy pauses, Americans are prone to surge in with numerous interruptions.[4]

Shocked Japanese are surprised to learn that the American appears to have far less patience for pauses and believes that an "extended" silence gives them the right to seize a turn.[5] In actuality, the length of time considered appropriate for pauses during conversation is considerably longer for Japanese speaking English as a second language than for native U.S. English speakers. This lengthy silence is both a product of Japanese use of silences as an integral part of business communication and a result of the difficulty of having to translate mentally from English to Japanese and back to English during the course of pausing.

Moving from the business meeting into a broad arena of contact situations, expatriates find that some of their most cherished "truisms" governing talk and conversation are in violation of fundamental Japanese practices. Japanese are generally under less obligation to speak in situations where there is not much to say. At bus stops and train stations, Americans may believe that it is impolite or wrong not to speak with a stranger or acquaintance while Japanese remain silent.

In dire contrast, Japanese in early meetings with U.S. joint venture representatives, frequently engage in small talk, attempting to gauge the suitability of the American's commitment, character, and desire to associate with Japanese. But while such talk may flow freely (with the aid of afterhours cocktails), American expatriates should carefully investigate the rules regarding specific business and social situations with Japanese. Even though "less talk" is the general rule, more talk is expected in social situations reserved for getting to know one another.

Realizing that "too much talk" and an uncomfortableness with situations calling for Japanese silence creates numerous communication conflicts, American managers should strive to uncover the specific rules applicable in particular contexts. The great intercultural dangers are the twin forces of ethnocentrism and oversimplification. Ignorant of Japanese cultural and communicative codes, ethnocentric American managers mistakingly apply Western standards to conversations with Japanese. Based upon exposure to a few Japanese communication rules U.S. managers are sometimes too quick to generalize all contact with Japanese. Despite the fact that Japanese "talk less", it is vital to note important exceptions, especially during afterhours socializing.

Finally, without a cultural compass, Americans may continue to talk too much, out of turn, and to the wrong person, or misjudge Japanese verbal economy and miss the all important, rich terrain of Japanese body language and nonverbal communication. *For a study of Japanese business and social protocol uncovers that a high percentage of Japanese "messages" are extremely difficult for Westerners to discern—as they are unspoken, silent, and nonverbal.* Hence a natural consequence of learning more about Japanese talk and conversational codes is the need to make sense out of the accompanying, embellishing and powerful influence of facial expressions, gestures, movements, eye contact, and the entirety of body language. Some of the cues and implicit messages surrounding Japanese talk are contained in nonverbal expression. And you can be assured that Japanese nonverbal communication will *not* generally follow our Western expectations and rather reflects Japanese history, etiquette, and national culture.

"SILENCE IN SOCIAL AND BUSINESS COMMUNICATION"

Many intercultural communication experts carefully decode the cultural differences between Eastern and Western approaches to silence. Studies reveal that Japanese are more comfortable with silences and pauses—whereas U.S. communicators tend to want to fill silences with verbiage.

U.S. expatriates and business visitors should examine carefully the strategic use of Japanese silences, as knowing when "not to talk" is vital to Japanese business communication.

"THE STREETS OF NEW YORK"

HASEGAWA: You're in for a few surprises when you go to New York. You've never been to the U.S., have you?

MORITA: I've never been to the U.S., but I look forward to it.

HASEGAWA: Should I tell you about some of the good things or bad things to expect in New York?

MORITA: How about starting with the bad things?

HASEGAWA: Certainly. Do you like panhandlers? People who beg on the street for money? Or people living on the street?

MORITA: You mean like the beggars in Shinjuku station?

HASEGAWA: Well I guess you've had some experience... How about tipping waiters in restaurants, or going to an "all you can eat" brunch in San Francisco, where everyone goes to a central bar and chooses their own food?

MORITA: You mean I have to tip waiters? Or eat from the same food that a whole room of customers picks from? No thanks.

HASEGAWA: How about pay toilets? Or driving on the right side of the road? Wearing shoes indoors, in apartments? Having solicitors knock on your apartment door?

MORITA: I refuse to drive in America. I'll take trains. And I can't imagine paying to go to the toilet or wearing shoes inside someone's apartment. It isn't clean.

HASEGAWA: Clean? How about having a toilet bowl and a shower in the same room, right next to each other? Or no hot towels before you eat an American meal? And having to take quick showers because there may not be a bathtub in your room . . . if there is . . . it's shaped very peculiar . . .

MORITA: There must be some good things about New York?

HASEGAWA: How about American jeans, designer suits from Georgio Armani at half Japanese price . . . and large apartments and houses, double Japanese size, with cathedral high ceilings? You like great theatre? It's excellent. But don't take the trains, you might get robbed!

MORITA: Robbed! I hear so many stories! About violent America!

HASEGAWA: You have to have good directions on where to go and where not to go . . . anyway . . . you can drink great whiskey, big selections of beers, kona coffee is available, espresso cafés in New York, quick taxicabs, and even Japanese language newspapers. I've even heard of Karoake bars! And sushi is everywhere . . .

MORITA: Well I am happy you gave me this great briefing. I feel like you've spoken about at least a hundred items. I think I'll make my plane reservations.

HASEGAWA: I don't know if your company is paying or not . . . but airline tickets are sometimes cheaper in the U.S. than in Japan . . . you should check into what the Americans call "supersaver fares" and other discounts.

MORITA: My company will pay for my first trip. But when I am in the U.S. I will investigate these cheaper American airfares for future pleasure trips, perhaps to San Francisco or Hawaii.

HASEGAWA: I must excuse myself, as I have to get back to work. It was nice speaking with you but my lunchtime is over. Must get back . . .

MORITA: Thank you so much, Mr. Hasegawa, for telling me about the U.S. You are a regular cultural library.

HASEGAWA: Not really. I have only made several trips, but I read all I can . . .

MORITA: Where is the best place to find books on the U.S. and on business practices between Americans and Japanese?

HASEGAWA: I prefer Kinokuniya Bookstore in Shinjuku. They are also in New York City and San Francisco. Many Japan Times books are sold there that will discuss American culture.

MORITA: One final thing. I will be delivering a presentation at a convention in New York and also sitting in on several meetings with American doctors. Do you have any tips for me?

HASEGAWA: That is a very difficult and complex question. Perhaps we can discuss this on another lunch break. For now I can say that successful speaking style for Japanese in Japan may not be very successful with Americans in the U.S. The same with business meetings. They value different things than Japanese. Americans are very outspoken, and more direct than Japanese. They want people to get to the point, reach quick decisions . . . Well I have to run . . .

MORITA: Thank you again, Mr. Hasegawa. I have learned so much from you today. You are very kind.

HASEGAWA: I am pleased to assist you. I wish you very good luck with the Americans.

Analysis: Part of predeparture training and preparation for doing business with Japanese should include an appreciation and sensitivity to the struggles that Japanese face in dealing with Americans. This cultural drama depicts two Japanese businessmen discussing the "peculiarities" of U.S. social and business life, and offers insights into how Japanese tend to view the U.S. as guests. As much as Japanese are surprised by U.S. panhandlers, "all you can eat brunches," tipping, wearing shoes indoors, solicitors, toilets and showers in the same room, robberies and the unsafe U.S. streets, cheaper airfares, business meetings and public speaking venues, every Japanese culture shock supplies a "tip" for American expatriates or hosts.

The streets of Japan will be safer, tipping is rare, shoes are removed in homes, toilets and showers are separate, and Japanese have starkly contrasting standards for competently communicating at business meetings and through public speeches. Behind every contrast there are numerous "reasons," sometimes deeply entrenched within Japanese and U.S. history and culture.

Little should be taken for granted, as the "facts" of everyday life need to be constantly rethought, relearned and renegotiated in U.S.-Japanese business relations. Expatriate Japanese or Americans can learn to both gather information prior to trips abroad, and frequently ask questions on the other side of the Pacific. Polite questions, especially when asked in informal, social venues, supply answers to an endless array of bewildering codes. Anticipate that much of our initial communication will focus upon the strangeness and peculiarities of the other culture. Until some of these surprises are sorted through, joint venture conflicts will be compounded.

CHAPTER 8

Meishi

MEDIA BRIEFING

"JAPANESE SAY, 'NEW FRIENDS ARE BURDENS' "

While most Westerners believe that the more friends they have, the better off they are, the Japanese tend to shy away from additional acquaintances, feeling that each is more of a burden than a pleasure or a source of gain. Each requires much attention, and one can do only so much. Further, the social values involved are so delicate, so subject to varied interpretations and evaluations that the associations governed by them require the taut concentration of a tight-rope walker. To maintain each of several social relationships in proper balance and in a state of good repair is not, as the Japanese would say, an *"asameshi-mae no shigoto"*—an easy, "before-breakfast" job. They require much deliberation, concentration, time, worry, and expense.

(from Jack Seward, *More about the Japanese,* Tokyo: Yohan Publications Inc., 1988, 176.)

The Japanese term for business card exchange is *meishi*. The meishi ritual occupies a strategic place in Japanese business communication. Serving as part of business introductions, *meishi* allows Japanese and Americans to identify positions and rankings within an organization, offering valuable guideposts for interaction.

The *meishi* is a good example of the more restricted, rule governed codes of Japanese business communication.[1] A variety of expectations surrounding *meishi* should be noted. Beginning with the printing of the cards, U.S. managers, business visitors, and expatriates must take care in the preparation of the business card. The business card is more than a mere means for future correspondence, as Japanese meticulously examine a card for signals that will allow them to communicate appropriately.[2]

First of all, select an expert translator who has specific expertise in translating business cards, from English to Japanese.[3] Inasmuch as you will be preparing a two-sided card, offering identification in both English and Japanese language, it is paramount that your translator have skills in the subtleties of Japanese language, business and corporate culture. For instance, when having one of my business cards translated, I learned that a literal translation into Japanese may not be advantageous. On the English side I identify myself as "Dr.," while on the Japanese side I was strongly urged by my translator to drop the title. I was baffled. How could the title adversely affect the impact of the card, as it was intended for status conscious, hierarchal Japanese?[4] The response of my translator, a native Japanese and refugee of the business world, was that it is possible that restating the title in both English and Japanese language could constitute an act of overkill, indirectly requesting too much respect from Japanese associates. Additionally, since the majority of the Japanese I would be exchanging cards with do have English language proficiency, it is not necessary to repeat the full title, complete street address, etc.

Secondly, the *meishi* ritual necessitates specific interpersonal rules for exchange. In addition to presenting your card on the Japanese language side, in order to expedite easy reading (without having to flip the card over), it is also Japanese protocol to engage in a short bow during the exchange. At times a confusion unfolds as Japanese may extend their hands for a handshake while you are attempting to bow. Such cases of mutual attempts at adaptation are usually met with good will and humor. The card should be given and received with both hands, indicating respect. Care should be taken to keep the card received visible to you (by holding it or

placing it on the table surface directly in front of your seat) throughout the duration of the conversation. To rapidly insert the card in
a wallet or pocket and place it out of sight is widely considered
insulting.[5]

When offering a business card, recognize that the exterior,
packaging, or surface dimensions of business communication
(*tatemae*) carries much weight with Japanese. An attractively
printed card on high quality stock, enclosed within a quality leather
carrying case, communicates a positive message. It is a mistake to
dispel such seeming trivialities, for to do so is to dismiss the central
role of surfaces and veneers in a culture committed to the all important exterior of objects and people. Do not underestimate the attention paid to aesthetic minutia in business transactions by the
Japanese.[6]

When putting the card away, respectfully place it in your card
case or wallet and slip the card case into the inner vest pocket of
your suit or jacket. Placing a Japanese associates' business card
into a wallet to be positioned in the rear pocket of your trousers is a
subtle violation of Japanese business code. While the placement of
the card in the vest pocket signifies proper respect, slipping it into
the rear pocket shows disrespect, as the card will be literally "sat
upon" and is in closest proximity to the buttocks.

A minor footnote to keep in mind is that it is unthinkable and
inexcusable to run out of business cards. Keep an ample supply on
hand, with an additional several hundred cards ready and available
in your briefcase. Some business occasions call for handing out
cards to large groups of Japanese business people. Not having a
card to offer is an act of exclusion.

Also essential is the "struggle" to identify the approximate status and ranking of both parties through a *meishi*. The Japanese will
be interested in the company you work with, as the ranking of the
individual is closely related to the status of the company. Japanese
are more likely to view Americans as having greater esteem by virtue of their ranking with a top company, rather than through their
individual career achievements. A middle manager ranking with
a high status company such as IBM or Xerox will be seen as significantly higher than an equivalent ranking with a lower status
company.[7]

Finally, since it may be difficult to understand Japanese rankings from business card exchange, the following is a ranking in as-
cending order—identifying titles commonly utilized in Japanese
companies.

"SMALL vs. LARGE GESTURES"

Larger gestures more aptly fit the U.S. cultural script(s), while small gestures mirror the Japanese maxim: "the nail that sticks out gets banged down."

Titles Utilized in Japanese Organizations and on Japanese Business Cards

staff	ka-in
chief	shunin/kakaricho
deputy section chief	kacho dairi
section chief	kacho
deputy department head	bucho dairi
department head or general manager	bucho
director or supervisor	torishimariyaku
executive managing director	jomu torishimariyaku
senior executive managing director	senmu torishimariyaku
vice president	fuku shacho
president	shacho
chairman	kaicho

"TOO MUCH TALKING"

LEROY: I absolutely, positively guarantee you that I am the most formidable, experienced, polished, and excellent man for the position, Mr. Nakeshita. I am the best foreman you will ever find, sir!

NAKESHITA: Please tell me a little about your family life.

LEROY: Listen. I am divorced three times. Haven't had a lot of luck with my marriages. Have three kids. I pay alimony on two of them. And my third wife and I are still rather close. But . . . I don't want you to think that any of this personal family stuff has any bearing on the strength of my foreman abilities. I am a rock solid worker who always gets the job done and I deliver the goods. People call me the "mailman!"

NAKESHITA: The mailman?

LEROY: Yeah! Sure! The fellow that always comes around when he's supposed to. You know. The guy who delivers. Never any postage due? Get my drift?

NAKESHITA: It has been very pleasant speaking with you Mr. Leroy, and I will have my staff communicate with you regarding our decision on the foreman position.

LEROY: Do yourself a favor, Nakeshita. Hire me! I'm the man.

Analysis: If Leroy wants to learn from this interview, it would be helpful to take note of some of the communicative and cultural problems contained in this cultural dialogue.

Leroy is far too talkative for Japanese tastes. Only the most Westernized of Japanese could conceivably be favorably disposed to the verbose Leroy. Japanese tend to view the "fast talker" or verbal eloquence as far less important than do Westerners. *Leroy must understand the value of pauses, silences, and listening. The interview is dominated by the interviewee; this is not good.*

Leroy also is supplying too much personal information, too soon. While his personal scenario may not be that unusual within Western corporate culture, it is far less common among Japanese corporates. It is difficult if not unlikely for Japanese management to suddenly suspend its values and attitudes surrounding multiple marriages, and the greater state of experimentation and flux in the West.

In addition, Leroy is "guilty" of utilizing English slang or idioms when using the phrase, "the mailman." It is important to communicate in a simple fashion, and to avoid idioms with Japanese.

Finally, Leroy is boastful. His ego can easily be interpreted as a great barrier to becoming a team player. Overall, Leroy will be rejected and Nakeshita is likely to give his reason as "talk, talk, talk."

CHAPTER 9

First Contacts

"JAPANESE AND U.S. APPROACHES TO RANK, STATUS, AND HIERARCHY"

It is hardly coincidental that Japanese language excels in verbiage designating rank, status, hierarchy, seniority, and reverence . . . as well as a complex vernacular for multiple intricacies of politeness.

This "li" dimension of Confucianism makes extraordinary demands upon U.S. and other Western business associates who find that despite facing fluent Japanese English speakers, that many of the subtleties of hierarchy continue to prevail.

In addition to a knowledge of *meishi*, Western business visitors and corporate expatriates in Japan can profit from a knowledge of "first contacts" with Japanese.

The ordering of introductions is important. From a Western perspective it is proper to first introduce the senior member of a negotiating team, proceeding to the members of lower rank. But Japanese business etiquette begins with the introduction of the junior member, proceeding to the senior.

As indicated through the earlier discussion of *meishi,* the opening minutes of first business contacts are characterized by a probing for status, ranking, and affiliations. Until the rank and accomplishments of a visitor or expatriate are known, Japanese are at a disadvantage, not knowing precisely how to interact or address this individual.[1] Prior to establishing the status of the American, Japanese usually work on the assumption that s/he may be of a significantly higher ranking than themselves. If the American turns out to be of a lower rank and younger age than a Japanese counterpart, the Japanese may quietly "dismiss" or lower the level of respect accorded to the Westerner, in contrast to showing more serious reverence for a senior.

In extended first meetings, including initial table negotiation meetings, it is necessary to understand typical Japanese hierarchy in group communication settings. For instance, some U.S. negotiators may misinterpret the sparse contributions of the senior member of a Japanese negotiating team.[2] As first time strangers to Japanese group etiquette it is commonplace to expect that the senior will lead talks, but Japanese top management usually designates junior colleagues as the primary spokespeople or communicators. *The senior commonly refrains from speaking and through silently closing his eyes during the talks is communicating his approval of the negotiations.* At most, the Japanese senior will make a concluding statement and offer some guidance regarding the scheduled agenda and direction of the meeting.

Guided by their own cultural scripts and business protocol, Western expatriates are quick to jump to faulty conclusions. From a Western perspective, it is likely that the senior member of a negotiating team is expected to take a leadership role. The lack of interaction on the part of the Japanese senior is readily interpreted to be aloofness, lack of concern, and a blow against the Western team. Unknown to some U.S. business negotiators is the fact that Japanese meetings follow a different set of communication rules.[3] In the event that this meeting was to explore a U.S.-Japanese joint venture candidacy, the inability of both the Japanese and the American negotiators to identify each other's rules for communicating at business meetings could easily result in a "no go."

"MANZAI RIDICULE UNATTRACTIVE PHYSICAL APPEARANCE OF JAPANESE"

. . . . . Quite often when a *manzai* pair (a pair of comedians) appears on stage, one of them insults the partner by pointing out his or her unattractive and ugly physical features and then laughs; then the partner who has been ridiculed counter-attacks by pointing out the detractor's unattractive and ugly features. This may involve a part of the body which has nothing to do with racial differences such as obesity or baldness. In fact, it is common in Japanese culture as a whole to laugh at people by pointing out unattractive physical features. This has no particular relationship with the level of education or occupation or income. I have seen many university professors who talk like *manzai* . . . . . .

(from Michio Kitahara, *Children of the Sun: The Japanese and the Outside World*, Sandgate, Folkestone, Kent, England: Paul Norbury Publications, 1989, 118.)

"COMMUNICATING THROUGH INTERPRETERS: A LESSON FOR JAPANESE AND AMERICANS"

MR. NAKASONE: The Americans have problems communicating through interpreters, and the Japanese have trouble understanding.

MR. JAMIESON: Please explain this further.

MR. NAKASONE: For example, many considerate Americans . . . culturally considerate . . . determine that it is most polite and efficient to employ an interpreter when conducting business in Japan.

MR. JAMIESON: But I thought that the majority of Japanese politicians and corporate people know conversational English.

MR. NAKASONE: Many have a working knowledge of English. But unless you have specific experience or information about the Japanese you will be communicating with, you should always be very careful, and ALWAYS have an interpreter hired and ready.

MR. JAMIESON: My company did just that. We hired an excellent interpreter and it turned out that we really needed her! Many of the Japanese politicians we spoke with in Tokyo, did not have sufficient English knowledge, and they preferred Japanese. But we had other problems.

MR. NAKASONE: What kind of problems?

MR. JAMIESON: We did not know how to speak English in a way that made it simple and efficient for the translator?

MR. NAKASONE: Can you be more specific?

MR. JAMIESON: For example, we were speaking in very long sentences, and oftentimes we broke our sentences up with pauses. The interpreter told us to speak in short, complete sentences.

MR. NAKASONE: You mean that when a sentence is cut into short chunks that the interpreter has a hard time putting it into Japanese, accurately?

MR. JAMIESON: Exactly. Due to the fact that English and Japanese construct sentences in almost opposite ways, the interpreter had to know what the end of the sentence was before she could interpret it to Japanese.

MR. NAKASONE: Because the words at the end of the sentence in English language may be the word at the beginning of the sentence in Japanese?

MR. JAMIESON: Exactly! So now I explain these interpreter difficulties to both my American and Japanese associates. It helps to make everyone sensitive to a delicate language translation situation.

MR. NAKASONE: And you must really spend time with your interpreter to work closely and effectively with her in bridging the peculiarities of both our languages!

Analysis: Many U.S. corporations and expatriate negotiating teams are unfamiliar with the use of interpreters. It is essential that Americans pay ample attention both to the choosing of an interpreter (do not necessarily leave the choice up to Japanese associates) and to their ability to work with the interpreter.

Few U.S. business people recognize that the interpreter's job is a delicate and important one. It is a good idea to delete slang, use of idioms and metaphors, and to avoid constructing lengthy, difficult sentences. As indicated in this cultural dialogue, it makes the interpreter's job easier and more effective by speaking in shorter, more concise sentences.

Moreover, it is important to make ample use of lengthy pauses and silences between sentences and phrases. You will need to determine how the specific interpreter works and to allow them a maximum amount of time to perform the translation.

It is also a good idea to get to know the interpreter, their capabilities, intercultural expertise and experience, and whether they are just "bilingual," or also "bicultural." The more broad based the interpreter, the better it is for translating sometimes ambiguous concepts, notions and feelings.

Finally, view the interpreter as more than a "machine" or "narrow translator." An interpreter is in actuality a more significant player than is usually recognized. It is not unusual to find an interpreter favoring one "side" or the other, withholding information from the less favored side, and even acting as an agent for a given faction. Although this is a cynical view, a view of interpreters that such professionals would most likely vehemently reject, it is nevertheless my personal experience at U.S.-Japanese negotiating tables.

CHAPTER 10

Nonverbal and Intuitive Communication in Japanese Business and Management

It is oftentimes debated, on both sides of the Pacific, in U.S. and Japanese companies, among line workers and CEOs, how Japanese use of conversational English is sharply different from U.S. usage. As emissaries of an old and far reaching national culture, contemporary Japanese managers do not fully or necessarily shed their Japanese skin or conditioning when learning English as a second language. Note that English does not adequately accommodate the hierarchal, status conscious, collectivist messages of the Japanese mind, business or social ethic and that many bilingual Japanese managers tend to utilize English in a very Japanese manner.[1]

Japanese Managers Utilize a "Japanized" Version of English

Japanese managers seek out English language substitutes for the elaborate system of Japanese honorifics, rapidly familiarizing themselves with English terms and phrases offering maximum indirectness and ambiguity, and opportunities for articulating cohesiveness, solidarity, group spirit, and apology.[2] As already pointed out, only the most international or Americanized of Japanese business or political leaders would incorporate the more adversarial, aggressive, individualistic, exaggerating, direct use of English—widely promoted in the Western world.[3] Japanese managers are more comfortable with a transference or infusion of Japanese cultural principles into the workplace use of English.[4] Despite Japanese belief that English is crucial for successful joint ventures with Americans and other Westerners, the carryover of Japanese culture presents numerous problems of meaning for U.S. expatriates.

Japanese Skepticism toward Spoken Language

It is also broadly recognized that Japanese have traditionally held a certain skepticism toward spoken language.[5] Confucianist and Buddhist philosophies, for example, have been extremely influential in directing attention toward the limitations of spoken language and logic, and the need to distrust the eloquent speaker or communicator.[6]

Verbal Expression a Poor Substitute for Nonverbal Communication

Japanese widely believe that verbal expression is a poor substitute for intuitive and nonverbal communication.[7] This reliance upon a language of facial expression, gesture and bodily language (kinesics), sound and inflection of the voice when speaking (paralanguage), spatial arrangements of offices, workplaces and furniture (proxemics), and use of silences—is strategic to Japanese business and social communication.

Ironically, international business people are far more aware of the blatant cultural conflicts when using two different spoken or written languages (Japanese and English), than they are conscious of contrasts in nonverbal communication. Yet the unspoken language of the body, space arrangements, facial expression, and intuition are also culturally based.[8]

In U.S., Nonverbal Communication is Secondary to Verbal

In the U.S. and throughout the West, the importance of verbal communication frequently minimizes or trivializes the impact of the nonverbal. Despite an avalanche of recent "body language" books out on the popular market, and the advent of nonverbal specialists in the academic disciplines, nonverbal communication largely remains an enigma in culturally diverse workplaces and in U.S.-Japanese joint ventures.[9] Why? Body language and eye contact on the factory line, in offices, and at negotiating tables and interviews is a "natural expression" of culture, is taken-for-granted, and is difficult to accurately understand when crossing ethnic, racial or national boundaries.

Japanese Use Subtle, Indirect Nonverbal Communication

Japanese and American managers learn nonverbal language, much as they learn an alphabet, a spoken and written language. At negotiating tables, U.S. diplomats from Los Angeles and New York City are products of a more individualistic approach to body language. In contrast, Japanese managers are far more restricted, subtle, indirect in their nonverbal communication. Japanese rely more on intuitive or nonverbal communication to express their objectives and intentions, and to read the motivations of their American counterparts. Americans are more forceful, direct, assertive, argumentative and overtly expressive with their vocal inflection, gestures, and facial interaction. Japanese study American nonverbal cues and practice a far more subdued silent language.[10]

Japanese Silence: A Source of U.S.-Japanese Conflict

Studies reveal that the central and ample use of silence, as a vital component of Japanese nonverbal communication, is not shared by U.S. business people.[11] Japanese silence is comfortable, readily meaningful, and a time for intuition, thought, and careful analysis through the senses. U.S. expatriates find the lengthy, repeated, strategic use of Japanese silence as a major source of discomfort.[12]

While consulting and training Japanese corporates in Japan, I witnessed numerous misunderstandings and conflicts originating in the profoundly different uses and perceptions surrounding silence and verbal eloquence. The fact that U.S. politicians and business leaders, secure in their stateside eloquence, could not get a rise out of Japanese audiences and negotiators, was a source of significant concern. Unaware of the unique and piercing role of Japanese silences (termed *ma*), *U.S. expatriates find themselves in an upside-down world—where silences are precious, and verbal eloquence can cheapen the message and speaker.* This typical scenario surrounding the intercultural challenge of silence is captured by Michihiro Matsumoto:

> I am reminded of an occasion when I accompanied a particularly intelligent labor leader of the AFL-CIO. He was one of the most articulate lecturers I have ever interpreted for. The man, proud of having been a good orator in the United

States, asked me why there was no feedback from the Japanese audience. At a loss to explain in detail the meaning of *ma* in English, I answered, in an overly-simplified manner: "Because you were articulate." My comment was obviously inadequate. For what I meant was this: "Your speech was so neatly organized that the Japanese audience, deprived of *ma*, didn't know how to identify with you non-verbally, much less to relate to you verbally."[13]

Matsumoto's example rings true. Business or managerial eloquence is simply not transferable between U.S. and Japanese social, business, political or corporate cultures. Especially problematic for Americans is the mastery of Japanese silences, whether in the course of speaking, or in the silent, effortless gestures, facial expres-

---

MEDIA BRIEFING

"NAKASONE ON U.S. AND JAPAN BASHING"

It has been increasingly said in recent years that there are some fundamental and irreconcilable differences between our two societies, but what's most important is to recognize the fundamental need for both countries to accept common rules by which the game is to be played. While there is an understandable temptation to dichotomize the argument in dire black-and-white for the sake of added emphasis, we ought to be paying much more attention to the basic premises we share rather than some particular differences . . .

Last, but not the least important, is the communication between the national legislatures of both countries. There is much room for improvement in this area due mainly to the barriers of language and geographical distance. There ought to be several new channels of communication open for two-way information flow.

(from Yasuhiro Nakasone, "Beyond *kenbei*, anti-U.S. Sentiment and Japan-bashing," *The Japan Times*, May 25–31, 1992, volume 32, #21, 9.)

sions and movements of the skilled negotiator. As further pointed out by Matsumoto, "Western conversationalists listen to the words between pauses, whereas Japanese . . . listen more attentively to the pauses between the words and gestures."[14]

Japanese Eloquence is Nonverbal: The Sophisticated Communicator

Japanese eloquence is primarily nonverbal. The words of the expatriate do not carry the same weight with Japanese hosts that they have with the parent company in San Jose, California. In the face of the Japanese practice and view of a nonverbal sophistication, the reservoir of verbiage is easily heard as a subterfuge, as superfluous. Japanese social and business protocol devaluates a needless chatter that does not serve primary understanding.

Japanese use of nonverbal communication is viewed as more sophisticated than verbal utterings because the subtle, indirect messages of the face, eyes, body, voice, spatial arrangements and silence depend upon an unspoken empathy and intuitiveness between sender and receiver. The incessant use of direct, overt, adversarial, verbal messages is seen as somewhat barbaric or uncouth.[15]

The Ringi System

The subtle nonverbal communication engaged in within the Japanese social and corporate world is witnessed in the Japanese use of the *ringi* system of decision-making. Japanese affix their personal "seal" to a series of printed proposals (called a *hanko;* used in lieu of a personal signature or initial)—attempting to gauge the degree of agreement or disagreement for a pending company-wide or negotiating table decision. In place of a Western public meeting where corporate members voice their views, Japanese *ringi* system offers a quieter, less combative, more discreet channel for reaching consensus. Shunning public disagreement and debate, as both are viewed as a vexation to the spirit and detrimental to individual and group face (*kao*), *ringi* allows a personalized, private venue for decisions. Specifically, the imprints of the personal seals represents the views of the participant. This silent, visual mode of expression is even more subtle than originally meets the Western eye. If in complete agreement, the player fixes the seal, upright; if in complete disagreement, the seal is fixed upside down; if in partial agreement or disagreement, the seal is imprinted sideways. The very, very minor twisting of the seal, perhaps two to three degrees to the West or East reflects a minute amount of concern and perhaps 1/100th agreement or disagreement.[16]

Subtle, Nonverbal Communication in the Japanese Home

In the same manner, the Japanese homemaker may make an extremely minor alteration in the flower arrangement—with something in the configuration appearing mildly in disorder. This "minutia message" is indicative of a wife quietly expressing her displeasure to a husband or with a mother-in-law in residence. Since Japanese will not readily express adversity, publicly, the deviation in the flower arrangement is the crux of the message— offered through a rarefied nonverbal channel.[17] As pointed out by Professor Takiyama Lebra, such subtleties in nonverbal expression require extremely empathic communicators, people who are unusually fine tuned to the smallest and most delicate of messages.[18]

Japanese High Context Communicators

Likewise, within the company setting, Japanese men and women workers are meticulously encultured or trained to communicate in terribly intricate, precise and unobtrusive manners. Japanese who have so much in common (termed a *high context culture* by Edward T. Hall),[19] freely send the facial, vocal, bodily, and spatial arrangement equivalents of the "flower arrangement message," during the course of the organizational day. Not only is this nonverbal exchange considered refined, it also serves the crucial purpose of sidestepping direct, verbal, face-threatening, group provoking verbal communication.

Seated across the table from Japanese negotiators, U.S. diplomats, however, clearly miss much of this very Japanese nonverbal code, and both misread these messages and overwhelmingly attend to the verbal content.[20] It is vital to redirect Western expatriates' attention to this nonverbal interplay, as just the base realization that there is a silent language operating is invaluable.

"COMMUNICATING EMOTIONS"

Whether emotions should be aired or expressed in public, business situations, is central to U.S.-Japanese communication. U.S. culture allows for a broader expression of emotions while Japanese expect that emotions will remain more private and controlled.

The flaring of tempers, use of exaggeration and overall communication of overt feelings are more suited to U.S. than Japanese public arenas. Conversely, the control of emotions is hardly considered concealment on the Japanese side of the Pacific. To publicly reveal emotions is considered by Japanese to be a sign of serious immaturity.

The cultural backdrop of Japanese development of nonverbal communication as a primary vehicle for business and social messages is further understood vis-à-vis American culture. The high context Japanese culture, characterized by a sharing of a common heritage, philosophical and religious systems, language, history, and widely followed cultural codes, makes it possible to communicate more intuitively than Americans. With so much in common, there is less need to put business or managerial messages explicitly into verbally stated forms (e.g., memos, orally, face-to-face communication).

Within the high context Japanese organization, greater focus is placed upon the development of a silent language of ambiguities, silences, and subtleties. In comparison, U.S. business people have less in common, come from a plethora of racial, ethnic and national groups, and must rely more upon the spoken word. The broad diversity necessitates that Americans spend great efforts on clearly articulating, through verbal and print media, as precise and specific a message as possible. In effect, the great empathy and intuition that closely links Japanese management and workers, and prioritizes nonverbal communication, is somewhat alien to U.S. business visitors and expatriates.

Nonverbal Applications in U.S.-Japanese Joint Ventures

If as a U.S. business representative, you are motivated to want to adapt to Japanese organizational practices, sensitivity to nonverbal protocol is instrumental. To begin with, the mission of more effectively communicating with Japanese is not just a verbal challenge; it is primarily a nonverbal challenge.

In negotiations with Japanese, perhaps your chief objectives are to establish good will, lay the groundwork for a longterm, personalized relationship (*ningensei*), and bridge the distance or cultural gap. Assume that this cannot be accomplished through verbal channels alone. It will call upon an ability to establish a nonverbal, silent closeness, a rapport.

The setting for communication is important. An understanding of the central role of communication in conducting business with Japanese should lead you to seek out informal venues, afterhours. Contrast the cold formality of sitting across a table negotiating with Japanese associates, eye to eye, with the closer, more intimate proxemic arrangement of sitting on *tatami* mats in a traditional restaurant. Or consider the informal camaraderie that prevails at an *akachochin* (a "red lantern," Japanese eating and drinking establishment, a counterpart of the British pub) as Japanese and Americans pour drinks for each other (Japanese custom), sit flush against one another, and Japanese are allowed to thoroughly enjoy the role of hosts.

The closeness of the social setting spills over into business negotiations, even when business is not discussed. Sitting elbow to elbow, knee to knee, on a *tatami* or in an *akachochin,* is the appropriate environment that allows for vital nonverbal communication—an exchange strategic to silently bridging or adjusting conflicts, differences and distances. It is a nonverbal, Japanese alternative to the American passion for "talking your way" out of differences.

Another nonverbal application is the subtle use of vocal inflection and nuances as a vehicle for delivering negative, face-provoking, potentially disruptive messages. Maybe you want to express a certain displeasure with Japanese distaste for having their middle managers serving under a younger U.S. expatriate.

MEDIA BRIEFING

"WORDS AND SPEECH ARE DECEPTIVE"

The inner self is symbolically localized in the chest or belly ... whereas the outer self is focused on the face and mouth which are socially addressed. At the center of the inner self is the *kokoro* which stands for heart, sentiment, spirit, will or mind. While the outer self is socially circumscribed, the *kokoro* can be free, spontaneous, and even asocial. Further, the *kokoro* claims moral superiority over the outer self in that it is a reservoir of truthfulness and purity, uncontaminated by circumspections and contrivances to which the outer self is subject. This association of the *kokoro* (or inner self) with truthfulness gives rise to the paradoxical notion that the "real" truth is inexpressible. Thus words and speech as means of expression are often regarded as potentially deceptive and false, and silence as indicative of the true *kokoro*.

(from Takie Sugiyama Lebra, "Self in Japanese Culture," in T. Lebra, editor, *Japanese Sense of Self*, Cambridge, United Kingdom: Cambridge University Press, 1992, 112.)

One of the "all-American" U.S. approaches is to tactfully voice the displeasure, usually in a somewhat direct, forthright fashion. But if you are interested in sincerely attending to Japanese protocol for expressing disagreement or troubled concern, it is more interculturally effective (and competent) to use an ironic, slightly "wounded" vocal inflection when stating that Japanese reaction to your U.S. expatriate was "unusual," and "genuinely interesting." In line with the subtlety of the homemaker's slightly altered flower arrangement, such out of the ordinary inflection may be quite effective in getting the message across.

The strategic intercultural point is that through recourse to a nonverbal channel, acting a bit surprised or wounded—or a troubled inflection in the voice—a potentially awkward or damaging public and verbal blunder can be diverted. While these subtle

MEDIA BRIEFING

"JAPANESE EQUALITY FOR WOMEN"

... American and Japanese women differ in their view of equality ... In terms of rights, Japanese women believe, as do their American counterparts, in equal pay for equal work, equal opportunity, and so on. What appears to be different in their concepts of equality is that in Japan equality is not sought on principle, and part-time working women and full-time housewives in particular consider themselves equal to their professionally or vocationally employed husbands ... Not only do women see themselves as equal to their husbands but their husbands willingly admit their dependence on women (in a sense, their inferiority.) This is not merely private lip service but the stuff of public opinion ...

(from Sumiko Iwao, *The Japanese Woman: Traditional Image and Changing Reality*, New York: The Free Press, 1993, 3.)

shades of nonverbal meanings and expression are not uncommon among closely knit American family members or lovers (appears to be universally true), they are far more prevalent in Japanese than U.S. management and organizations. By literally "switching codes" to a more Japanese-like format of sending and receiving messages, expatriates can avoid some of the cultural collisions so notoriously publicized in U.S.-Japanese popular media.

Nonverbal Postscript: On "Trading Places"

Some American expatriates may find this use of a more Japanese approach to nonverbal communication inappropriate, uncomfortable or akin to "play acting." I rather strongly advocate a growing appreciation of Japanese styled body, facial, and paralanguages. If, for the sake of politeness and relationship building, some Japanese styled *tatemae* is appreciated (surface, superficial communication), I believe that it is just a simple matter of *increasing* your intercultural range and competency—specifically regarding nonverbal interaction in business. Keep in mind that Japanese associates generally struggle to learn the international language of English and it is usually understood that the Japanese partner will supply the translators (as needed) when conducting business with Americans. Few American corporates reciprocate by studying Japanese—although some of this intercultural deficit can be offset by intercultural predeparture training.

I invite U.S. expatriates to appreciate both the efforts made by Japanese in speaking the English language and learning about American culture, and to conversely acknowledge and accommodate business and social protocol of Japanese associates. The typical nonverbal behavior experienced in U.S. business is going to be a source of friction with Japanese—and preventative damage control is one of the goals of successful communication, management and diplomacy.

"THE BUSINESS INTRODUCTION—MEISHI"

U.S.: I am very pleased to meet you Mr. Sato. (The American extends his hand for a handshake).

JAPAN: (extending his hand and shakes hands with a weak, limp grip) So pleased to meet you, Mr. Rogers.

U.S.: This is my first time in Tokyo, and I look forward to our business association . . . shall we begin our meeting?

JAPAN: (puzzled). Excuse me. (reaches into card case and presents his card to Rogers). Here is my business card . . .

U.S.: (Rogers takes out his wallet immediately and puts Sato's card in it after quickly glancing at both sides; he fumbles through his credit cards looking for a business card) . . . I'm sure I have a card here . . . somewhere . . .

JAPAN: (acting hurt) Do not go to any trouble . . .

U.S.: (Finds one) . . . Ah, here's a card . . . (he hands Sato a bent card).

JAPAN: (Sato graciously accepts the card and reads it very carefully, and turns it over to its flip side and it is blank . . . he is puzzled . . .)

U.S.: Is there something the matter? (He sees that Sato San is uncomfortable).

JAPAN: Not really.

U.S.: Shall we begin our meeting?

JAPAN: That would be very nice, but perhaps we can first speak about ourselves a little bit . . . such as our positions in the company?

U.S.: Oh. sure . . .

JAPAN: (Sato has kept Rogers' card in front of him all this time, holds it with his two hands and keeps looking at it . . .)

Analysis: This cultural dialogue introduces many commonplace problems facing Americans who lack background and insight into Japanese business practices.

Anywhere in the world, business introductions and greetings have a special significance. Social scientists in recent years have sometimes referred to introductions as "foot in the door" behaviors. In first contacts with Japanese, the *meishi* ritual is of real significance.

In the cultural dialogue, it is quite problematic that Mr. Rogers is unskilled in *meishi.* Apparently he is unaware that there should always be a Japanese language "side" to a business card. He has undoubtedly disappointed Mr. Sato, when he discovers that he has no Japanese language point of reference.

Furthermore, Rogers does not attach any importance to the exchange of cards; if he did, it would be extremely unlikely that he would be caught with a "bent card." In fact, the importance of surface communication and appearances (*tatemae)* cannot be overstated when interacting with Japanese. Ideally, Rogers would have a crisp, two-sided Japanese and English language card, housed within a very attractive leather card case. Once cards are exchanged it is common Japanese style practice that you communicate respect by nonverbal behavior—holding your associate's card in plain view, in front of you, and glancing at it from time to time. You should not immediately discard it or put it away in a wallet.

In addition, Rogers does not understand that many Japanese associates do not view a first meeting and introduction as a time to immediately get down to business. It is also a time to get to know each other and to "feel out" who you will be doing business with. At the end of the dialogue Rogers appears to want to get on with the task, while Sato is still staring at Roger's card, not in any particular hurry. Sato wants to explore 'relationship' before task.

Cultural Abyss at the Negotiating Table: U.S. Expatriates Facing Japanese Associates

"HOW JAPANESE AND AMERICANS SAY 'NO' "

Although "yes" and "no" appear to be instrumental in the communication arsenal of any U.S. or Western business leader, there is a centuries old adversion to either/or responses in far Eastern cultures. More comfortable with indirect forms of expression, keeping their options open, and favoring a public ambiguity over a disconfirmation, Japanese are extremely skillful in wanting to actively sustain a healthy level of uncertainty. In contrast, the uncertainty reduction tactics of the U.S. business communicator is aimed at more rapidly getting to the point in public, whereas Japanese primarily offer private, drawn out, hesitant replies.

A cultural abyss continues at U.S.-Japanese negotiating tables despite efforts on both sides of the Pacific to bridge the gap. The shocks of misinterpreting Japanese intentions and motives are commonplace, and numerous management books, cross-cultural studies, and decades of corporate and political diplomacy have not alleviated problems continuing into the 1990s.[1] Deeply rooted cultural values, beliefs, and attitudes breed Japanese and U.S. communicative styles that are fundamentally different, at odds, juxtaposed, and stylistically distant.[2] The distance, void, gap, or *cultural abyss* between Japanese and Americans at negotiating tables necessitates probing, synthesizing analysis, and accompanying innovative and practical solutions. Specifically within the realm of the public small group format of negotiating, Japanese and Americans struggle to understand respective communication styles for pressing agendas of trade, deficits, joint ventures, sales and marketing, investments, subsidiaries, relocations, diplomacy and public relations, and mounting problems of expatriations.

Under the overwhelming influences of their respective world views or *weltanschauungs*, Japanese and U.S. communicators at negotiating tables oftentimes struggle more with communication itself, than with the content or substance of proposals at hand.[3] U.S. representatives may be particularly baffled as they face Japanese speaking high level conversational English, dressed in stylish European clothes, yet communicating in a very Japanese manner.[4] Japanese, on the other hand, may be surprised to experience the confrontational, verbose, argumentative, rhetorical style of Americans at negotiating tables, unprepared for a cultural alternative to a Japanese conciliatory, indirect, non-confrontational communicative style.[5] Throughout sometimes lengthy negotiating processes, both Japanese and American spokespeople and diplomats face seemingly unreconcilable cultural differences. As a microcosm for the communication conflicts that plague Japanese and Americans, the negotiating table presents a unique challenge to theorists, consultants, and negotiators alike. Can cultural "strangers" meet through a commonly agreed upon language and create bridges, not walls?

The U.S.-Japan Negotiating Table: Prototype for Intercultural Communication

U.S. business visitors and diplomats are frequently seated at formal negotiations with Japanese and struggle to decode Japanese verbal and nonverbal communication. Americans who lack experience with Japanese negotiators overwhelmingly anticipate direct and to-the-point statements, are prepared for some public confrontation and adversarial discourse, and expect the negotiating table to be a format for here-and-now decision-making.[6] Yet what U.S. ex-patriates find are Japanese who send verbal and nonverbal messages in an indirect, non-adversarial, and ambiguous fashion, with negotiations characterized by longer-term, delayed decision-making procedures.[7] Negotiating difficulties are further compounded by the fact that most American business players are not particularly conscious or aware of how they communicate nonverbally.[8] Many expatriates express themselves in what Japanese perceive as exceedingly bold, assertive, projecting, and imposing gestures.[9] *The large U.S. movements of the arms, pounding of the fists, waving of the hands, stretching out of the body over a large area, all tend to signify an aggressive or informal posturing for Japanese.*[10] On the other hand, U.S. negotiators find it a confusing task to decipher or unmask Japanese nonverbal behavior at meetings. Small, restricted, formal, rigid, tightly controlled body language and facial expression seem to be too subtle, rehearsed or contrived, passive, and masking true intentions.[11]

Japanese-U.S. negotiating tables also call attention to intercultural differences regarding what constitutes the "good" or "successful" business communicator. Trained in contemporary manifestations of a several thousand year old rhetorical tradition, many U.S. negotiators assume that skill in forensics, debate, argumentation, persuasion and oratory are highly desirable within decision-making groups.[12] But as pointed out by U.S.-Japan intercultural expert Roichi Okabe, the Western rhetorical lineage, valuing persuasive speaking skills in public arenas, is quite alien to Japanese culture.[13] Accordingly, a common intercultural scenario includes the brilliant CEO, who has been a "shining star" of a negotiator for the American team, only to be privately shunned by Japanese as overly verbose, self-congratulating, too loud, egotistical and aggressive.

Evidence of cultural naivete, blindness and misperceptions abound in the experiences of international negotiators, business people, and sojourners, and is repeatedly documented in the study of U.S. and Japanese communication researchers.[14] Americans ethnocentrically decode Japanese "evasiveness, ambiguity, and superficiality," in the face of Japanese interpretations of U.S. "threats, attacks, ultimatums, impatience, rude provocations, and surprise agendas."[15] Numerous questions lurk as to whether Japanese and U.S. communicative styles can in fact be "bridged," and peacefully coexist.[16] Surely the data suggests a continuing plethora of conflict and misunderstanding at Japanese-U.S. negotiations.[17]

Culturally Juxtaposed Views of Table Negotiations and Decision-Making

In approaching the negotiating table, both U.S. and Japanese representatives have usually been briefed on the agenda and proposals to be covered and decisions pending. Problems commonly arise, however, when U.S. negotiators, for instance, demand decisions that the Japanese team is not prepared to make during a given meeting or time frame. Americans may encounter what "appears to be" Japanese ambiguity, delays, and resistance when new, unscheduled items are suddenly, abruptly introduced at the table—without warning or foreshadowing. Operating from a Western paradigm of direct adversarial communication, Americans may not anticipate the general Japanese adversion to public argument, or reluctance to tackling unannounced agenda items.

From a Japanese vantage point, sensitive issues or face-threatening communicative style is not appropriate within public, formal situations, such as at the negotiating table. Japanese rather conceive of the "table" as a time and place for informing Americans of intraorganizational decisions already made, or as a venue for niceties, ritualistic conversation and surface communication or *tatemae*.[18] U.S. probings of the intricacies and subtleties of the Japanese position, the prospects for compromise, or points of dispute—are not usually fitting topics for public discussion.

In contrast, Americans are moderately to strongly inclined toward favoring public showdowns, heated debates, public arguments and controversy.[19] Media depictions of top U.S. governmental negotiators, for expample, frequently report of American displeasure with Japanese negotiators who "refuse to get down to the nitty gritty," and "decline to talk turkey," or get to a "bottom line."[20] American business sojourners and expatriates want results "now," while Japanese negotiate according to a different "cultural clock," a time frame of longer duration and orientation conceived apart from public scrutiny.

Soto and Uchi: Public and Private Negotiating Arenas

From a U.S. perspective, Japanese communicative behavior is "limited" at the intercultural negotiating table by virtue of cultural dictates for formal, public situations.[21] For Japanese, the negotiating table typifies a communicative situation that may be described

as *soto* or in the "outside, external, public world," and *omote,* referring to "what is exposed to public attention;"[22] Japanese respond by
normatively "selecting" ritualistic, formal, rule-governed behaviors
at the table. Inasmuch as more spontaneous, candid, emotional, adversarial, exploratory interactions are largely designated to *uchi*
(in, inside, internal, private) and *ura* situations (back, hidden from
the public eye), there is little leeway for Japanese "candor" when
facing U.S. representatives at meetings.[23] Whereas U.S. negotiators
bring aspects of celebrated jurisprudence-adversarial models of interaction to meetings, Japanese prefer to voice differences of opinion and persuasion within the face-saving arenas of *uchi* and *ura.*[24]
In contrast, Americans may insist upon a direct dialogue, a public
testing, and airing of views within the context of a public forum,
sometimes before the cameras of the international media. To "speak
up," and be publicly verbose, witty and argumentative is deeply
structured into paradigms of Western communicative style. And
under the heat of deadlines, it is difficult for Americans to resist
a Western based deciphering of "obstinate" Japanese, who lack
willingness to reach decisions or reply in an appropriate, timely
fashion.[25]

A Campaign Approach to Decision-Making: Behind and Beyond the Negotiating Table

Behind the public negotiating table behavior of Japanese lurks
the world of *ura* and *uchi,* where private, intraorganizational communication is integral to the decision-making process. A long-term
campaign approach to decisions is precipitated via *nemawashi* or
"rootbinding," and a corresponding, formal consensus process
termed *ringi.* For crucial contractual, policy making, joint venture,
relocation and subsidiary decision, the Japanese intraorganizational process of securing complete solidarity and a united front
may take long periods of deliberation, with one year or more not being that unusual. Yet, as is well documented by U.S. repatriates,
once Japanese *finally* decide, they are very fast to implement and
voice such decisions.

Once the agenda of an upcoming Japan-U.S. meeting is known,
numerous face-to-face, informal interactions transpire between all
organizational players involved. Known as *nemawashi,* frequent
chats over lunches, dinners, drinks, and during social events serves
as a congenial, informal context for discussion of proposals, possible

courses of action, decision-making, and potential negotiating table strategies. This process is formalized through *ringi,* as a go-between or mediator circulates printed proposals and positions to be taken at upcoming negotiations. Each player responds by affixing his/her seal in a prescribed manner (a personalized seal is used in lieu of a signature): upright, for agreement; upside down, for disagreement; and sideways, for partial agreement—with reservations and qualifications to be further voiced. Through a series of modified proposals, reflecting the feedback of organizational participants, and resubmitted by the mediator to each participant, complete agreement is finally reached prior to company representatives meeting with U.S. representatives.

Japanese spokespeople are subsequently bound to the intraorganizational or in-house decisions reached, and all communication with Americans must reflect this group consensus. Accordingly, any surprise issues, new developments, contingencies, modifications of original proposals cannot be resolved or acted upon by Japanese negotiators in face-to-face, public meetings. Such developments would necessarily result in postponements and require additional meetings at later dates. Bound to a prescribed approach to decision-making, Japanese negotiators are usually not at liberty to publicly speak or forge agreements without an intraorganizational return to *nemawashi,* and the achievement of a *ringi-sho* (complete, 100% consensus).

U.S. negotiators are oftentimes unfamiliar with the in-house decision-making processes of Japanese *nemawashi* and *ringi,* further contributing to a *cultural abyss* at the negotiating table. Placing a higher priority upon the *soto* and *omote* dimensions of the negotiating table than Japanese, American communicative style is geared toward the public, individualistic forum for debate. As opposed to Japanese coming to the negotiating table in the aftermath of lengthy *nemawashi* and *ringi-sho,* Americans rely more upon the setting of the negotiating table itself, and the skills of individual negotiators, as the vehicle for reaching final decisions. Japanese communicative style at the negotiating table clearly reflects unanimity of opinion, and little can be said by Americans to unsettle consensus reached inside the Japanese organization (*uchi*), hidden from the public eye (*ura*). U.S. negotiators are geared up for some Western style argumentation and debate but only find congenial Japanese negotiators, hardly willing to openly confront substantive issues, and more likely to invest in relationship than task communication.

"SIGNING AND NEGOTIATING JAPANESE-U.S. CONTRACTS"

Shall firm, explicit, printed contracts guide U.S.-Japanese business ventures? Or shall a more "Japanized" oral, ambiguous, inexplicit, contingency agreement prevail? Negotiating contracts is a mine field for U.S. and Japanese associates.

Toward a Bridging of the Cultural Abyss at Japanese-U.S. Negotiating Tables

In 1990 Japanese and U.S. trade negotiations between representatives of former President Bush and Prime Minister Kaifu suffered from the *cultural abyss*. Japanese proceeded at a slower pace, requesting more meetings and time-consuming clarifications of U.S. and joint objectives. Americans "accused" Japanese of delaying tactics, not getting to the point, and purposely diverting U.S. demands for timely decision-making, concessions, and a more open-door trade policy. Threats of Gephardt-style U.S. protectionism hovered in the background, as Japanese publicly stated (once again) that they will not be reprimanded or bullied by U.S. confrontational strategies. And the familiar scenario was once again repreated when Bush and the team of U.S. auto executives, including Lee Iacocca, pushed a showdown in Japan during January 1992, as a multitude of demands were made of Japanese. Although the American media reported a mixed bag of success and failures, on the Japanese side there was new grist for the mill of extremists and right wing Japanese nationalists. Once again, the Americans were publicly "dictating" to Japanese and blaming the trade deficit on allegedly clandestine, Japanese activities—rather than facing the shortcomings of U.S. productivity, competitiveness, and motivation.

Apart from the substantive issues at stake, concerning whether Japan has engaged in dumping or unfair trade practices, is the *manner* in which Americans are communicating their frustration and objectives. *Is a Western styled confrontation the "best" negotiating strategy to employ with Japanese, or will this pushing and battering style continue to play poorly before Japanese politicians, CEOs, and constituencies within Japan?*

Is there any way of bridging the abyss, the gap, the perpetual repetition of conflicting Japanese-U.S. communicative styles revealed at negotiating tables? Or are the problems faced by Japanese and Americans more directly related to fundamentally antagonistic business, political and corporate goals—exigencies quite separate and apart from issues of intercultural communication?

The bridging of the *cultural abyss* at Japanese-U.S. negotiating tables *is* essential. Even in instances where Japanese and U.S. corporate or political objectives are on a collision course, the differences are *further extended and aggravated* by an ignorance of intercultural communication differences. In many cases Japanese and U.S. goals are not far apart, and concessions, compromises, and creative decision-making is directly contingent upon the communicative abilities and innovativeness of negotiators—to bridge the *cultural abyss*. Too often the *cultural abyss* is needlessly deepened due to intercultural incompetency of negotiators—and accompanying intercultural inexperience, insensitivity, and ethnocentrism.[26] Despite 1985, 1990, 1992, and 1994 ultimatums publicly issued to Japanese by U.S. trade negotiators, President Clinton and Western media, there is no simple way of suddenly erasing the deeply rooted *uchi* and *ura* dimensions of Japanese decision-making. Nor is there any abbreviated manner of disembodying the adversarial style of negotiating embraced by Americans and representative of a several thousand year old rhetorical and forensic tradition at the podium, pulpit, and board meeting table.[27]

Is it not the *voice of the abyss* when U.S. negotiators are ignorant of or ignore Japanese intraorganizational consensus building and a slower campaign approach to negotiating? And why should Japanese negotiators and the Japanese media, on the other hand, continue to act surprised when Americans want to rush Japanese into decisions, confront and argue at public negotiating tables, and make adversarial announcements at press conferences? Why aren't Japanese prepared and predisposed to be increasingly tolerant of U.S. interactions? Are both Japanese and Americans that oblivious to repeat, command performances, to the obvious clash of East and West?

Although continuing exposure over a period of years is one of the best remedies for ethnocentrism, much of the damage done

MEDIA BRIEFING

"THINLY VEILED RACISM IN THE MEDIA"

. . . Mitsuko Shimomura, editor-in-chief of the *Asahi Journal,* and Jackson H. Bailey, a professor of history at Earlham College, criticized the media for heightening perceptions often based on ignorance that both countries harbor against each other, including the subtle but volatile issue of racism.

"There is a certain amount of animosity among the Japanese public that is a reflection of their arrogance toward the United States. Journalists under pressure from their editors in both countries have fanned these fires, Shimomura said.

Shrill negative rhetoric in the press has also made it easier for thinly veiled racism to appear in the media.

"It appears in both societies," said Dr. Bailey. "Behind that is a public attitude in both countries we must speak out against. This is epitomized by those in Japan who say foreigners should never be allowed to become yokozuna in sumo and is matched by Americans who say, 'Oh, no, you cannot buy the Seattle Mariners.' The source of both attitudes is fundamentally a racist response. That is a hoax," he said.

(from John Cobb, "New glue needed to strengthen the U.S.-Japan relationship," *The Japan Times,* April 27–May 3, 1992, volume 32, #17, 9.)

in U.S.-Japanese relations is a result of inexperienced, cultural strangers, who are unprepared novices in a potentially lethal arena. It is also particularly problematic when the press enters into this bashing mold and further sets the agenda for intolerance, exaggeration, polarization and condemnations. Having culturally naive, inexperienced, or "bashing" members of the media reporting on already trying table negotiations, proliferates a negative climate on both sides of the Pacific, and can be seriously detrimental to adaptation and compromise.

Z-Communication Bridges

Whether the abyss is fueled by ignorance and/or convenience, inexperience or ethnocentrism, there are approaches to bridging Japanese-U.S. differences, already under consideration. Okabe and Goldman, for example, posit the prospect of a Z-communication hybrid, whereby theorists, trainers and practitioners strive to create communication blends of Japanese and American workplace interaction, public speaking, interviewing, negotiating and the whole range of joint-venture human relations.[28] Within the framework of negotiating, a Z-communication amalgam has been suggested by Goldman, consisting of a joint Japanese-U.S. involvement in *nemawashi* and *ringi* processes.[29] Goldman contends that Japanese or Americans may initiate an intercultural and interorganizational approach to decision-making and a longer term negotiating process, by opening the doors to informal communication. Frequent meetings, socializing, conference calls, faxes, letters, memos, dinners, cocktails, computerized communication exchange, videotaped data, teleconferencing, and other links help to establish a more congenial, total relationship oriented "atmosphere" for the negotiating process. Requiring the opening of sometimes closed Japanese corporate doors, and the enthusiastic desire to enter on the part of Americans, the resulting bridge can serve as a counterpoint to the usual abyss.

An obvious question to be raised is the degree to which Japanese or Americans make communicative and negotiating concessions with each other. Surely the answer is contingent upon situational variables. Depending upon seniority, who is serving as host, precedent, and a multitude of power dimensions (majority stock holder, who is in the position of greater power, etc.), Japanese and American negotiators may construct communicative bridges, amalgams that fit the particulars of the situation. What is important is the need to pay attention to the communicative styles of negotiators, rather than an exclusive preoccupation with the task at hand.

Both Japanese and U.S. negotiators must increasingly work with the cultural mandates dealt them. Communication itself, especially in the intercultural arena, must be reflected upon and studied, cross-culturally. It is paramount that both Japanese and American negotiators nurture a fundamental understanding of cultural differences in verbal and nonverbal communication styles, approaches to public and private negotiating and decision-making,

MEDIA BRIEFING

"JAPANESE STANCE OF 'UNIQUENESS' IS BARRIER TO INTERCULTURAL COMMUNICATION, MANAGEMENT AND DIPLOMACY WITH AMERICANS"

. . . . Japan's shared culture may be the richest and oldest on Earth and it gives you ample reason for immense pride. But this great strength can also be a great weakness in the international arena. Why? Japanese often believe, and openly state, that they are different, unique, apart from the rest of the world, and cannot be understood by foreigners. This attitude, I guarantee you, will be the most difficult obstacle you will experience in communicating with Americans. Although you may have strong reasons for this pride in the uniqueness of the Japanese, it will quickly separate you from Americans and will not serve your goal of successful *inter*cultural communication. . . . . it is much better to be open-minded, flexible and as international as possible in attitude. . . . you must be ready to construct a bridge between the American and Japanese cultures. You must think like an open-minded anthropologist, who attempts to temporarily forget his/her home culture and see a new, foreign culture with the open-minded eyes and ears of a child. . . .

(from Alan Goldman, *For Japanese Only: Intercultural Communication with Americans*, Tokyo: The Japan Times, 1988, 5–6.)

and the relationship between negotiators and their organizations. Only when differences are identified and appreciated can Z-communication bridges be approached.

In Response to the Cultural Abyss

It is recommended that a *negotiating of the negotiation process may sometimes take priority over the substantive U.S.-Japanese negotiating table agenda.* A preventative alternative may be found in intercultural training for both Japanese and Americans. Training specifically devised to enhance communicative skills in areas of negotiating, business and management, gender communication, public speaking and presentations, everyday social life, and verbal and nonverbal communication can be extremely helpful to active Japanese and U.S. players. Overall business and managerial communication skills for both Japanese and U.S. expatriates should be developed along intercultural lines—breeding communication skills strategic to both Japanese and U.S. corporate life.

The *cultural abyss* is further crossed or bridged by a concerted effort to merge theory and practice. As Japanese and U.S. universities, corporations, and governments increasingly recognize the importance of communication between our countries, it is time to crack through narrow cultural boundaries,[30] and conclusively challenge national prejudices, limitations, ethnocentrism, and enter the global village. As the Japanese have so aptly illustrated, it is quite possible to remain thoroughly true to one's primary or native culture, while embracing the ways of "strangers."[31] Perhaps it is a time to construct bridges, not walls, a time to give ample attention to the negotiating tables on both sides of the Pacific, a time to narrow the *cultural abyss* and invest in intercultural bridges. Japanese and U.S. negotiators await the impetus and direction of communication theorists, practitioners and pedagogists. I personally invite you to enter tomorrow's news and work toward the minimizing of Japanese-U.S. conflict by addressing research and practice to current and pressing urgencies, to the demands of the *cultural abyss.*

"SOFT SELL vs. HARD SELL PRESENTATIONS: JAPAN-U.S."

U.S. business communicators are more acceptable of the adversarial, confrontational "hard sell." The "softer sell" is more reflective of the collectivist, high context backdrop of Japanese national, social and business cultures.

To push too hard, to be overly confrontational or bold is to bring potentially negative dimensions of "face" into play. Without paying homage to the relationship prerequisites, U.S. hard sell negotiators or salespeople may unwittingly enter into face-provoking, face-challenging interactions. In contrast, the softer sell of Japanese leaves U.S. associates searching for bottom lines and suspicious of a misconstrued "evasiveness."

"HONNE AND TATEMAE IN JAPAN-U.S. CORPORATE JOINT VENTURES"

John Riggs was fairly new to Japan-U.S. business. He was only beginning to learn about Japanese culture. In several of his early encounters with Japanese management, he was baffled. Frequently on assignment in Tokyo, Riggs represented his U.S. corporation in a joint venture with a Tokyo company.

When it came time for informal talk regarding upcoming decisions that had to be made, Riggs found that the senior manager, Mr. Yokota, despite his position as an upper-level manager, was not the man to whom to speak. This confused Riggs. He was gently told that Mr. Sato and Mr. Saito, who both held lower positions as managers, were the men to whom he needed to speak. Mr. Riggs could not understand how Japanese of lower rank, Mr. Sato and Mr. Saito, could be in a decision-making capacity, whereas the higher-ranked man, Mr. Yokota, was being "upstaged."

Mr. Riggs was disturbed to the point that he saw the chief executive officer of the Japanese corporation, Mr. Fuji, in an effort to get to the bottom of his dilemma. Mr. Riggs was quite upset and said to Mr. Fuji, "I do not see why I should be discussing important ongoing venture matters with Mr. Saito and Mr. Sato when I have been speaking with their superior, Mr. Yokota, all along. I refuse to deal with his subordinates unless you give me an explanation." Mr. Riggs was quite annoyed and was initiating a conflict between the U.S. corporation and the Japanese corporation. Mr. Fuji very politely handled the matter by saying that "this is a difficult situation and perhaps you are not aware of *honne* and *tatemae*." Mr. Fuji went on to say "sometimes in Japanese corporations the superior may be superior in name or title, but not in actual power. It is not that unusual for middle-managers beneath an upper-manager to have decision-making power, competency, and understanding that their superior does *not* have."

Mr. Riggs was quite surprised and had not expected a lesson in *honne* and *tatemae*. But Mr. Fuji's patience and explanation of Japanese culture helped Mr. Riggs to understand the subtleties. He now realized that the "pretense" or outer shell was *tatemae* and that in essence was what Mr. Yokota's title and position was about. But when it came to the essence or substantive matters, it was Mr. Saito and Mr. Sato, the underlings, who wielded the true decision-making power.

Analysis: Rank and hierarchy are strategic to Japanese business and the American representative in a U.S.-Japan joint venture, John Riggs, is struggling to understand the unwritten organizational chart and the appropriate channels for communication.

Riggs, like most Americans, is intent upon addressing his joint venture concerns with the higher ranking Japanese official, Mr. Yokota, but discovers that communication should be held with two lower ranking managers, Mr. Sato and Mr. Saito.

What Riggs discovers via the CEO, Mr. Fuji, is that there is a subtle, in-house distinction between formal and informal power, or the "outer shell" (*tatemae*) and "true inner workings" (*honne*) of Japanese decision-making.

Hence, it is vital for U.S. business, political and corporate players to both learn the organizational charts and the *tatemae* of power and decision-making, as well as the informal *honne* of a Japanese company. While rank and hierarchy *must* be outwardly acknowledged and respected, the underlying channels of communication and decision-makers should also be sought out.

CHAPTER 12

Verbal Communication with Japanese

BICULTURAL

"PUBLIC SPEAKING FOR JAPANESE AUDIENCES"

One of the most influential forms of communication is public speaking. It is well known that public speaking is rated as one of the top five fears of Western business executives. This communication apprehension is compounded by Westerners having to face cultural strangers, largely unaware of their expectations of the public speaker.

In Japan, speech and oratory are less explored subjects, as Japanese do not have the equivalent of our Greco-Roman rhetorical tradition. Japanese do not have much experience as public speakers as this is a highly individualistic activity.

Regarding style and delivery, U.S. public speakers in business and political spheres alike, follow a more projective, assertive, individualist format than do Japanese. Japanese speakers and audiences are more restrained.

Verbal communication, the talk and conversations of everyday social and business life, is strongly tied to cultures. How we converse with seniors, subordinates, insiders, outsiders is all contingent upon communication rules followed by members of national and corporate cultures. Even on commonground, business and managerial communication can be problematic. Managers are not understood by subordinates, ambiguous use of language is misinterpreted, and workers' productivity, motivation, efficiency and relationships are intimately entangled in the quality of communication relationships.

Clearly the complexity of human communication is tremendously compounded when U.S. expatriate managers must communicate on a daily basis with Japanese associates. Talk in factory work areas, in white collar office rooms (containing dozens of desks positioned in a room without walls or partitions), at negotiating tables, over the telephone, and other channels, is a source of constant trouble.

Japanese English speakers in U.S.-Japan joint ventures can be better understood by spending the time to prepare for the differences that are typically found between our codes of communicating. Turning to the spoken word, it is vital to identify how the U.S. manager can anticipate workplace conflicts before they arise. In other words, certain rules are in operation in Japan—broadly accepted codes—that direct how Japanese speak in the marketplace.

Silence

Japanese silence is well known. Expect to be caught off guard by prolonged, pregnant pauses and silences. Silence oftentimes carries more weight than "needless" talk.[1] If in doubt concerning whether you should speak more or less with Japanese associates, notice the quantity of verbiage coming from Japanese. The senior sets the agenda. If s/he appears comfortable with less talk and frequent, lengthy silences, do not feel obliged to fill up these "empty" spaces. For the unspoken pauses are hardly "empty" for Japanese— they are meaningful.[2]

Seniority

When approaching verbal communication with Japanese management, assume that the initiation rites rest with the senior. Simply, seniors are usually the initiators. Avoid too much chatter, frequent questions, or attempting to lure seniors into conversation that they may not be interested in. Carefully study nonverbal cues, the tone of voice, and the communicative styles of seniors. This is difficult to adjust to, as U.S. national and corporate cultures more readily value the importance of "speaking up." Controlling the American "virtues" of assertive, aggressive, emotive, provocative speech, is necessary. For when crossing Japanese national or business boundaries, these sterling Western attributes can be transformed into intercultural liabilities.

In-Group/Out-Group

Whether speaking English as a second language, or native tongue Japanese, Japanese tend to display their own peculiar version of ethnocentrism. Termed the *nihonjinron syndrome,* Japanese managers and workers frequently assume that foreigners (*gaijin*) could not possibly understand the motives, productivity, work style, culture or use of language by Japanese. In essence, Japan is for Japanese, and cannot be understood by outsiders.

Serious implications can be derived from the *nihonjinron* beliefs of Japanese.[3] Japanese managers typically assume that the visiting expatriate manager could not "really" understand the meaning contained in Japanese messages. For example, when Japanese speak English and refrain from saying "no," (but say 'no' via vocal or bodily innuendo) there are very few Japanese who would miss the unstated message that they had been "turned down." In effect, the connotative meanings behind and between the words are missed by members of the Western out-group.

During my time spent in Japan I began to become quite familiar with the "kiss of death" phrases uttered by very cordial Japanese middle and upper managers. As soon as I heard such phrases as: "that is a little difficult;" "this probably calls for further questioning and consideration;" or "I am not sure about this;" I was certain that I was being denied my request.

Closely tied in with the Japanese socialization process, it is obvious to Japanese that preservation of face (*kao*), and group harmony (e.g., *wa*), requires that direct, definitive denials or negation be avoided in public. Unknown to many American expatriates, they go rushing back to their home offices, or fax memos to U.S. superiors, convinced that Japanese are "seriously considering a proposal," or said "yes," when in actuality they were turned down.

Direct and Indirect Use of Language in U.S.-Japanese Business Communication: The Art of Ambiguity

Verbal communication with Japanese, whether through English or via an interpreter, is terribly indirect. Our preference for direct use of language is antithetical to Japanese codes for communicating.

Avoiding a clearcut use of "yes" or "no," Japanese skillfully dance a "dance of ambiguity." Especially in face-to-face interaction in the organization, ordinary language is not thought of as a precise, reliable instrument. *Japanese assume that language can be extremely unreliable, inaccurate, and conjures up an illusion that understanding has taken place.*

From the perspective of Japanese (who have not been significantly altered by repeated and longterm contact with Americans), the imprecision of spoken language cannot be avoided. More important than a nebulous exercise in using language for clarity is the strategic use of language to preserve and nurture rank, order, seniority, feelings, relationships and the appearance of groupness.

Unaccustomed to this indirect use of language, Americans may press Japanese for a more specific response to a business proposal, or a firm articulation of a Japanese position. Rather than publicly stating Japanese management's mind in definitive words and phrases, Japanese skillfully walk a verbal tightrope. It is the "fine line" of public communication at public negotiating tables and workplaces. Why say anything that smacks of certainty, when indirect responses are better at preserving the peace, the harmony?

Moreover, indirectness in verbal communication keeps more options open—keeps everyone guessing. *Much as the Japanese language allows the user to delay use of the verb until the very end of a sentence, so does the CEO or senior negotiator measure the atmosphere of all players involved before committing.*

Indirectness also permeates Japanese verbal agreements on the printed page. Contracts are typically ambiguous, indirect, lacking specificity and preciseness. *The vague wording of contracts is a highly purposeful Japanese verbal strategy.* Saying too much, being too specific, or anticipating too many contingencies can later cause conflict, loss of face, and differences.

Verbal communication is, at best, an *approximation* of intentions and motivations, obligations and understanding. Japanese organizations prefer that a situational ethic guide verbal agreements, an ability to resolve problems as they arise. Not being bound to an explicit verbalization of all terms and issues is pivotal for Japanese management—and the source of culture shock for U.S. organizations.

Turn Taking and Cooperation in Group Communication

The vital role of business meetings and negotiations in U.S.-Japanese business relationships provides another occasion for analysis of verbal communication. How do Americans know *when* to speak at meetings with Japanese? How does seniority operate? Is there some way to begin to understand when to take a turn, yield a turn, interrupt, etc.?

MEDIA BRIEFING

"JAPAN VIEWS U.S.' 'THIRD WORLD PROBLEM' "

Diversity is a source of strength in the United States, as it is in the rest of the world. But are the Americans extracting strength from the diversity of their own country? In many American cities, African Americans live in urban centers, while the white middle class has moved to the suburbs to get away from the rest of the people.

But a United States that remains divided by race and class will not have a healthy future. We hope that the Clinton administration will come to grips with solving what might be called the Third World problem within the United States itself.

(An editorial, *Asahi Shimbun Japan Access*, November 9, 1992, volume 3, #43, 9.)

Practical questions are not easily answered in the study of intercultural communication and its interrelationship with business and management. Even a straightforward question – response format at a U.S.-Japan meeting sometimes requires insight into the backlog of culture and language codes.

When to "switch on" or "switch off" the flow of verbal communication, for example, is a subject matter that fascinated the social anthropologist and intercultural communication pioneer, Del Hymes.[4] At international business meetings in Tokyo and New York, Japanese and Americans may share a knowledge of conversational English, a grasp of strategic management and global marketing, but lack a simple understanding of how to *use* the language at a business meeting. *To speak up at the wrong moment, to the wrong person, or to interrupt, are all sources of social and business conflict.* The prospects for these violations are dramatically enhanced by the cultural precedents guiding Japanese and Americans.

As a rule of thumb, Japanese are far more restrictive and exacting in the etiquette of business conversations and cooperation.[6] Without briefings on the hidden cultural and communicative rules governing Japanese, U.S. expatriates are engaging in a high risk interaction. Although Americans certainly have a sense of seniority, respect, and appropriate forms of address, there is less of a national or commonly agreed upon modus operandi.

Regarding who speaks first, there is little doubt among Japanese corporates, that the highest ranking senior official has the floor (even in silence). The apparent Japanese egalitarianism of seniors and juniors dining together in the company lunchhall, or having equal footing in the corporate parking lot, does not spill over into the hierarchal sanctuary of verbal language.[7] Opening statements are usually reserved for seniors or *appointed* spokespeople. If an American outsider or junior would be so bold as to "break the ice" in a formal business meeting, a breach would undoubtedly be underway. Although Japanese might not directly articulate that you had spoken out of turn and out of rank, the nonverbals around the table would be devastatingly clear to the Japanese constituency.[8]

In some business meetings, Japanese have a tacit agreement to cover a specific order of agenda items in a pre-agreed and arranged fashion. Following opening statements by a senior or spokesperson, each member present in the room or at the table would be expected to speak and make a contribution on the cited topic.

I have witnessed U.S., European, and Australian expatriates who were frustrated and confused by this extremely orderly speaking arrangement. It appeared too rule-bound, constricting, and prefabricated. Missing for the Westerners is any semblance of give and take, especially the combative, spontaneous exchange of words, ideas and suggestions.

It sometimes eludes Westerners that the Japanese ordering of who speaks, in what order, and about what topic, is quite intentional. I have seen Americans jump to the conclusion that Japanese wanted to "gut out" American opinions and free expression from these formal gatherings. Others complained that the Japanese did not know how to argue, debate, or put themselves on the line.[9]

There is some truth in all the objections, as well as degrees of ignorance. Japanese have purposefully restricted the free flow of ideas at such formal, public venues—*because* they are out in the open. *Japanese may not want there to be an egalitarian flow of verbiage, as to do so could prove detrimental to cooperation, harmony, and the balance of groups and relationships.* Whereas, U.S. expatriates are dying to spurt out their personal observations on why productivity is down at a U.S. subsidiary, or why the U.S. press is recently crucifying the *keiretsu* ("families" of Japanese companies in close alliance with one another—usually portrayed as "cartels" in the U.S. press) system of Japan, Japanese do not necessarily want to invite such talk into *this* room.

Ironically, knowledge of Japanese use of public and private venues for communication could lead the disgruntled expatriate into realizing that although it is taboo to inflame a formal meeting, such probings may be quite appropriate away from the eyes of the group and the press. Talk in the trenches, at afterhour spots, can be a fertile terrain for the expression of more controversial, potentially face-provoking verbiage.

Briefly returning to the formal, public meeting, it is also essential for expatriates to decode further rules regulating Japanese taking and yielding of turns in conversations. If a Japanese senior is holding the floor, a lengthy pause or silence is frequently misinterpreted as an "invitation" for American or U.K. visitors to interrupt. Proceed with extreme caution. I have personally coached and trained Japanese on the minutia of business meeting protocol, and was regularly drilled regarding this very issue of pauses and interruptions. *Japanese wanted to know exactly how many seconds they were "permitted" to pause (by the "rules" of U.S. business decorum) before they should expect an interruption from Americans.* As you know, explicit rules are not existent among Americans, but there is an unwritten code in Japan allowing for extensive pauses and silences in business meetings, workplace conversations, and other superior-subordinate interactions. To interrupt someone while they are still in the midst of attempting to speak, is an act of "verbal seizure."[10] Japanese expatriates visiting the U.S. for the first time are in a state of culture shock when they are constantly interrupted by Americans. They are surprised that they must "do battle" in order to finish a sentence, and typically perceive American conversational partners as overly combative and competing for the floor.[11]

Whether communicating with Japanese in English or via an interpreter (or in Japanese), do not forget about some of the subtler, hidden stumbling blocks in conducting a conversation. In addition to contrasting codes surrounding opening and closing conversations, taking turns speaking, changing the conversation, who to address, yielding a turn, and interruptions, there is a long inventory of unconsciously practiced cultural rules for talking. Japanese frequently respond adversely to: abruptly raising the volume of the voice; speaking too rapidly; gushing with emotion and excitement; words that exaggerate, boastfulness, and other verbal gymnastics experienced by Japanese as too excessive or direct. Acknowledging Japanese verbal and conversational preferences and expectations is not an easy feat for expatriates as it is quite possible that behaviors rejected by Japanese are part of the strategic communication for success arsenal practiced in the West.

Subtleties of Verbal Communication with Japanese

As will be indicated at the close of this chapter, Japanese are seemingly more concerned with following rules and appropriate form in verbal communication, than in using words in a pursuit of "truth." As an American cross-cultural trainer in corporate Japan, I learned about Japanese communication rules—the hard way.

Thoroughly entrenched in the U.S. version of the business or university classroom, I assumed that a Socratic question and answer approach to training was the way to go in Tokyo. In all truth, I didn't even give it much thought. I asked for Japanese corporate trainees to volunteer their answers to a series of questions. I had no responses. I called upon individual Japanese assembly line workers and managers—they were extremely reluctant to answer my questions. I praised several Japanese men for astute performances in classroom exercises—and they appeared embarrassed. I was baffled.

One afternoon I agreed to meet with one of my corporate trainees over lunch. During this luncheon he told me that I was breaking many of the "rules" of Japanese communication. He informed me that I was using very "direct" language in the classroom, and I was "forcing" trainees to respond to questions. He politely coached me on the differences between using language and conversation in an egalitarian versus a hierarchal fashion. To begin with, I was speaking to the "wrong" trainees. I was unaware that questions should have been directed to the spokesman (he was my luncheon partner), rather than to the class-at-large. Compliments should not be directed to individuals, only the entire group. By directing my words to individual trainees I was unwittingly using the language of "individualism" rather than the language of "collectivism." Even if the trainee knew the answer, s/he was not likely to answer, as it was the spokesperson who was designated to speak. I was reminded of the status, rank, and hierarchal rules at the negotiating table. There were obvious parallels.

As I slowly adjusted my language and interaction style to the corporate Tokyo classroom I also found out that Japanese workers and corporate trainees *do* gradually adapt to more Americanized rules for verbal communication—given time and repeated exposure to U.S. ways. For instance, several months into a training session, Japanese began to exhibit a little more individualistic, outspoken tendencies in corporate training. They spoke up more, interrupted, and were less hesitant at voicing a few controversial ideas before the entire group.

At the same time, I was also changing and becoming increasingly more "Japanese like" in my leadership behavior. I used the language in a more ambiguous, indirect fashion, always conscious of turn taking, turn yielding and the importance of observing Japanese rank and ordering of conversations.

This mutual adaptation is observed over time in the joint venture factories and corporations in the U.S. and Japan. We slowly, sometimes unconsciously begin to tone down those verbal behaviors that alienate our partners and workers from the other side of the Pacific. This merging of characteristics of Japanese and American styles of business communication has been termed "Z Communication," and reflects the broader trends in "Z management."[12]

Years later, I realized that I had finally internalized the important rules of verbal communication with Japanese by having successfully adapted to Japanese expectations. As an author of a number of books sold in Japan that address U.S.-Japanese business, communication, management and organizational behavior, I utilized a "Japanese version" of English. The tone of my words, the use of honorifics, reverence, status, ambiguity, and other variables added up to a use of the English language that is readily digestible by Japanese English speakers.

I became aware of my successful crossing of cultural and national boundaries when I was told by a fluently bilingual Japanese that he was surprised to learn that the book, *For Japanese Only: Intercultural Communication with Americans,* was *not* written by a Japanese. He explained that my English language usage was "very Japanese" and this was "surprising." I took this as a compliment of the highest order.

Violations of Verbal Language Usage

While a majority of Japanese managers and workers follow Japanese culture rules when utilizing English as a second language, there are some serious exceptions.

As a corporate trainer in cross-cultural communication, I trained a Mr. Fukuzawa, with Japan Victor Corporation. Mr. Fukuzawa was a factory line supervisor who dramatically "changed" when offered the opportunity to communicate in English before a large group.

Mr. Fukuzawa emerged as a class clown, but for reasons that are not easily understood from an American expatriate's perspective. Fukuzawa vaguely knew that communication is far more democratic, less rule governed and more egalitarian among English speakers in the U.S. Whenever he had a turn to address our training group, Fukuzawa spoke in an obnoxiously abrasive, loud voice, spewing insults and cuss words. Research into Fukuzawa's background revealed that he was a very well mannered employee when conversing in Japanese language with other Japanese.

Apparently, Mr. Fukuzawa felt that it was a big joke to be speaking in English. Much as a child who wields great power by uttering some cuss words, Fukuzawa was very powerful in his new found English language laboratory of cross-cultural training. He was *finally* able to be the bold, crazy, outspoken man that he secretly desired to be. The strict Japanese rules kept much of this suppressed. In the English speaking venue, he believed he had complete license to "be free" and state anything he wished, in whatever style and manner he chose.

Fukuzawa *polarized* the freedom of choice and combative, jurisprudence tendencies of American English usage in the marketplace. In his mind, the less restricted Western code of *how* to communicate offered him a nihilistic carte blanche for screaming out anything he fancied.

Words for "Substantive Meaning" or "Good Form"?

Japanese rarely exchange words for substantive meaning alone. In fact, there is much in Japanese cultural lineage suggesting that words have serious limitations, and verbal discourse should not be taken too seriously.[13] *Japanese are fond of saying that Americans are rikutsuppoi, or too logical and rational.* And this Western shortcoming is largely a result of our trusting attitude toward language.

When doing business via language, we are not just dealing with the difficult task of translations of verbal languages, we must also address underlying attitudes toward those languages. *There is much agreement among Japan experts that Japanese have a deep and fundamental mistrust of the spoken or written word.*[14] Japanese take words with "a grain of salt," and view spoken language as more indicative of the surface world of *tatemae* than of the essential world of true motivations or *honne.*

Perhaps the most difficult lesson of all is to adjust to this Japanese skepticism toward language, in the course of conducting business. The Western inclination to search for the precise phrase or language to voice a motive, secure a deal, state a negotiating position, or word a contract, is more of a U.S. and Western European inclination. Japanese marvel at the empassioned investment in words—as they mask a communication of the inner self (*kokoro*), and of the stomach or gut (*haragei*). Japanese critic BenDasan, for example, expressed that Japanese search out relationships, true intentions, and commitments that *cannot,* in their estimation, be found in spoken or written language. BenDasan states that for Japanese

> . . . symbolic representations like law, words, and reason remain only secondary; the Japanese thus are cognizant and respectful of . . . "words behind words," and "reason behind reason."[15]

Hence verbal language, Japanese or English, is not the primary or most trustworthy vehicle for communication.

In the midst of struggles for meaning, learning Japanese as a second language, and utilizing interpreters, it is a strange and ironic lesson to learn of the Japanese view of verbal communication. Perhaps it is a sobering reminder of the findings of nonverbal communication researchers who indicate that up to 93% of human interaction is *not* verbal. Or it is a contemporary practice of the anti-verbal rhetoric of ancient Confucianism.[16] But however the late twentieth-century Western manager, expatriate, or corporate affiliate views it, it is an essential "revelation."

On one hand, we struggle for verbal meaning, strive to cross the cultural abyss of a tower of Babel. On the other hand, we are ironically forewarned that words lie and Japanese look for the meaning behind the words. What that leaves us with is a far greater stress upon nonverbal communication. But it also brings the American businessperson back to the observation made by a myriad of intercultural researchers: that Japanese are typically more concerned with "good form" than with "substance." Assuming that true meanings take time, and that motivations will unfold in due course, the emptiness of words is accompanied by an almost artistic pursuit of aesthetic style and form.

Perhaps you do not readily understand the English usage of your Japanese business partner. You may very well find yourself in a double bind. It is somewhat predictable, that unless handled with the utmost form, that it is very difficult to interrupt Japanese. Shall you strive for meaning, and tell him that you don't understand, or keep the harmony and social graces flowing by keeping your mouth shut and head nodding? Many Japanese will not admit or interject that they do not understand you—unless they have become Americanized and place substance above form. Afterall, since words are so limited anyway, why interrupt, ask for clarification or elaboration? Isn't silence and careful observation more reliable than more words?

"THE WRAPPING OF GIFTS"

The wrapping of gifts and packages has played and still plays an important part in Japanese life. Experts and retailers agree that people will continue to place as much importance on the packaging as what is inside it.

Kunio Ekiguchi, author of "Gift Wrapping," and a teacher of wrapping styles, suggests that the concept of wrapping has broad-based and deep roots in Japanese tradition, encompassing everything from enshrouding gods in a family alter to wrapping gift money in special, ornate gift envelopes.

(from "Wrap Artists, Japan Demystified," *Asahi Shimbun Japan Access*, August 3, 1992, volume 3, #29, 12.)

"GIFTS AND BONUSES"

It may be better to give than to receive, but in Japan, gift-giving obligations can ravage a family budget. According to a recent survey, the average Japanese household spent a painful $1,790 (¥229,164) in 1991 on presents and monetary gifts for weddings, funerals and other occasions . . .

It is customary to present mid-summer gifts and year-end gifts to those to whom one feels indebted, such as teachers, company superiors or important customers. Department stores profit enormously during these two gift seasons, while many families use their semiannual bonuses, which are received just prior to these two periods, to partially offset their expenditures . . .

(from "Obligatory gift-giving strains family purse," *Asahi Shimbun Japan Access*, June 29, 1992, volume 3, #25, 9.)

CHAPTER 13

Print Communication with Japanese

In the course of conducting business with Japanese, print communication should not be overlooked. Both obvious and subtle cultural and communicative differences create difficulties for expatriates and for both Japanese and American home offices.

Thank You Letters

When writing letters of "thank you" to Japanese hosts for hospitality extended at a recent visit, feel free to utilize English. *Especially within the Tokyo corporate community, many Japanese would rather receive an eloquent English letter than a second-rate Japanese language correspondence.* Japanese hosts find receipt of an English language letter as an opportunity to practice their English skills.

Greeting Cards

It is essential to follow up rapidly on business visits and other U.S.-Japanese associations with letters of gratitude and thanks. Other writing occasions may include the sending of holiday cards during the Christmas/New Year season.

It may be a worthwhile networking strategy to also send greeting cards to Japanese not well known to you—but individuals with which you have engaged in a *meishi* (business card exchange). I recently received a holiday greeting card from the newly appointed JETRO representative of New Mexico and Arizona. I only briefly met the gentleman several months prior during a local Japan-America Society meeting. Surely this act of print communication establishes a precedent for future relations and a longer term communication campaign of correspondences. Along these lines, the prescripted greeting card message may be accompanied by a few personalized sentences making reference to the initial encounter, constituting an informal note rather than a more formalized letter. It is Japanese style to refer back to the last meeting or correspondence when communicating.

Business Letters and Faxes

When preparing letters or faxes it is relevant to determine the level of English language proficiency and familiarity with American culture held by the Japanese being addressed. It is safest to assume that, even though the Japanese addressee has conversational English proficiency, s/he will be most comfortable with some allegiances to Japanese rules of business communication.

Similar to face-to-face communication in the workplace, the print channels are best utilized in an indirect fashion. Purely bottom-line, to-the-point letters are less effective than those able to quietly engage a more human touch. Care should be taken to partake in *tatemae,* as Japanese expect surface communication, niceties, and some "softer" material other than sheer business talk,. In cases where the last business contact was recent, some reference to same is usually appreciated—similar to the opening of interpersonal conversations. Moreover, some small talk regarding weather, holidays, your last trip to Japan, Golden Week, or guesting or hosting experiences with Japanese, serves as a social lubricant prior to getting down to business. Even in the fax letter do not overlook the importance of some general chatter and beating around the bush.

In frequent fax letter correspondences to Japanese associates in Tokyo and Nagoya, I rarely plunge directly into my *honne* or true intentions. I rather utilize at least an entire paragraph of *tatemae,* attempting to create pleasantries, warmth, and a pleasant atmosphere before getting down to business. Even when I finally articulate my purpose, I will refrain from being overly direct, assertive, or demanding. When corresponding with Japanese I utilize a lot of "probably" words and phrases, such as:

"I am not sure;"
"Perhaps"
"I was wondering if. . ."
"I hope this is not too bold a request but. . ."

CORPORATE COMMUNICATION: GENERALISTS vs. SPECIALISTS

To a certain degree due to their higher context, more collectivist national culture, Japanese managers and workers have been ushered into "generalist" roles within their organizations. Their naturally derived approach to team building has been a cornerstone of Japanese total quality management. Slowly, U.S. management (particularly in those organizations interested in TQM) has attempted to convert the more territorial, private, individualist, specialist U.S. worker into more of a generalist. But in the majority of U.S.-Japanese joint ventures, the generalist/specialist distinction potentially wreaks havoc on factory lines, between engineers and supervisors and throughout organizations. U.S. expatriates should prepare for this clash of national, professional, and corporate cultures.

Memorandums

As an expatriate in Japan I discovered that there was less need for frequent interoffice memorandums and the usual flood of internal paperwork characteristic of U.S. organizations. Largely due to a much more personalized face-to-face interaction between workers and management, closer workplace proximity, and an extremely rapid information flow, in-house print communication is not necessarily a top priority for everyday work product. Bound by walls, doors, partitions, secretaries, gatekeepers and formidable physical obstacles and distances between departments and co-workers, the U.S. CEO and manager is very dependent upon a constant reservoir of memorandums and reports. In comparison, *the more rapid flow of information and increased accessibility and teamwork within Japanese companies renders the trail of paper correspondence to a more secondary line of communication.* Oftentimes, printed interoffice correspondence is generated as a backup to important face-to-face contacts. Expatriates should brace themselves for an unprecedented and unexpected level of constant interaction with staff and management, greatly diminishing the Western manager's reliance upon print.

When memorandums are called for, it is important to remember that Japanese etiquette still prevails, even when dictating or typing an English language message. As suggested throughout this book, keep your print communication somewhat ambiguous, indirect, non-confrontational, and respectful of Japanese status and hierarchy principles. It is also a good idea to utilize a sufficient percentage of *tatemae* language when composing a memo, as it is a breach to be too bold, abrupt or forthright about your true intentions (*honne*).

A Note on Written Reports

Despite a Japanese propensity for surface communication, and the secondary status of print to oral communication within certain business situations, do not overlook the importance of written reports in other venues. When making business proposals, supplying marketing and consumer data, partaking in precise engineering communication, or presenting other quantifiable proposals, Japanese expect extensive print reports and documentation. As a supplementary and tangible appendage to a negotiation, business meeting, or oral report and proposal, it is customary to have a comprehensive typed report. This report allows Japanese associates to dissect the proposal and reach decisions and consensus—in part based upon the document provided. It is best to present the documentation, evidence, surveys, and quantification in an objective fashion, sidestepping Western style persuasive tactics.

Receiving Japanese Print Communication

On the receiving end, Americans may find that there are numerous spelling, grammatical, structural and organizational errors in Japanese composed English language memos, letters, faxes and other business correspondence. Although your Japanese associates may have ten to fifteen years of English language training, many Japanese lack practical or marketplace experience in their second language. Tolerance should prevail as it has been an extraordinarily difficult task for Japanese to learn the English language. It is only with the rise of Japanese industry and the emergence of Japan as a world economic power, that we have even contemplated reciprocating by learning Japanese.

In addition, *Japanese messages will not necessarily follow what we think of as a systematic arrangement or organizational scheme, nor will they be exemplary of Western logic.* More "true" to Japanese language and rules of communication than to English rules or American culture, Japanese business writers tend to meander and to fit their English usage into a Japanese format.

Conventional Japanese Letter Writing: Business and Personal

As you have probably suspected, Japanese letter writing does not get right down to the task or reason for taking pen in hand. The communication menu for letter writing begins with obligatory references to weather, seasons, cherry blossoms, health, and like topics. *In the event that the writer wants to circumvent the tatemae, s/he may begin the letter by stating, "formalities omitted."*

Following the formal, ritualized opening to a letter, there is a shift from the surface message to a truer motivation for the correspondence. This transition is usually signaled by an expression such as "and concerning business," or "by the way." These transitional phrases in Japanese (e.g., *tokoro de* or *sate*) are usually utilized by Japanese English language writers, as it is natural to carry over such print etiquette between languages. Only the more experienced, bicultural or Americanized Japanese writer is apt to drop such deeply grounded Japanese practices. Once the reader receives the "by the way" signal, you have been given a "red flag" that the business, real message, or *honne* is about to unfold.

Both business and personal letters allow Japanese a channel for communicating that is considered discreet, and in some respects, safer than face-to-face relations. Especially if there is any concern over face (*kao*), print communication allows for less complete engagement and contact, and subsequently reduces the propensity for embarrassment. In some situations, letter writing provides an indirect outlet for expression of thoughts and emotions that would not otherwise be communicated in person. It is not unusual to find that business associates, lovers, mother and daughter, speak of feelings, private ideas, and other classified thoughts never before expressed between them. There is a certain safety that protects the Japanese letter writer, allowing for self-disclosure not permissible in the corridors of the organization or within the walls of one's home. Do not overlook the medium of letter writing as a potentially important means of communication with Japanese.

Preparing for Japanese Print Communication

The following list of suggestions may help you prepare for Japanese print communication. Keep in mind that this briefing is based upon the assumption that a majority of Japanese maintain the print and interpersonal etiquette of Japanese culture when using English as a second language. You will notice that the items cited all reiterate some of the basic tenets of Japanese communicative practices already examined within other business contexts.

Briefing List on Characteristics of Japanese Print Communication

1. Extensive use of *tatemae* or "surface communication" in memos, faxes, and letterwriting;

2. *Tatemae* usually precedes the true objectives or motivations for the correspondence; expect the *honne* to follow the *tatemae;*

3. Use of indirect, ambiguous language;

4. Reference to personal and social events, last meetings between sender and receiver and other pleasantries;

5. Communication that gingerly deals with touchy issues, sidestepping face (*kao*) threatening topics;

6. Use of understatement;

7. Use of probabilistic, tentative language;

8. Because of extensive face-to-face communication in the marketplace, there is less reliance upon interoffice, inhouse memorandums;

9. Thank you letters and greeting cards are important print communication vehicles in the course of developing business relationships;

10. Japanese print communication is more circular, sporadic, and meandering than Western correspondences; do not expect to find clear, to-the-point, well organized correspondences following the rules of Western logic;

11. Japanese take written reports quite seriously; when making proposals, or delivering a significant oral presentation, Japanese expect a highly detailed written/typed report with elaborate evidence, quantification, etc.;

12. Japanese are very concerned with appropriate form when engaging in oral or print communication; proper form can be more important than the substantive issues at hand; and

13. Letter writing sometimes provides a channel for Japanese to more discretely self-disclose than is permitted via face-to-face contact; this is due to the indirectness of print versus human interaction.

"JAPANESE ATTACH PRESTIGE TO ENGLISH EXPRESSIONS"

. . . . .The prestige attached to English or English-sounding expressions seems to be effective in influencing people not only for making people buy commercial products, but also for making people vote, changing opinions, or impressing people. Politicians like to use English words in political speeches, but often they dig up very rare or obsolete words from a dictionary so that what they are saying is unintelligible or meaningless even to a native speaker of English . . .

(from Michio Kitahara, *Children of the Sun: The Japanese and the Outside World*, Sandgate, Folkestone, Kent, England: Paul Norbury Publications, 1989, 121)

CHAPTER 14

Corporate Persuasion: Communicating with Japanese Audiences

BICULTURAL

"NATIVE PUBLIC SPEAKERS vs. SECOND LANGUAGE SPEAKERS"

Far more Japanese are able to conduct business in English language than U.S. counterparts are able to speak Japanese.

U.S. associates may unconsciously expect Japanese to utilize English in a Western fashion—forgetting that the majority of second language speakers retain many of the behaviors strategic to their native language and indigenous culture.

Great care must be given to facilitate mutual understanding in the conversing through second and primary languages—as it is essential to U.S.-Japanese business transactions. Interpreters may occupy a unique role in helping to decipher differing uses of the English language.

U. S. managers and multinational corporations regularly engage in various forms of "persuasion" in the course of conducting business with the Japanese. Persuasive presentations, videos and mediated messages are delivered by CEOs before live Japanese constituencies and television cameras. Negotiators attempt to argue the merits of utilizing more U.S. nationals in a Nagoya based subsidiary, and Americans and Europeans travel to Tokyo intent upon soliciting Japanese investment in Western based joint ventures, all to be accomplished in part through persuasive and eloquent messages. Unfortunately, the majority of Western CEOs or managers fail to adequately examine whether their usual arsenal of persuasive techniques utilized at home will prove as effective with Japanese clients. Additionally, the same members of U.S. top management teams may lack briefings in how Japanese persuade Japanese—hence, Japanese persuasive style.

Roots of Western Mistakes

"When in Rome, do as the Romans do" is a useful maxim to keep in mind when engaged in international attempts at persuasion. Yet it is particularly difficult for Western executives to adjust to Japanese predispositions. For instance, it is somewhat of a cultural shock to discover that Japanese do not have an equivalent of our adversarial, combative brand of "hard sell" communication tactics. Behind closed doors, in the halls of the Diet, or other designated venues, it is common to find Japanese engaged in heated, verbal arguments. But in a majority of public business situations, the overt, manipulative, strategies practiced in the West are largely unacceptable to Japanese.

In contrast, Confucian tradition has trained Japanese to seek out the spirit and true intentions (*honne*) behind the loud, verbose exclamations of Western persuaders. A softer sell, with the true motivation subtly and quietly veiled, is more a Japanese style.

Corporate and Cultural Bridges

Assuming that U.S. multinationals adequately value their Japanese associates and markets, it is reasonable to consider alternative means for corporate persuasion. For instance, Westerners may begin by recognizing that there is quite a gap between the moot court, jurisprudence style of persuasion popularized in the West, and the more disguised, indirect, group oriented persuasion used in Japanese business. When in Japan, it is advantageous to master a more Japanese mode of persuasion.

Cultural Briefing

The following is a brief list of suggestions (followed by further qualification) for Western organizations intent upon supplying expatriates, negotiators and representatives with a blueprint for addressing Japanese management, workers and markets.

Persuasion Techniques to be Avoided
with Japanese Associates

1. Relying upon a single persuasive speech, negotiation, talk, telephone conversation, print or electronic message as a means of convincing Japanese;

2. Short term communication of several days, weeks, or even months;

3. Using bottomline, direct persuasion aimed at calculated goals or objectives, without taking time to get to know Japanese associates, or engage in preliminary pleasantries;

4. Highly argumentative, hard-sell, persuasive strategies aimed at overt, immediate influence;

5. Overly verbose, eloquent speeches or negotiations;

6. Ultimata, inflexible or sudden deadlines and other non-negotiable, confrontational methods;

7. Any public communication strategy or statement that might cause Japanese to lose face.

Persuasion Techniques Appropriate
with Japanese Associates

1. Proceeding slowly, viewing persuasion as a long-term campaign, rather than a short-term act of salesmanship;

2. Expressing the fact that the corporation is interested in its Japanese associates and is willing to invest in a long-term business relationship;

3. Valuing a congenial atmosphere for speaking, meeting and conducting business over the Western tendency to convince Japanese of the merits or superiority of the company's propositions;

4. Learning how to be less verbose and making ample, comfortable use of silences and pauses;

5. Careful monitoring of feedback from Japanese associates; cultivation of listening skills and observation and decoding of Japanese body language, facial expression, and inflection;

6. Listening and observing Japanese responses beyond the more obvious verbal messages;

7. Always allowing Japanese to save face in public communication settings; refraining from face-provoking persuasion;

8. Growing to accept Japanese ambiguity, delays and inconsistencies in offering responses or feedback;

9. Utilizing non-business, social settings for conducting a "gentle" form of corporate persuasion, devoid of briefcases, paperwork and documents, and intent upon establishing a trusting climate for building business relationships.

Further Elucidation

Persuading the Japanese requires extensive patience, long-term communication in the "social trenches" and a finely tuned ability to shift out of the verbose, confrontational mode of the advocate. It is essential that Western organizations begin to examine every aspect of their native and corporate communication style, and to recognize the Japanese preference for subtlety, formality and emotional control in public, as well as long-term commitment. There is also a great need to nurture personalized relations. The cultivation of a "relationship" based on reciprocal good feeling, trust and compassion cannot be overstressed, as this is a precursor to serious business ventures.

Telephone calls are not a viable replacement for face-to-face interaction, as frequency of meetings with the same faces will expedite relations. Moreover, the Japanese prefer to develop relations with specific individuals, and Western tendencies toward rapid employee turnover and transient management will adversely affect the prospects for corporate persuasion.

CASE STUDY

"U.S. POLITICAL SPEAKER SHOCKS TOKYO AUDIENCE"

A celebrated U.S. political speaker addressed a Tokyo audience last week, and was ill-received by the Tokyo press. Local Japanese and English language press stated that the U.S. politician had very substantive, enlightening points of view. But the press was unanimous in stating their surprise at the U.S. politician's fiery rhetorical style. Various press accounts exclaimed that the U.S. politician was extremely bold, loud, almost screaming, confrontational, and nearly hysterical in his speaking style. They questioned whether a more subdued, subtle style might be more appropriate for speaking on political issues that require serious thought, patience, and sophisticated decision-making. The speaker was also labeled as being very "evangelical" and TV preacher-like in gesture and delivery.

Upon being approached for his reaction to the Japanese press' slamming of his speaking style, the politician stated "in the U.S. of A. we say it big and bold, and I have a ferocity to what I say. The Japanese seem to like everything real quiet and subtle-like." He went on to say "different strokes, for different folks."

Analysis: The U.S. political speaker is ethnocentric and appears unwilling to adapt to Japanese audiences.

An evangelical, TV preacher style is particularly harsh, confrontational, and too exaggerated for most Japanese audiences. It is not surprising that the Japanese press labeled the politician as "hysterical."

It is vital that U.S. speakers learn how to anticipate the expectations of Japanese audiences. It is not enough to know your subject matter or to have had continued success with U.S. and Western audiences. Speaking before Japanese warrants a revamping of style and delivery, as the presentation is crucial to Japanese.

Japanese lack an adversarial oratory tradition and rather favor speeches that build solidarity and relationships, avoid public arguments and confrontations and work in a subtler fashion. The U.S. political speaker should carefully examine Japanese styled public speaking and no longer assume that a Western style is automatically transferable to Japanese expectations.

CHAPTER 15

An Intercultural View of Eloquence: U.S. and Japanese Approaches to Public Speaking

MEDIA BRIEFING

"JAPAN BASHING"

They save; we spend. They produce; we consume. They have a surplus; we have a deficit. They have little crime; we have a lot. They study our language; we don't study theirs. We condemn their trade surplus, but not ours with other countries . . .

When the English bought Holiday Inn, no one cared; but when the Japanese invest here, we resent it . . .

The Dutch own about as many of the American assets as the Japanese; no one complains about them. The British own twice as much and no one complains . . .

Our bashing is sour grapes, envy, scapegoating, self-delusion, arrogance, pettiness, xenophobia, prejudice, hypocrisy, and double standards . . .

(from Al Garner, "On Japan Bashing," Letters To the Editor, *The Japan Times,* June 1–7. 1992, volume 32, #32, 11.)

One of the top five fears of U.S. business, political and corporate leaders is fear of public speaking.[1] Speech anxiety, communication apprehension, and communication avoidance is further compounded when U.S. expatriates face foreign audiences.[2] As a "stranger," the speaker frequently lacks an understanding of how non-Western audiences view eloquence or communication competence.

This chapter will specifically focus upon the cultural and communicative barriers faced by U.S. speakers in addressing Japanese audiences. American business and political speakers are provided with a non-Western, Japanese approach to eloquence. The unparalleled U.S.-Japanese strategic corporate, political, and economic relationship generates an escalating number of public speaking engagements requiring that U.S. speakers develop a working knowledge of intercultural communication. Within the corridors of joint venture organizations, Americans frequently are called upon to deliver oral reports at meetings and negotiations, and in-house presentations to workers and management. As "cultural strangers," many of these U.S. expatriates are in dire need of briefings on adapting their Western style of eloquence and speaking to Japanese expectations. The following will prepare you for Japanese audiences.

Crossing Cultural Borders: U.S. Standards of Eloquence Don't Apply

It is particularly interesting to take note of some of the unique cultural and communicative challenges facing Americans when they must speak in public forums with Japanese. In essence, a vital component of successful business relations with Japanese is contingent upon an ability to cross cultural borders and deliver an oral report or a speech that moves, persuades and informs Japanese. Japanese express in private that Americans are oftentimes too logical and rational (*rikutsuppoi*), too much in a hurry to persuade audiences, unaware of Japanese stress upon establishing interpersonal relationships and gut communication (*haragei*) as a prerequisite to doing business, oblivious to Japanese interdependencies (*amae*), and overly independent.[3]

Expatriate U.S. managers in Kyoto need cultural preparation concerning how to address their Japanese workers. *Visiting U.S. business and trade representatives require briefings on how to effec-*

tively make an oral report to a group of senior Japanese managers who are potential investors. A myriad of possible speaking venues mandate predeparture training as premature returns of U.S. expatriates, stalled negotiations, fractured joint ventures and damaging international media coverage are just a few of the lethal cross cultural conflicts or scenarios to be anticipated.

Success as a public speaker before Japanese audiences is inseparable from an understanding of how Japanese experience speeches and speakers, and how they respond to words, arguments, logic, body language, emotions and facial expression. Quite simply, many U.S. standards of eloquence do not apply with Japanese audiences.[4] The intercultural challenge of public speaking necessitates cross cultural skills—an ability to be flexible enough to both comprehend Japanese communication etiquette and partially adapt to Japanese standards of eloquence.

Fear of public speaking certainly increases when American business representatives are called upon to deliver a winning oration to a Japanese audience. Uncertainty and a desire to avoid the responses and interpretations of an "unknown," poorly understood audience magnifies the perceived difficulty of the task.[5] U.S. business people traveling to Japan and American expatriates (in Japan) regularly face a multitude of cultural differences impinging upon or influencing the prospects of delivering an effective presentation. The challenge is one of developing intercultural competency when speaking to Japanese audiences.

Language Barriers and Translators

Beginning with the language barrier, it is crucial to identify how many members (or what percentage) of your Japanese audience are English speakers. Despite the fact that a majority of Japanese corporate managers in Tokyo do have English language proficiency,[6] in certain situations it may be necessary to employ a translator.[7] If this is warranted (due to a large number of non-English speaking Japanese to be addressed), it is advisable to employ a hands-on approach to the selection of a translator. Your oral presentation can be greatly aided or diminished by the skill and style of the translator. In controversial situations involving joint venture conflicts, or when suddenly surprised by the need for a translator, it can be advantageous to personally select a translator (with the assistance of your organization and/or a Japanese language expert from a local university), rather than delegating this to your Japanese hosts.

Through my consulting work in Japan I found out that translators for American business speakers and negotiators are not always "neutral" and may assume the covert role (intentional or unintentional) of an "advocate." Keeping this in mind, *it is vital to contract a translator who is sympathetic with your business mission and objectives, criteria not always met by allowing the translator to be chosen by your Japanese associate or affiliate.* For without any Japanese language ability, you may find yourself in the role of an American speaker who has no idea, whatsoever, regarding the accuracy or tone of the translator's Japanese interpretations of your presentation. Moreover, if you are to be completely dependent upon the translator, you should be able to trust that this professional translates both your words and the Japanese language responses of your audience with truthfulness, allegiance and fidelity.

Japanese Judge Speeches via Native Cultural Standards

Even when speaking to a Japanese audience well-versed in conversational English, do not assume that they understand or utilize the language in an Americanized way.[8] Assuming that you are primarily addressing Japanese who utilize English as a second language, there is a wide body of research indicating that Japanese maintain an "allegiance" to the rules, customs, practices and precepts of their native culture and language.[9]

In other words, Japanese audiences and public speakers tend to speak and listen to English in a Japanese manner. Many Americans mistakingly assume that Japanese English usage will closely parallel American usage, meaning that there need not be much thought given to *how* we communicate through English.[10] This is a costly error for the American business person in Japan or the U.S. born manager delivering a speech to recently arrived Japanese expatriate workers in a Tennessee automobile plant or an Arizona automobile testing facility.

Without extensive contact with American culture(s), many Japanese unwittingly anticipate that public speakers will follow Japanese guidelines for business and social decorum, even when communicating in English; or Japanese may be very unfamiliar and unappreciative of American norms guiding the model, effective public speaker.[11] It is not surprising when a false sense of security arises as otherwise apprehensive American businesspeople are briefly able to reduce their stage fright when learning that their

Japanese audiences in Tokyo are fluent English speakers. The cross-cultural stage fright rapidly escalates, however, when it becomes apparent that Japanese will not respond on cue (according to U.S. based speech and response cues). Culture shock follows as the American speaker is confronted with the fact that Japanese speak and hear a very different version of English than Americans.

Japanese preferences in communication may be very deeply ingrained within Japanese language. For example, Japanese language tends to be indirect, vague and ambiguous with the use of verbs usually reserved for the end of sentences. Japanese lacking ample contact with Americans experience a series of cultural shocks when they hear a "true" American speak an Americanized version of English. Despite having learned conversational English through ten years of training in the public schools and continuing in-house corporate training, few Japanese are prepared for the more emotional, combative, face-threatening manner that many American speakers employ. Whereas Japanese language nurtures group relationships and has a plethora of words and phrases for preserving face, English language has cultivated an articulation of independence, debate and individuality.

The seasoned American expatriate business speaker in Japan learns that many clues are contained within Japanese culture and language—guides instrumental in adjusting to Japanese. In Japanese language there are a large number of pronoun variations dependent upon the stature, rank, position or status of the person addressed. Americans can heed this to be a strong sign that speakers should not be too informal before Japanese audiences and strive to discern how to address corporates of varying ranks. When in doubt, the American business stranger should always refer to Japanese individuals during an oral report by use of the last name and title, completely refraining from first name usage. Crucial is the understanding that even when Japanese do converse or listen to a U.S. speaker communicating through English, that it is quite difficult or even impossible to shed the thick influences of their native language. The clash between languages and cultures is largely inevitable, but can be significantly alleviated or offset by predeparture preparation for Japanese audiences.

What Persuades an American Audience
may not Score with Japanese

What persuades an American audience may not score with a Japanese group. The hard hitting, opening argument or persuasive speech so successful with an American jury or group of investors depends upon the speaker's insights into the minds, emotions, logic, values, and assumptions of his U.S. audience. Much of the identification or relationship established by the eloquent public speaker is built upon shared beliefs, attitudes and values between speaker and audience—assumptions held in common prior to the speech. Devoid of a background in Japanese culture, the same public speaking techniques are very likely to fail with Japanese business partners in Osaka—unless the Japanese audience is thoroughly enculturated and Americanized or the speaker is able to establish a warm, interpersonal relationship.[12] For although Japanese English speakers may understand the denotative meaning of words and sentences, the connotative meaning is dependent upon a common cultural identification and overlap between speaker and audience.

The culturally naive business speaker overlooks this vast sea of cultural differences, assuming that Japanese will be able to adequately understand most of what is intended. The experienced U.S. expatriate devotes herself to examining many facets of Japanese history, society and etiquette—ultimately utilizing this information as a solid basis for creating commonalities with Japanese associates.

Speechwriting and Speaking for Japanese Audiences: Avoiding American Idioms and Humor

Closely related is the need for a cognizance on the part of U.S. public speakers that they should strive to write speeches that are simple, utilize short sentences, and avoid humor or American metaphors and idioms. Many repatriates tell ugly war stories surrounding the impossibility of translating American humor to Japanese English speaking audiences (English as a second language). Widely substantiated by international business and intercultural communication researchers and consultants,[13] it is necessary to "throw out the window" all the advice of Western speech coaches celebrating the use of humor.

Since humor does not hold up well when crossing Japanese cultural borders, be extremely cautious before uttering the one liner in the opening sentence of your speech. If you insist on utilizing humor, then this urge can be sensitively satisfied by obtaining a consultant briefing on Japanese humor, or looking up cross cultural U.S.-Japanese intercultural communication research studies on the subject.

Similarly, American idioms are a particularly deadly form of intercultural expression and can ruin an otherwise strong speech.[14] Within the confines of the Japanese corporation, middle managers, supervisors and CEOs are actually studying American idioms in their on-site conversational English classes—taught by imported native English teachers. But if you are concerned with probabilities, then I strongly urge you to avoid the usage of popular baseball, military and other extended metaphors and idioms commonly developed in U.S. corporate and national culture.

Expatriate Preparation: Merging Business and Anthropology

Idioms such as "he's a longball hitter," or "let's go for a touchdown on this one" are usually a source of bewilderment and embarrassment for both American speakers and Japanese audiences. As a cross-cultural trainer and consultant for Japanese corporates, I frequently spent up to an hour explaining the cultural, historical and corporate origins behind a single idiom or extended metaphor.[15]

BICULTURAL

"FOLLOWING-UP ON COMPLETED JAPANESE-U.S. BUSINESS TRANSACTIONS"

Is a business transaction to be viewed as a singular event or as part of a longer term campaign? As slower, more patient, longer term practitioners of business, Japanese are particularly skilled in "following-up." Shorter term, more rapid paced U.S. business associates are faced with having to produce faster results and may not be as considerate when it comes to "following-up."

This highly effective tool for American speakers facing U.S. audiences, is an intercultural disaster before Japanese. The only exception would be if you were speaking with Japanese who have spent years living and working with Americans and have mastered Western national and corporate culture.

Pivotal is the necessity of viewing public communication from both U.S. and Japanese perspectives—as there is no way to penetrate a Japanese associate or audience without a knowledge of their expectations. This ability to speak at least in part according to Japanese communicative standards mandates that the business person of the 1990s be willing to unravel some of the cultural background lurking behind the practices of day-to-day business. For even the act of giving a speech before a room full of Japanese investors, engineers, workers or managers, is an assignment in both business and anthropology, requiring that you know how to speak, think, listen, respond and reason from both a U.S. and a Japanese perspective. Consider, for example, the plight of the U.S. expatriate manager who in the course of delivering a short motivation and appreciation speech to Japanese factory line workers, makes the cultural blunder of profusely complimenting the work of an individual worker. The Japanese worker's face turned colors, thoroughly embarrassed that he had been singled out from the group for praise. Now armed with some additional cultural insight, this same manager will have learned that Japanese socialization makes it largely taboo to call attention to the individual—even for praise. All future addresses of the American manager focused upon group issues, with individual assessments handled only through private venues.

Rethinking the Assertive, Bottom-Line U.S. Speaking Style: Recognizing the Multicultural Tower of Babel

A majority of U.S. business people have been raised and taught to "speak up," be assertive, project and "state their mind." This "bottom line," adversarial orientation prevalent in mainstream U.S. business is to a large degree a taken-for-granted model of how to inform or persuade an audience. Without the benefit of reflection and cross-cultural preparation it is likely that even the extraordinarily expressive U.S. business speaker will find that his verbose, animated, argumentative speeches are inappropriate, alienating and failures before Japanese audiences.

Surprisingly, Japanese do not have a speech and oratory tradition and they may find Western standards of eloquence to be alien and distasteful.[16] Japanese rather view public speaking as a primarily Western mode of communicating, and position it as a surface or superficial means of expression (*tatemae*), as opposed to a communication of true intentions (*honne*)[17] or the gut (*haragei*).

In preparing for public business communication with Japanese, it is essential to first reflect upon this deeply rooted U.S. assumption—that it is best to express business objectives in a bold, direct, to-the-point, clear and unambiguous fashion. Even within the continental boundaries of the U.S., there are significantly contrasting cultural and communicative styles operating between New York and Chicago corporate players, rural Appalachian factory line workers, Alabama business negotiators, and inner city Los Angeles Hispanics and Afro-American entrepreneurs. The rich tapestry of

MEDIA BRIEFING

"ABOUT ETHNOCENTRIC ARROGANCE"

Growing emotional conflicts between Americans and Japanese within Japanese firms in the United States are largely being aggravated by the insensitivity of Japanese expatriates to the changing view of Japan and the Japanese held by many Americans.

For Japanese companies, the disintegration of the once-mighty General Motors and other giant American enterprises should also serve as a sobering reminder of the outcome of ethnocentric arrogance on the part of a corporation or a nation.

(from Yoshihiro Tsurumi, "Japan for Isolation from Rest of the World," *The Japan Times*, June 8–14, 1992, volume 32, #23, 11.)

cultural, ethnic, and racial groups within U.S. businesses and workplaces is expressed in verbal and nonverbal communication patterns and preferences and starkly contrasting public speaking styles.

Before heading to Japan for expatriate assignments, Americans have their hands full deciphering a seeming Tower of Babel at

home. It is only recently that intercultural research scientists are
discovering verifiable contrasts in verbal styles and facial expressions among various U.S. ethnic and racial groups. For example, research indicates that when listening to a speaker, Afro-Americans
tend to make far less eye contact than do their Anglo counterparts.[18] Ironically, however, the same Afro-Americans may make far
more eye contact than Anglos when they are the speakers.[19] Much
as American business should thoroughly prepare for the micronu-
ances of Japanese speech and body language, so are we challenged
by diversity within U.S. cities—a multiculturalism that can lead to
workplace conflicts, grievances, litigation, turnover, and corporate
image crisis.

These cultural differences experienced on the U.S. homefront
are generally accelerated and exaggerated when U.S. businesses
face Japanese workers, managers, negotiators, politicians and
CEOs in Japan or the United States. It is no simple matter to speak
to Japanese audiences who are "strangers"[20] to U.S. culture, history, and value systems. Unless Americans are dealing with experienced, U.S. wise Japanese sojourners or expatriates, it is quite
likely that the assertive, aggressive mode of delivering presentations and oral reports will not be terribly well received. Why? Multiple forces operating within Japanese lineage, social and business
etiquette, virtually castigate or banish the verbose, eloquent, argumentative speaker.

Cultural Background and Views on Japanese Public Speaking: Confucianism, Buddhism, Nakasone, Morita and Ishihara

A brief diversion into Japanese history unveils that Confucian
and Buddhist influences have made a clear imprint on the Japanese
business psyche. Presentational skills and manner are tempered by
teachings emphasizing collectivism.[21] Inasmuch as the group has
been heralded over the individual, the soloist must speak in a fashion that advances the team, village or organization. Modesty, few
words, deference to superiors and a thorough disdain for overly vocal, argumentative speech is widely recognized throughout Japan.

At stake is not only a recognition of bold cultural clashes between Japanese and Americans vis-à-vis public communication, but
the issue of whether adaptation is in order. It is extremely difficult
for thoroughly Westernized American business people (especially

those with limited experience with Japanese culture) to even begin to fathom a Japanese approach to public speaking. For many American expatriates and business sojourners, Japanese views of public communication represent an elaborate code of rules glorifying the quiet, self-effacing, reluctant speaker and castigating our U.S. and Western European models of eloquence.[22]

Inasmuch as preparation for speaking before Japanese audiences and media necessitates a sensitivity to the culture and background of Japanese associates, it is important to take note of how they view the challenge of addressing the American public. From the Japanese side of the Pacific there are indications that there is a new breed of Japanese corporate player and politician, epitomized in such international figures as former Prime Minister Nakasone, and Sony CEO Morita. Particularly in the case of Yasuhiro Nakasone, he has systematically and repeatedly developed a cross-cultural form of speechwriting and public speaking. A study by Notre Dame professor Sister Dei indicates that Nakasone dramatically shifted his speech scripts and speeches when facing either Japanese or Western audiences.[23] He "switched codes" when needed, speaking in conciliatory, nationalistic, subdued tones before Japanese audiences, and turned more outspoken before European, Canadian and U.S. audiences.

A large majority of Japanese, however, do not appear to be following Nakasone's lead. With the startling exception of Ishihara and Morita's U.S. bashing book, *The Japan That Can Say "No"* (experts attribute the confrontational rhetoric largely to the staunch nationalist, Ishihara, rather than the more mild centrist, Morita),[24] most Japanese continue to find the fast talking, argumentative U.S. executive and politician mildly objectionable to repugnant.[25]

Yukichi Fukuzawa's Struggle to Introduce Western Styled Speaking to Meiji Period Japan

The Japanese aversion to what Western communication experts refer to as an adversarial, jurisprudence styled model of communication can be more comprehensively appreciated by a recognition of the earlier struggle of the Japanese educational reformer and maverick, Yukichi Fukuzawa.[26] Shortly following Commodore Perry's entrance into Japanese territory, Japan succumbed to U.S. and Western pressure to open its ports and people to Western goods, business, trade and civilization. This was expedited under the reign of Emperor Meiji, as the celebrated Japanese period of Westernization, from 1868–1912 is termed the "Meiji Period." In the early years of Meiji modernization, Fukuzawa made numerous trips to Europe and the United States. Foremost among his attempted "imports" from the West was the Greco-Roman tradition of public speaking, oratory, argumentation and debate.[27]

Fukuzawa told his Meiji period audience that it was time to reconsider the Buddhist and Confucian grounded Japanese rules for public communication and speaking. It was vital, in his estimation, that Japanese educators, students, businessmen and politicians learn the celebrated and prestigious oratory and persuasive speaking style first articulated in Aristotle's "The Rhetoric"—a tradition developed by the Greek Sophists, the Socratic dialogues, the Roman rhetorics of Cicero and Quintillian and through centuries of reinventions by clergy, politicians, actors, and elocutionists.[28] Fukuzawa argued that there was a compelling gap in the Japanese understanding of Western communication, as during the early Meiji Period there were no Japanese language words for "speech," "public speaking," or "debate."[29] He contended that without an ability to speak forcefully and eloquently, or to participate in the art and science of debate and persuasion, Japanese would not be able to be competitive within the emerging world market. Fukuzawa struggled to convince his contemporaries that the archaic, ethnocentric, Confucian rules governing public interaction would prevent Japanese from effective participation in international trade, commerce, world political forums, and in development of a British styled parliament (now the "Diet").

Although the intercultural challenge of Fukuzawa was instrumental among the new voices of the Meiji Period and his educational innovations and private school paved the way for a Tokyo university, he had limited success with his communicative mission. Adversarial speaking and debate remains more confined to private Japanese venues, the Diet, nationalistic protests and rarely surfaces in public international settings. For every Nakasone or Ishihara there are tens of thousands of Japanese who prefer a non-Western style of communicating in public.[30]

Public and Private Speaking in Japan: Reagan, Bush and the Detroit Trade Convoy

Perhaps it was the softer, more effeminate speaking style of the great communicator, Ronald Reagan, coupled with the aggressive

Western speaking repertoire of Nakasone that got through to both Japanese and American audiences. And conversely, the more confrontative, face-threatening public blasts of Iacocca, Bush and the U.S. automobile group of January 1992, represented a series of severe cultural code violations—perpetrated on Japanese soil.[31] Magnified many times over by adverse international media coverage, the Bush convoy literally steamrolled into and through Japan, with arguments and showdowns constituting the chosen mode of communication. The issue here is not whether Japanese are unfair trade partners but rather whether the American tactics of communicating were optimal and productive means for voicing both Detroit's and the U.S.' collective frustrations, demands and objectives. Did the public statements and speeches of the U.S. trade team further American goals or serve to alienate Japanese consumers?

In my estimation, the confrontation may have been more successful if conducted primarily in private, secluded, face-to-face interactions, rather than flaunting U.S. disgust in public. Although there is not a precise or conclusive way to dissect this January 1992 U.S. visit or debacle (depends on your frame of reference), I believe that a more "two dimensional" approach was appropriate. By respecting Japanese distinctions between private and public speech, the U.S. delegation could have displayed both public respect and private determination and persuasion. For as pointed out by Japanese experts Barnlund,[32] Doi,[33] and Nakane,[34] it is extremely fundamental to Japanese business and social protocol that every effort be made to avoid challenges of face or confrontations in public arenas. When an aggressive, argumentative form of speech is necessary, Japanese expect that such abrasive words be altogether avoided, communicated indirectly through implications and innuendo, or at least spoken in utter privacy—away from the cameras and the eyes of the media. By respecting this distinction between private and public communication, the American delegation could have been far more consistent with Japanese national and corporate culture and communicative expectations, perhaps yielding better results.

Adapting to Japanese Audiences' Expectations: Code Switching and Z-Communication

In the most fundamental sense, we must consider whether Americans should conform or adapt to Japanese codes governing public speaking? Or should Japanese adapt to U.S. cultural codes?

In my view, based on research and cross cultural consulting and training work for Japan, the U.S. and the U.K., it is most appropriate and advantageous for Americans or British to adapt to Japanese codes when we are guests in Japan or within parent companies, subsidiaries, consortiums, mergers, or joint ventures with a dominant Japanese ownership or interest. But although the host is less obliged to substantively adapt (Japanese hosts are obliged to profusely adapt to U.S. business visitors and expatriate guests—but this is largely an act of *tatemae* or surface, polite communication), some adaptation is extremely helpful and well received in business with Japanese. Accordingly, the more subdued, indirect, ambiguous, non-argumentative and conciliatory American speaker is particularly welcomed by Japanese businessmen, even if that speaker is not well versed in Japanese social or business practices. A willingness to adapt to Japanese protocol is of great importance to Japanese associates as it is *indicative of good faith.*

Some very astute, experienced international Japanese and Americans are able to fluidly switch gears as public speakers—depending upon whether they are in the U.S. or Japan, speaking to Americans or Japanese. This "code switching" skill allows the speaker to more fully exist and participate in both Japanese and American worlds—as a bicultural business communicator. As bicultural public speakers they full well expect that Americans will assertively argue and "bottom line" audiences while Japanese remain distrustful of the eloquent speaker, saying more through nonverbal nuances, than the word. Although such Japanese and Americans may not prefer the other's approach when in the company of their fellow countrymen/women and nationals, they nevertheless are prepared to switch voices, judgment, culture, and expectations when crossing the Pacific or at joint venture podiums.

Another approach of adaptation to Japanese public speaking expectations is the Z-theory of communication advanced by Goldman[35] and Okabe.[36] From this perspective, a natural convergence or blending takes place between Japanese and Americans over repeated exposures and interaction. With prolonged contact through speaking engagements, joint ventures, negotiations, expatriations and repatriations, there may be an inclination to combine both Japanese and American orientations. Americans may become less verbose, aggressive, assertive, and vocal in their public speaking style with Japanese audiences and gradually encompass a more indirect, ambiguous, conciliatory, face saving communicative style.[37] This can produce the bicultural American speaker who reduces her adversarial tendencies by thirty percent and becomes twenty-five percent more Japanized.

Predeparture Training for Establishing Common Ground with Japanese Audiences

A growing familiarity with Japanese national and corporate culture allows the American business speaker to begin to approach the content and style of speeches from a Japanese perspective. This adaptation, in part viewed as "code switching" and "Z communication," can be further understood as a task of establishing common ground with Japanese audiences.

Finding what an American speaker may have in common with Japanese is of course contingent upon the specifics of the situation and how well known participants are to one another. An American business person on a first visit to Japan is obviously at a disadvantage, as less is known of Japanese culture and a given audience than is available to the longer term expatriate. The expatriate speaker's objective should be to find out as much as possible about Japanese culture in general as well as about the specific audience. It will usually be in the best interest of the American speaker to concentrate upon opening the doors for a relationship with Japanese during the first few presentations or contacts. The persuasive mission is best perceived as one of convincing Japanese that you are genuine and sincere in wanting to do business. A patient, thoughtful sensitive acknowledgement of social, cultural and business factors may be more relevant than a strict getting-down-to-business speech. *The initial focus with Japanese is much more interpersonal and relational than "talking turkey."* If specific proposals must be communicated to a Japanese audience, this may be best left for a hand-delivered printed report or a later speaking engagement.

For American strangers it is particularly valuable to seek assistance prior to a speaking engagement with a Japanese audience, as a cross-cultural trainer, human resource manager, or Japan expert can help you with preparation. Through use of a cross-cultural speechwriter and public speaking expert, you will be briefed on how to approach Japanese audiences, how to communicate objectives, when to speak your mind, what to reveal or withhold, and the all important sense of timing. Predeparture training usually prepares Americans for a longer term approach to doing business, one that utilizes speeches, meetings and presentations as a means for establishing relationships—enroute to meeting longer range projected goals. For much of establishing common ground entails small talk, expressing noble intentions and trustworthiness, a commitment to an association with Japanese, and an appreciation of Japanese culture. Even the most serious minded speech or oral report can usually draw upon the weather, food, baseball, fashion, restaurants, etiquette, cultural challenges and other generalized, relatively safe topics of conversation.

These public speaking topics may be further substantiated by repeatedly agreeing to socialize with members of the Japanese constituency. Much as an oral presentation may help to set the agenda, follow-up involves frequent socializing at cabarets, restaurants and local *yakitori* eateries. By viewing public presentations as interrelated with social communication, the U.S. expatriate can continue talk after hours and ultimately convince Japanese of the worthiness or suitableness of a business connection.

Predeparture training for public speaking before Japanese audiences should also include several months of exposure to Japanese publications, literature and media as a source for tapping Japanese business and national culture, as well as topical issues. By sampling as eclectic a mixture of Japanese information as possible, American business speakers will have a greater repertoire to draw upon when attempting to establish identification or common ground with Japanese audiences. This preparation may include such diverse options as:

1. Scanning English language Japanese newspapers, magazines, and international publications;

2. Familiarity with *The Japan Times* newspaper (largest English language newspaper in the Far East—published out of Tokyo); a weekly U.S. edition is also available;

3. Regular viewings of the programming of the Japanese cable television network in the U.S. and internationally televised Japanese news reports; do not overlook T.V. advertising spots;

4. The reading of popular books pertaining to Japanese business, communication, culture and management;

5. The sampling of current or recent popular motion pictures depicting the meeting of Japanese and U.S. national, busi-

ness, and corporate cultures. Highly visible movies help to set an agenda and a mind-set regarding U.S.-Japanese relations.

A comprehensive plan for briefings on Japanese culture is extremely important to the American business stranger as it will help place your personal and company objectives within a larger context. By beginning to examine what is behind the potential responses of your Japanese audience you understand how to strategize a speech or series of speeches. This contextual background can in part be found in popular newspapers and media, briefings from repatriates who lived and worked in Japanese sectors relevant to your concerns, and through more targeted examinations of the specific corporate culture and history of the company or audience being addressed. *If addressing members of a single company, obtain English language translations of strategic, recent corporate newsletters and other print communications—even if this requires that you solicit the services of a translator.*

Your broader base for speaking evolves from a growing penetration of Japanese business and social precedents. Knowledge of protocols surrounding everyday Japanese life is invaluable as context information for speechwriting or impromptu speaking.

And if the situation appears to warrant a carefully scripted and sculpted speech text, I urge you to engage a speechwriter with expertise in Japanese business. Hardly a frill or luxury, this service can help you "melt the ice" with Japanese who are not readily trusting or open to outsider business people. This slower "melting" process, not to be confused with the more immediate or shorter term U.S. idiom of "breaking the ice," may require that you have a go-between, and receive appropriate introductions to your audience before delivering the speech written by your consultant behind-the-scenes. And it is also of use to note that there is little hope of making a dent in Japanese audiences through a single speech or oral report as it will most likely take your Asian listeners a significant period of time to "make their minds up" about you. In a real sense, your speaking engagements will serve as tests, auditions, and raw data for Japanese who discretely and acutely attempt to decipher your innermost motivations. This intuitive sense of "reading" speakers is widely recognized in Japan and is termed *haragei* or communication of the stomach or gut.[38] Expect that your Japanese audience is predisposed to believe that words serve as a kind of superficial, surface form of communication (*tatemae*), acting as a smokescreen or diversion for the actual objectives (*honne* and *haragei*).

Finally, inasmuch as Japanese hosts are notoriously nurturing, they expect the U.S. business visitor or expatriate to be extremely dependent on them. Expect that a precise itinerary and a social and business schedule will be part of the plan. Be prepared to follow some unanticipated but well intended rules that will emerge at your speaking engagement. Maintain flexibility and try not to be smothered or offended if your hosts appear to make too many decisions for you. As a guest you are the exclusive responsibility of your hosts and you should accept this dependency as an example of Japanese *amae*.

Public Speaking Tips for American Expatriates

As a specific aid in training U.S. managers, leaders and expatriates for oral reports and public speaking before Japanese audiences, I have compiled the following list of "Public Speaking Tips for Americans Facing Japanese Audiences."

This list is followed by a second list specifically preparing U.S. business people and expatriates to evaluate more competently the presentations of Japanese business speakers. The second list is entitled "Tips for American Business Audiences Listening to Japanese Speakers." These tips may be used in cross-cultural training programs offered by intercultural consultants or human resource managers and as part of a predeparture agenda.

Public Speaking Tips for Americans
Facing Japanese Audiences

1. Assume that successful U.S. and Western public speaking techniques do not readily apply to Japanese audiences.

2. *Verbally economize* when addressing Japanese. Overly verbal and eloquent public speakers are held in suspicion.

3. Recognize that the group orientation of Japanese prevails, meaning that individual skills as a speaker call too much attention to the self. This may be interpreted to mean that you are not a team player, not to be trusted.

4. Carefully investigate the English language proficiency of your Japanese audience prior to speaking.

5. If it is necessary to utilize a translator, it is best to choose your own rather than allowing your Japanese host to do so.

6. Consider consulting with a Japanese-U.S. intercultural communication and business specialist for assistance with speechwriting, oral reports and presentation style.

7. Realize that since Japanese have more in common than Americans, they have less need to verbalize. Much of the Japanese speaker's message is found in the subtleties and nuances of nonverbal communication.

8. Carefully examine your facial expression, eye contact, body language and the sound and inflection of your voice (paralanguage) for compatibility or incompatibility with Japanese audiences' expectations.

9. *Speak slowly* as members of the audience may be mentally translating from English to Japanese as you speak.

10. *Utilize long pauses* and silences while delivering a speech, allowing Japanese time to digest and translate your words and ideas.

11. *Communicate warmth* and nurture a business "relationship" through your speaking rather than a strict concern for task and objectives.

12. Recognize that Japanese listeners regularly attempt to unveil the "gut" or "stomach communication" behind the words of a speaker (*haragei*). This is examined by audiences closely scrutinizing your feel, atmosphere, the sound of your voice, the gestures of the body, facial expression and eye contact.

13. Do not attempt to state your full business objectives via a single speech or presentation as Japanese prefer a longer term campaign approach to doing business. View a single presentation as one in a series of presentations.

14. Strive to establish common ground with Japanese audiences through predeparture training and briefings, and an eclectic exposure to Japanese newspapers, publications, media and specific corporate print communications.

15. For important speaking engagements with Japanese audiences, *contract with a cross-cultural speechwriter and public speaking coach with specific expertise in Japanese business culture.*

16. Although Japanese audiences will make allowances for your inexperience with Japanese business and cultural protocol, strive to incorporate aspects of Japanese communicative style into your presentations: ambiguity, indirectness, conciliatory language, avoid confrontations or issues resulting in loss of face (*kao*), refrain from overly bold or exaggerated terminology, and develop subtle, subdued bodily language and facial expression.

Tips for American Business Audiences Listening to Japanese Speakers

1. Japanese English speakers tend to be modest and apologize regarding their limited English language ability and knowledge of a subject matter.

2. Japanese speakers tend to speak more slowly, especially when they are speaking English as a second language (they may be mentally translating languages as they speak).

3. Anticipate long pauses and silences from Japanese speakers.

4. Expect Japanese to be verbally economical.

5. Carefully examine Japanese body language, facial language, and eye contact as part of the unspoken message.

6. Understand that most Japanese view public speaking as an exercise in *tatemae* or surface, polite communication, rather than *honne* or true communication of the heart.

7. Anticipate Japanese English speakers to be somewhat vague, indirect, ambiguous and not very prone to get to the point. This does **not** indicate a strategy of deception and is rather rooted in Japanese national culture and language.

8. Recognize that much Japanese public speaking is more concerned with establishing good will and building and maintaining face and relationships than with persuading an audience or achieving a specific business objective.

9. Anticipate that Japanese public speakers tend to avoid exaggerations, boastfulness, strong language, definitiveness, commitments or power language.

10. Japanese businessmen may communicate more of their substantive, definitive agenda and objectives via submission of a printed report—rather than through a speech or oral report.

MEDIA BRIEFING

"KISSINGER ON U.S.-JAPANESE RELATIONS"

About two years ago, I had the good fortune of being bottled up in a hotel in Hawaii with Dr. Henry Kissinger for three consecutive days discussing a wide range of subjects. At that time, he said to me: "Look at the Japanese greeting. One bows always lower than the other and never at the same level as equals. I suppose this is a good measure to show how difficult it is for us to deal with the Japanese as our equals."

(from Yasuhiro Nakasone, "Beyond *kenbei,* anti-U.S. sentiment and Japan-bashing," *The Japan Times,* May 25–31, 1992, volume 32, #21, 9.)

Conclusion

By actively pursuing an understanding of Japanese standards of business speaking and how Japanese evaluate American business communicators, U.S. expatriates and leaders will be in a better position to culturally adapt and overcome intercultural stage fright. I have provided background on some of the more significant differences in U.S. and Japanese expectations surrounding business speaking and moreover offer the two sets of "cultural tips" as part of predeparture training or training for bicultural workforces. Preparation for public speaking engagements in Japan or before Japanese audiences in the U.S. and around the world, is essential, and is best approached by seeking assistance from a cross-cultural expert in speechwriting and presentation style. Finally, an appreciation of Japanese culture is a key to developing skills as a speaker before Japanese audiences and as an audience to Japanese business communicators.

"INCIDENT AT NAGANO MOUNTAIN HOT SPRINGS: TO TRUST OR NOT TO TRUST"

Golden Week: The National Holiday

During a springtime escape from Tokyo, during the celebrated Golden Week (late April, early May), I visited the breathtaking Nagano Mountains. The rugged terrain reminded me of parts of the Colorado Rockies and the Swiss Alps. The mountains of Nagano Prefecture offered a stark, naturalistic contrast to the technology, crowds and grey skies of Tokyo.

En Route: The Bullet Trains and Bento Boxes

Traveling to Nagano on the Shinkansen (bullet train), I sampled many bento boxes (boxed Japanese lunches) along the way. The brief stops of the train offered an opportunity to experience the prepared box lunches at each station. Many fish, rice, pickle and surprise delicacy combinations graced every box. By my fifth month in Japan, I was not only a lover of Japanese food, I was getting adventurous. I no longer turned to the high priced Western food offerings for *gaijin* and tourists. I had finally acquired a real taste for the hundreds of variations of bento box sushi and pickles.

The Corporate Morality of Taking a Vacation

I noticed that much of Japan was in transit during Golden Week. While I learned from my friend, Mr. Sato, that there were many business people who did not take a holiday, there were millions of others who were en route to rest and relaxation. I questioned Suda San about those who declined vacations due them. Suda explained that it was "unwritten," but many Japanese salarymen considered that they would appear "selfish" or "uncommitted" if they chose a vacation over work. It was all related to the extremes of loyalty.

A Nagano Family Hosts their First Western Guest

In Nagano, I first stayed with a wonderful Japanese family who had never hosted a Westerner before. Utiko, her husband, their parents, and children, collectively served as the storybook hosts. I struggled not to be too fumbling of a guest.

The bath was set apart from the living area in a separate little structure, somewhat like a tiny U.S. guesthouse. After receiving briefings from Utiko on bathing etiquette (I had not yet forgotten my lessons learned from the Sato family of Nagoya), I finally entered the bathwater. It was scalding hot. I let out my loudest "hot water scream," arousing the entire family. I tried to smile my way through it. I spoke about my lack of toughness, that they shouldn't believe all the myths about the American men being "John Waynes." This in turn led to a discussion of American movies. They were particularly fond of Westerns, although they also approved of the James Bond, "007" series of films.

Nagano Mountain Hot Springs

To continue with the subject of bathing—a terribly important topic in everyday Japanese life—I will now shift to the hot springs of the Nagano Mountains. Driving up into the magestic Nagano Mountains we finally found our way to the hot springs. We parked about a half-mile away from the springs and hiked in. It was a beautiful site. The population at the hot springs was shockingly coed. Lovely Japanese women shared the springs with the gentlemen. I was, of course, the only resident *gaijin*.

No Security, No Lockers

I soon lost sight of the drama and aesthetic beauty of the setting and the people, and focused upon issues of security, theft, and "things." To begin with, I was carrying the equivalent of approximately $1,000 in yen. Japan is a "cash and carry" society, and it is far less common to utilize personal checks or credit cards. It is common practice to withdraw significant amounts of cash before the weekend or holidays, always expecting to pay with yen.

I was totally unprepared for the fact that there was no means of security at the hot springs. There were only wire baskets provided for each bather. When stripping down to the nude, it was expected that you leave all your clothing, wallet, and possessions in the basket, in plain view, within a designated open room. Hundreds of people freely walked through this little room, and from my Americana perspective it was a security nightmare.

I was more than mildly uncomfortable with this situation. I was petrified and furious. How was I to leave about $1,000 in cash, all my credit cards and identification, and $1,000 worth of camera equipment, unlocked and ready for robbers?

A Westerner Panics: Someone will Steal my Money

Explaining my upset to my Japanese friends, they were extremely amused. I blamed them for not informing me of the security policy.

> If you had told me that we had to leave our valuables unattended, without any locks, lockers, or security . . . I would have left everything in the trunk of the car. Why didn't you tell me? Why?

Suda san realized that I was quite serious and he attempted to heal the intercultural shock and dilemma. He assured me,

> No Japanese will take your money, camera, credit cards or clothes. Why are you so worried? Perhaps you should be more calm and realize that you are not in America where such terrible things always happen.
>
> After making a scene, I finally attempted to divert my attention to the sights of the hot springs and take the plunge. I was immersed in the hot springs, the bodies, the mountains, for several second intervals—interwoven with my *security mania*.

I excused myself long before the others, obviously more concerned with protecting my things than experiencing the springs.

Suffice it to say that everything was still there, nothing had been moved. When my Japanese friends emerged I took a memorable array of photos that I look at every few weeks. They remind me of the safety, security, and absence of theft in Japanese society. It also reminds me of my inner turmoil, and the projection of American theft and dishonesty upon the Nagano mountain terrain.

Implications for Westerners: Security on Both Sides of the Pacific

Not only should Americans and Europeans be aware of this highly safe and secure situation in Japan, they should conversely address how Japanese must feel upon receiving reports of theft and violence abroad, and arriving in Berlin, Paris, Amsterdam, London, Rome, New York, Los Angeles and Miami. I ask my fellow Westerners to consider such factors when hosting the Japanese, courting Japanese investment, providing U.S. or U.K. sites for diplomacy, and doing business with Japanese. Also, when in Japan, you need to be more concerned about the non-Japanese in the country. Otherwise you are as safe in Japan as we like to think the Eisenhower fifties were.

"VERBAL JABS: IMMATURE U.S.-JAPAN DIALOGUE"

The verbal jabs exchanged recently between some prominent leaders of both countries (U.S. and Japan) fall far short of being a mature dialogue, and should not have been given such public attention. President George Bush visited Japan in January accompanied by the top executives of the Big Three auto manufacturers voicing open criticism of Japan . . .

(from Yasuhiro Nakasone, "Beyond *kenbei,* anti-U.S. sentiment and Japan-bashing," *The Japan Times,* May 25–31, 1992, volume 32, #21, 9.)

PART IV

Unveiling Japanese Culture and Communication

"CULTURE SHOCK"

Attention to the potential danger abroad was refocused Oct. 17, 1992, with the shooting death of sixteen year old Yoshihiro Hattori, a Japanese exchange student in Baton Rouge, Louisiana. Hattori was shot to death while on his way to a Halloween party. Hattori and his American friend mistakenly went to the home of Rodney Peairs, a few doors away. Hattori was shot to death by Peairs, who came out with a pistol and shouted, "Freeze."

Some have said that Hattori did not understand the intention behind the order "Freeze." Others were shocked at the use of a handgun in a seemingly innocent confrontation. Whether the differences are cultural, linguistic or simple naivete . . . Japanese need to be more aware of the risks they take when they leave Japan.

(from "Going Abroad Now Means Playing It Safe," *Asahi Shimbun Japan Access*, November 16, 1992, volume 3, #44, 7.)

CHAPTER 16

Tatemae and Honne: Surface and True Communication

MEDIA BRIEFING

"JAPANESE REACT IN ROUNDABOUT FASHION"

(Regarding the U.S.-Japanese joint venture company National Steel)

Confrontations with Japanese executives are more trying than with Americans. American executives may be gruff when employees speak up, but usually they will listen. In Japan, the proper procedure is for superiors to initiate discussions and for subordinates to accept what they say and patiently wait until they wind up in their boss' job to change things. Thus, when we protested, the Japanese reacted in a roundabout fashion.

(from Susan Goldenberg, *Hands Across the Ocean,* Boston: Harvard Business School Press, 1988, 178.)

Communicating with Japanese business associates is riddled with a quagmire of cultural rules. Foremost, is the importance of exteriors and appearances. How you express yourself, saying the appropriate phrase to suit the occasion, is initially more valued than a revealing of true intentions. Veneers, form, style and presentation are the "packagings" of business communication. Your agility with Japanese depends upon a mastering of surface graces and a knowledge of pleasing words, phrases and conversational openers. The shell of your business and managerial performance carries great weight, as clothes, gesture, and manner communicate as well.

This prioritizing of surface communication, saying the right thing, on cue, and predictably participating in ritualized meetings and conversations, is central to *tatemae*. Roughly translating to "surface or outer communication," *tatemae* is a testimony to the aesthetic dimension of Japanese social behavior: the packaging of a gift, business manager, or consumer product. Although the content and true intentions are also of significance, the indirect manner of Japanese speech, the distrust of verbal communication, the reliance upon implicit meanings, brings performance to the main stage. *Since a heart-to-heart communication is not easily achieved, Japanese have cultivated a refined communication of appearances*—a ritual of exchanging pleasantries, preserving group harmony and the status quo, and perhaps smoothing the way for a later unveiling of deeper motivations and objectives.

Tatemae requires that expatriates explore the ritualized, rote, characteristic catalogue of Japanese business expressions and interactions appropriate to specific venues. Acknowledging status, when to speak, whom to speak to, what to say, where to sit, is all part of *tatemae*. In a broad sense, much of the *meishi* ritual (business card exchange and introductions) is *tatemae*. To prematurely speak of bottom lines, true motivations, or to request privileged information of superiors, may be attempts at *honne* (true communication), when *tatemae* is the far more appropriate level of contact. Everything in its due time. *To rush into an underlying agenda, to ask gut level questions of an organization or top management, may be a symptom of the expatriate's insensitivity to tatemae.*

Tatemae is both polite, surface, ritualized expression, as well as the less scripted, small talk, and polite conversation. *Tatemae* provides a communication channel for business associates to feel each other out, examine the style and manner of players, and see whether there appears to be a comfortable, personal basis for proceeding into *honne*.

Tatemae may also be viewed as the "window dressing" in a conversation.[1] *American and European business visitors commonly take the superficial aspects of an introduction, negotiation or contractual talk, literally, not realizing that Japanese may only be say-*

ing what they think you want to hear.[2] In actuality, the smooth, graceful and aesthetic surface of the business transaction is primarily *tatemae*. It takes some contact hours to know how to detect the lurking, nearly invisible *honne*.

In an account of a business trip to Japan, the late and prolific Mark Zimmerman spoke of a mission centered around determining the *tatemae* and *honne* of "Japanese licensing and marketing strategy and plans in South Asia and the rest of the world, especially with regard to licensing out to foreign companies."[3] Zimmerman goes on to describe the warm greetings he received from senior management of one Japanese company, culminating in a lavish night out at a *geisha* house. The splendid hosting was *tatemae* due to the fact that Zimmerman "knew that my visit did not call for this kind of treatment; they were entertaining me lavishly because the Japanese company had other plans for their commands in South Asia but did not want to offend me because I was a valued friend (this was *honne*, or the true situation)."[4] In Zimmerman's subsequent interpretation he recognized that he was able to discern what the Japanese company was up to, and from the perspective of *tatemae* and *honne,* there was no unethical, misleading, or questionable behavior on the part of the hosts. If Zimmerman did not come to this meeting with an understanding of Japanese *tatemae* and *honne,* as it relates to business communication, he would most likely have returned to his home office believing that the Japanese had all but agreed to the Americans' proposals.

In dealings with a Japanese corporation in Tokyo, I similarly stumbled upon another variety of *tatemae* and *honne*. There was a mix-up with my company and they booked me to go on a business trip to Seoul, Korea, for a weekend. When I received the call at home, I was told that the arrangements were already made, the trip was paid for, and my airline tickets were waiting for me. I was truly surprised. Once again I was shocked into the collectivist mentality of the Japanese company. Why was I not consulted?

To complicate matters, I already had a prior work engagement, locally within Tokyo, a consulting job for my parent company (same company booking me). Due to internal miscommunications, they were unaware of this booking and asked me to hold the phone line. Although we were both quite annoyed with each other, we spoke in niceties, politely and calmly, expressing the *tatemae* required to maintain the most important ingredient—the relationship between the *gaijin* trainer and the Japanese superior.

Further discussion resulted in the following: my superior came back to the phone (after most likely getting into a huddle with one or more of his superiors, immediately accessible via the open floor arrangements of office desks) and informed me that they would be cancelling the trip after all. I would only be responsible for paying one-half of the airline tickets and hotel reservations. Inwardly, I was slightly outraged. But, with my new found Japanese sensibility, I refrained from showing my anger (*honne*), and just kept up the surface appearances, hearing his preposterous proclamation out (*tatemae*).

Afterwards, I thought this through, dissecting the situation in dozens of ways. Detailed conversations and analysis with a close Japanese friend and confidant led to the pure and simple revelation. Part and parcel of business communication with a Japanese company is learning how to detect the role of *tatemae* in rites of passage. My Japanese boss and company surely knew that the source of the potential conflict was due to their own negligence, but the dilemma offered a perfect opportunity for a *gaijin test*. They were most curious about how I would respond to their unreasonable demand. More specifically, the *tatemae* of the exchange was the misunderstanding and the demand that I be responsible for payment of a trip that I did not book; also within the range of *tatemae*, I decided to react in kind. I graciously accepted this demand as if it was an invitation to a ballroom.

The *honne* of the manager and company was to conduct the test of the employee—seeing whether I was ready to yield to superiors, follow orders, and submit to an unreasonable demand. Most *gaijin* would fail this test. My *honne* was that I wanted to show them my loyalty, place the relationship above the seemingly ideological issue in front of my face, and establish that I was what the ex-heavyweight U.S. boxing champion, Evander Hollyfield, called himself, "the real deal." As a result of this highly strategized dance of *tatemae* I passed the test, emerged with a more serious status and worth, and my swallowing of the unreasonable demands left the manager and company in "debt" to me. Sure enough, months later, I very respectfully asked for a large favor, a significant cash advance on my salary and consulting fees without any collatoral; they gladly broke all company policy to favor my request. It was repayment in *honne* (money, respect, reinforcement, commitment) for the *tatemae* ordeal.

About Honne

As revealed throughout this book, decoding the *honne* or true intentions of Japanese business associations is not an easy task. It requires much reading between the lines, and an ongoing commitment to understanding Japanese style social maneuvering, organizational posturing, and subtle signals of underlying motivations.

For a starter, it should be clear that while surfaces are instrumental, they are but the "window dressing." *When a relationship is new, fleeting, or unproven, U.S. expatriates should not expect to experience much other than tatemae.* In addition to the niceties, the ritualized verbal expressions and surface politeness geared toward saying what the other wants to hear, Americans can be increasingly on the alert for the more invisible *honne* message. Most often it will just take time, patience, frequent visits and a business communication *campaign* to uncover the *honne*. Continued exposure to Japanese business culture and communicative style builds up experience in seeing the *honne* through the *tatemae*.

BICULTURAL

"COMMUNICATING PRAISE"

Shall praise be directed toward the individual or the group? When is praise appropriate? Inappropriate? Enter the complex intercultural arena of U.S.-Japanese communication.

Japanese Ningensei

Japanese use the term *ningensei* to refer to "human beingness." Not easily defined in English, *ningensei* expresses the Japanese interest in cultivating personal relationships. Extremely high priority is given to *ningensei*, both in social and business situations.

Central to *ningensei* is the belief that much of public life and business transactions are superficial or surface (*tatemae*). The Japanese business leader or manager with heart and vision is not satisfied with the appearances of people or things, and strives to find the person behind the words and the masks.[1]

Japanese experts BenDasen and Takiyama Lebra have spoken of the secondary reality of words, meaning that Japanese have a history and lineage that breeds skepticism of the spoken word. In working toward a *ningensei* relationship, Japanese try to get around, past, through, underneath, behind the endless babble of language that fills the corporation, diplomacy, marketplace, and business arena. Especially when dealing with Westerners, Japanese operate from the premise that the American, British, or Canadian is an outsider, and it is hardly cynical to want to look beyond the verbal eloquence they may display.

At negotiating tables or in afterhour cabarets and restaurants, Japanese study facial expressions, examine body language, and hear the sound and nuances of the voice. They observe and listen to find out the psychology and inner workings of the American expatriates with whom they are doing business. They examine whether the Americans are warm, trustworthy, distant, solid, insecure, dependable or selfish. Japanese in touch with *ningensei* know that words alone are not reliable indicators of motives and if a person can survive a business crisis.

Ningensei is also an ongoing process that puts the human being first. Powerful business alliances are constructed upon the foundations of solid human relationships. Over a long period of time, Japanese may offer favors, break rules, socialize in a free and uninhibited fashion, and subtly invite you to participate, reciprocate. A silent series of bonds, connections and interdependencies are formatted, and it is up to the Westerners to learn how to take cues.

Ningensei puts human feelings and relationships beyond the boundaries of words and logic. Contracts are suspect and always subject to revision. Logic and idealism are secondary realities, alongside words and eloquence, as the human bond that develops is the key to a *ningensei* styled business association.[2]

"CULTURAL ADAPTATION: RINGI"

There is . . . the possibility that the Japanese company may be altered as a result of its own operations abroad. It might be thought, for example, that the *ringi* system of decision-making would have to be modified, because it would appear cumbersome and even unintelligible to senior foreign employees. This sort of hypothesis underestimates the ability of foreigners to adapt to practices which, though superficially different, are in many ways analogous to their own. It also underestimates the ability of Japanese to preserve their customs. After all, firms like the trading companies and the Bank of Tokyo, which must surely employ as many foreigners as Japanese if all their subsidiaries and affiliates are taken into account, conduct their Japanese operations, at least, in a quintessentially Japanese manner.

(from Rodney Clark, *The Japanese Company.* London: Yale University Press, 1979, 253.)

CHAPTER 18

Japanese Public and Private Communication

Understanding how Japanese managers, workers, politicians, and business people express themselves depends upon an ability to distinguish between public and private communication, and public and private selves. Unlike Westerners, Japanese tend to keep more of their true intentions, inner feelings, and deeper motivations, away from the public eye. According to communication researcher Dean Barnlund, Japanese share less of their private selves in communication.[1] They rather develop a "public self" for communicating in everyday business situations.

In a strong sense, it is not unfair to say that Japanese regularly construct communication barriers or *smokescreens,* carefully chiseled to keep the private self, private. Especially in the earlier stages of business introductions, meetings, and interviews, the *tatemae* (surface communication) form of expression is dominant.

U.S. expatriates may be stumped in a variety of ways. Some Americans or Western Europeans have the inclination to get right down to business and "talk turkey." In typical fashion, Japanese business communicators meander about with small talk, and generally engage in an exploration of the personalities, preferences, backgrounds, attitudes and allegiances of potential associates. Despite the adversion to "bottom lining," Japanese social talk and conversation is rarely a venue for revealing actual motivation. The light social chatter, characteristic of virgin business links, is a probing method for getting to know the *gaijin* (foreigners) or outsiders.

The private side of the social or business self is guarded, preserved, only revealed as the Westerner is gradually accepted as a partial "insider." There is no way of rushing this inevitability. It is a time consuming process that Japanese stretch out over many meetings. The private world of individual business people remains invisible, as does the inner sanctum of the corporate world.

Japanese public communication, oftentimes fluffy, playful and ritualized, can serve the function of a jousting, fencing match. It is the only direct face-to-face channel readily open to Japanese to try to determine whether a given American or Western organization is a good match for a Japanese joint venture, subsidiary or investment. *By steadily courting and investigating the man or woman behind the Western business mask, Japanese discover whether this person or company should remain an outsider—or should be slowly ushered into "insider" status.*

Within every Japanese person and company there is an inner self called the *kokoro.* Unlike Westerners, there is a sharper and deeper distinction between the "outside" or *soto,* and the *kokoro.*

There is a long, treacherous road at times to cross from the outside to the inside, from the public to the private. Many tests, rites of passage, and questions may be directed by Japanese investors toward Western expatriates. Bottom lines are not just discerned from hard data contained on spreadsheets, they are also sought in relation to the personalities and motivations of the Westerners. So while Japanese are dreadfully slow at revealing their private selves, much of their public communication is nevertheless slowly and methodically trying to tap into the heart of the Western outsider.

The *kokoro* is also thought by Japanese to be closely linked to the heart. The greater, truer, more successful business alliance is surely that which is capable of a heart-to-heart communication. It is a level of commitment that can only be reached when private selves are finally being unfolded, and Westerner and Japanese increasingly trust one another. It is a kind of empathic communication most closely associated with lovers, close families, and tightly knit groups. Consider that it is no accident that Japanese competitiveness and total quality management is viewed the world over as a consequence of unprecedented levels of team work.

To add a little paradox to this description of private and public selves, Japanese view *kokoro,* the core of the private self, as not particularly communicable through words.[2] This quickly leads the Westerner to the citadel of Japanese *silence.*[3] Many researchers have spoken of the troublesome Japanese use of silence as a major method of communicating. Silence, more than spoken language, may be the expression of the private self. Talk of the heart, unveiling true motivations and intentions, these are private agendas not easily expressed in public conversations.

Japanese silence is the predominant channel or medium for *kokoro*. It is important that American expatriates become increasingly familiar, not only with the rites of passage, the movement from the public to the private self, but also with the leverage of silence. Silence is a powerful communicative device. *There are many types of Japanese silences, of varying intensities and durations.* As a Japanese negotiator observes your facial expression, breathing, and the pauses between your words, there may be a period where the sentences are meaningless. The Western reliance upon words fails Japanese. Words only go so far. They cannot necessarily open the doors of *kokoro*.

"NO CONTROL OF EMOTIONS"

WATANABE: Robbins showed great immaturity at meetings with our Japanese partners this week. I was surprised.

GOULD: Surprised about what?

WATANABE: I am very reluctant to discuss this as it is a criticism of Robbins . . .

GOULD: Yeah, yeah . . . and I know how you Japanese hate to criticize . . . but we've known each other for years . . . shared a lot of drinks and long nights . . .

WATANABE: O.K. But please be discreet about what I tell you . . .

GOULD: Promise. So how was Robbins "immature"?

WATANABE: Robbins got visibly upset. He shouted out loud. He nearly broke into tears. He looked at the Japanese with an angry, wild, emotional look. The Japanese representatives were in shock.

GOULD: Now I see. But he just had a lot of passion, a lot of emotion. He wants to see this deal go through . . . a quick decision be reached. There are millions of dollars at stake and many U.S. workers' lives depend on this joint venture.

WATANABE: I am sorry. I feel it's childish for a man to show such great emotions in public. No control!

Analysis: There is much at stake here, as U.S. and Japanese joint venture partners typically discover that they have radically contrasting approaches to communicating. While there is no readily available barometer or yardstick, Western business people do have a certain degree of latitude in expressing their emotions. It is not unusual to encounter an empassioned negotiator who raises her voice, waves his hands, points fingers, pounds on the table—and generally brings to mind a fire and brimstone styled trial attorney.

But for Japanese who have not been thoroughly Westernized, such displays of emotions as allegedly exhibited by Robbins, are sure to meet up with Japanese cultural shock and disapproval. Thousands of years of social training has discouraged the overt expression of emotions or feelings. Japanese are extremely reserved and constrained when it comes to communicating needs and feelings, particularly within public venues. It is quite unusual to find a Japanese business associate who speaks in a loud, assertive, argumentative tone of voice, or who freely displays bold facial expressions and gestures. Robbins has clearly violated these "codes."

"JAPANESE NEGOTIATING"

Culturally, there are sharp differences in the way Japanese and Westerners prepare for negotiation. The Japanese priorities are, first, to develop a working organization around a discussion leader, who will usually become the spokesman; second, to ensure that everyone has a thorough understanding of the issues; and, third, to develop a position on which everyone can agree. This position is usually arrived at in what we might call an intuitive way, for there is rarely any discussion of position options. The essence of the Japanese approach is organization, and they can be expected to come into a negotiation with a cohesive team, a single spokesman, a shared understanding of the issues, and consensus on one position even if they are ill-prepared in other respects.

(from Robert M. March, *The Japanese Negotiator: Subtlety and Strategy Beyond Western Logic*. Tokyo: Kodansha, 1989, 162–3.)

CHAPTER 19

The Omoiyari Culture: Japanese Empathy and Hospitality

As an *"omoiyari* culture," Japanese place high priority on empathy. Japanese views of empathy hold important clues for U.S. business and management, especially when assuming the role of "guest."

Japanese "host" empathy is expressed by taking almost complete responsibility for the guest. For example, the Western expatriate finds that

> The Japanese concept of hospitality is to have everything arranged ahead of time, including lodging, food, transportation, and detailed itinerary, rather than waiting to consult with the guest.[1]

The host has little need to inquire verbally as to the "wishes" of the guest, as it is expected that a well-tuned and developed empathy reveals what is appropriate.

U.S. and European visitors alternatively find this variety of Japanese empathy a source of pleasant surprise as well as discomfort. Within the boundaries of Western social and business venues, it is tacitly assumed that the guest should have significant say in their role as "guest." In American society, there is an overriding belief "that each individual knows what s/he wants and no one else can claim better knowledge."[2]

At stake is the sharp difference between a more active, interjecting "host knows best" axis of Japanese empathy versus the "guest knows best" orientation of Western hospitality. A mere scratching of the respective cultural surfaces unveils the recurring influence of Japanese collectivism and U.S. individualism.

American managers and visitors, especially in their early months of expatriation (or during their first few visits to Japan), easily feel "put upon or smothered," and may adversely respond to the Japanese onslaught of hospitality. Unsuspecting Westerners are unconsciously culturally 'programmed' to constantly exercise their prerogative of free choice, but find that Japanese place low priority on guest feedback or individualized agendas. It is assumed that it would be a poor Japanese host, one unskilled in *omoiyari*, who could *not* feel or intuitively grasp the needs of guests and respond. Moreover, Japanese CEOs, top management, diplomats and organizations naturally operate on the "we" principle, working toward a group defined notion of hosting. To pay too much attention to the individualist element is to break the prospects for *wa* (harmony).

Takeo Doi, a widely recognized Japan expert, was taken somewhat off-guard by the cultural precedent of U.S. hosts who displayed the antithesis of an *omoiyari* hospitality. The Americans placed an extraordinary amount of effort in extending a broad range of choices to Doi and other Japanese guests. Takiyama Lebra tells of Doi's confrontation and shock with a *non-omoiyari* style of hospitality:

> Doi writes about the American host, who, before offering anything, asks his guest, first, whether he would like a soft drink or hard liquor. If the guest decides to have liquor, the host then asks whether scotch or bourbon is preferred. And then how would the guest like it—on the rocks with water, and so forth—and how much? After dinner, the guest is again asked whether he prefers coffee or tea, and whether he wants cream and sugar in it. Having been the recipient of such hospitality, Doi realized that it was an American custom, but at the same time noted 'I could care less,' in reference to the choices offered.[3]

As pointed out by Doi and Lebra, there are significantly different views of hospitality and empathy in the U.S. and Japan, although both are similar in genuinely wanting to please the guest. The *omoiyari* culture strives to empathetically anticipate and fulfill the every need of the guest, a process calling on listening skills, care, intuition, and some specific personal data. The American's view of empathy is rather tied up in extending maximum individual choices to the guest, honoring them as a solo visitor with unique tastes.

Within the context of corporate dining in Japanese restaurants, U.S. business players should be forewarned. *Omoiyari* culture's teachings may not require Japanese hosts to ask their Western guests for preferences. This "father knows best" modus operandi results in uniform dinner orders at restaurant tables. The entire meal, from "A to Z," may be decided by the senior male host, and all diners will automatically, silently follow suit.

Throughout Japan, U.S. expatriates find the manifestations of *omoiyari*. The popular way of purchasing a meal at a neighborhood Japanese restaurant is to buy an entire dinner or lunch "set." A plastic replica of the "set options" are usually available in a store front window or display case, or are visually portrayed on the menu. All courses of the meal are included at a fixed price. There are usually no additional taxes or tips to be added—the price is inclusive. Bred on free choice, expatriates are quick to respond to this "total care" of the customer, wanting more input and decision-making latitude. But to speak up is to defy *omoiyari*.

On the other side of the Pacific, busy and/or fatigued Japanese business visitors find the American version of restaurant hospitality lacking in *omoiyari*. *Few U.S. business hosts offer the "full service empathy" of Japanese omoiyari and rather "burden" Japanese visitors with having to make many choices.* This is particularly inconvenient or even annoying and cumbersome for Japanese who are tired, and find it difficult to engage in an English language conversation with U.S. waiters. How simple it would be to have the Western host develop a bit of *omoiyari* styled hospitality and offer dinner "sets." In this way, Japanese visitors would have the option of not having to read and speak English throughout the meal, and to simply say "number two" when ordering. Little additional interaction would be necessary.

On a grander scale, Japanese business hosts will generally exercise *omoiyari* in providing a closely scripted, pre-planned, fully comprehensive itinerary for U.S. expatriates. Every waking moment may be meticulously accounted for by Japanese hosts, with little thought given to personal, individual time for the Americans. At the extreme, the *omoiyari* may border on *osekkai* or "meddlesomeness."[4] There is a fine line between the graciousness of *omoiyari* and the vice of *osekkai* hosting behaviors.[5] To Lebra, the *osekkai* must be accepted as the other side of the coin of *omoiyari*.[6]

The problem comes down to this: U.S. expatriates are understandably both surprised and resentful of the pleasantries and the outer limits of *omoiyari*. There is a strong tendency for American expatriates to perceive most Japanese *omoiyari* as a meddlesome *osekkai*. The intercultural challenge for Americans is to scrutinize the indigenous practice of Japanese empathy and see how it differs from American versions of hospitality.[7] Also, Japanese should be increasingly sensitized to the same, and the Westerners' adversion to overwhelming the guest with a "father knows best" itinerary. Japanese must be very careful not to "overly host" and show so much *omoiyari* that it is confused with *osekkai*.

MEDIA BRIEFING

"AGGRESSIVE AMERICANS, SELF-EFFACING JAPANESE"

The key to America's high-powered intellectual performance is motivation. U.S. scientists are driven by more than personal ambition. Imbued with a strong sense of mission, they try to live by their ideals and take the pursuit of scientific truth seriously. In Japan, by contrast, the social ideal is the hard-working, low-key craftsman. To maintain group harmony, we are encouraged to downplay individualism. Japanese society frowns on people who stand out from the crowd, who disrupt the status quo.

In the U.S., individuals are expected to take charge of their own lives. Self-expression is highly valued. And Americans, for better or worse, are aggressive. Quiet, self-effacing Japanese cut a poor figure in U.S. labs.

(from Professor of Economics, Yuji Harayama, Shinshu University; from *World Press Review,* January 1989.)

CHAPTER 20

Appropriate Rank and Order: Corporate and National Culture

MEDIA BRIEFING

"TQM BETTER SUITED TO JAPANESE THAN U.S. NATIONAL AND ORGANIZATIONAL CULTURES"

One of the highest-level hustles of our day is the great "total quality management" caper. Bombarded by news of a revolutionary style of management that propelled the Japanese miracle, we are constantly told how TQM is the cure to the ills, excesses, waste, inefficiencies and defects of the U.S. private and public sectors.

But scratch the trendy "management theory of the month club," and you will find that in our eagerness to stage organizational change, we are not sufficiently reflecting upon this panacea called TQM . . . TQM as practiced by the Japanese, is a kind of corporate socialism in which the company, the *keiretsu* and allegiance to the country is more important than the individual. But in the United States, TQM lobbyists have steamrolled over the fact that TQM cannot be separated from deeply ingrained beliefs, attitudes, and values of workers . . .

Having seen TQM in action in Japanese corporations, I find that there is little U.S. understanding of what TQM is, or whether it can "fit" or be transferred or modified for U.S. organizations. It is, rather, a conveniently empowering slogan for politicians and managers to magically, mystically, knowingly, and stoically proclaim that they are tightening company belts in the name of "excellence" and achievement of the ultimate organizational nirvana: TQM.

TQM is presented by high-priced consultants as a "culture-free" system that can cross national and cultural boundaries. Nothing could be further from the truth. The serious restructuring of government or Fortune 500 companies for a total group culture is the antithesis of Western individuality. As a cross-cultural trainer living in Japan, I found that Japanese TQM most closely paralleled the way Americans pulled together in the two World Wars, and is contrary to a civilian Western work force. . . . .TQM is far better suited to Japanese factories than to U.S. hospitals . . .

. . . . Without lifetime employment and complete care of workers and families by management, how could we conceive of long-term corporate or government teams? And even if we did realize that TQM was not a quick fix, and were willing to invest in expensive company-wide training, the rate of U.S. managerial and worker turnover is overwhelming compared to the naturally team-oriented Japanese . . .

. . . . In my estimation, having witnessed TQM on both sides of the Pacific, we should be flashing "caution" lights, red-flagging TQM salespeople and squarely addressing the "fit" of TQM in the West. I strongly urge that we resist and scrutinize anyone who seeks to restructure government or organizations abruptly in the name of TQM . . . We should see whether we are willing to pay the long-term price of creating a supportive TQM organizational culture, apart from American daily life and careers as we know them. We should proceed slowly, test the waters and implement some partial quality measures, rejecting the holier-than-thou hatchet transformation.

But it is more politically expedient for the naive, hungry, or calculating leader to hire TQM consultants as the experts who bless radical organizational change. Suffice to say that many of the consultants who serve governors and presidents with statistics for "quality change" are also lobbyists. . . .

(from Alan Goldman, "Take a Look on the Other Side of the TQM Curtain," *The Business Journal*, March 26, 1993, 3, 31.)

Appropriate rank and order are fundamentals of national and organizational culture among Japanese. It is very seldom that the appropriate order is broken or violated. Violations by Western visitors and expatriates are a deep source of conflict for Japanese hosts. By considering some key dimensions of rankings and arrangements central to Japanese national and corporate culture, U.S. managers and business people will be in a better position to avoid intercultural conflicts, insults, and misunderstandings.

Central to American managers' ignoring of Japanese rules of rank and order is the ethnocentric Western assumption that a certain degree of egalitarianism is a given. But one of the paradoxes of contemporary Japanese organizations is that many of the bastions of the old vertical culture are continued in the midst of the movement toward what appears to be more horizontal, participatory styles of management.

It is well known that in both U.S. and Japanese "theory Y" or "theory Z" organizations, managers more freely mingle with subordinates. Information is rapidly accessible and there is a propensity of "management by walking around" (MBWA). Although some of the traditional aspects of the tightly controlled, hierarchal company have given way to an environment where managers and workers talk, dine, and make decisions together, some of the old tenets of rank and order live on.

Rank is communicated through furniture and seating arrangements. The superior is generally understood to sit in a higher level seat than the inferior. Even within the close proxemics of white collar spatial arrangements, the seeming equality of group space is a bit deceptive. While working within Tokyo corporations I discovered that there was a somewhat invisible rank and seniority system operating.

I was highly uncomfortable with having to occupy a desk in a Japanese company without the privacy usually afforded a U.S. manager. The almost complete absence of walls, doors and partitions as a nonverbal, spatial expression of territoriality, placed me in what I initially experienced to be a Kafkaesque, existential sea of bland, identical office desks. The unobstructed space made everyone instantly visible to each other, highly accessible, and the rapid information flow seemingly defied the usual hierarchal, organizational chart.

A closer examination, however, depicted "choice locales" within the rows of what appeared to be hundreds of desks (actually about fifty). Gentlemen of rank were situated in the preferred corners, nearest to windows, and those of lower ranks clearly recognized this proxemic arrangement as hierarchal, ordered and purposeful.

Insight into corporate culture's continuation of some of the bastions of the old order or seniority system is found inside the Japanese home. Despite the Western press' insistence that Japanese national culture and management is rapidly democratizing, as reported in the group work, teams and solidarity of theory Z, and total quality management companies, it is revealing to observe that the female of the Japanese house of the 1990s *usually* follows traditional rank and order regarding service. At the beginning of the meal, for example, bowls of cooked rice are first served to those of the highest rank, with service descending to lower ranking family members. Japanese group structure is expressed in this ordered ritual as the male head of the household is served first, his male successor, second, followed by rice bowls for sons and daughters in accordance with their seniority and gender; the female of the house is finally served, with any woman successor to the woman head to follow (wife of male successor). To break the order is to defy the structure of the group.

Important is the contradictory, paradoxical nature of Japanese expression of rankings and arrangements. Whether in a Japanese home, at a table negotiation with a Japanese team, or involved in the daily factory or office life of a Japanese company, there are cues pointing in opposite directions. The breakdown of distances between workers, the tremendous accessibility of managers to subordinates, and the spatial arrangements of factory and office workplaces all appear to signal that the old hierarchy is no longer in operation. But additional *cues point toward the coexistence of the old and the new Japanese cultures.* There are specific seats reserved for senior Japanese at negotiating tables, and this is common domain to all Japanese workers. It is also necessary to understand that the egalitarianism of the doorless, group space arrangements are defied by the special reverence required by Japanese subordinates when addressing seniors.

Reserve and verbal economy is usually expected when conversing with those of higher rank. Although you may be inches from a superior's desk, as he does not have the claim to territoriality and privacy granted to Western managers, this does not mean that other forms of reverence are suspended. *Whether through seating and serving arrangements, or in the plethora of pronouns and Japanese language subtleties and nuances that speak rank and senior-*

ity, the hierarchy still stands. Even the initiating of workplace conversations between superiors and subordinates continues to be ordered and structured by rank. The unspoken rule is that the Japanese superior has the prerogative of initiating conversations. And during negotiations, the same senior may select to remain mostly silent. It is understood that the communication at the table is ordered via rank. Designated subordinates or juniors will be the mouthpieces for the senior. To directly request a response from the elder could very well summon notice as a violation.

As a fact of Japanese life, ranking orders are observed throughout corporate and social interaction. Rankings from the company are carried over into restaurant and street encounters, as appropriate honorific expressions and rules are observed. Japanese men of rank do not sit near entrances to rooms, they may speak first, and it is usually the senior who first laughs with subordinates following the lead. A complex tapestry of spatial arrangements, conversational rules, knowing when to speak and to remain silent, modes of address and honorifics, and the ordering of service and interaction, all permeate the companies and cafés of Japan. Whereas the Japanese senior may select silence in formal negotiations, in other social and workplace situations the senior may totally dominate conversation, as the junior is designated to the role of a listener.

Finally, the Japanese distaste for saying "no" or disagreeing in public business settings is particularly applicable to the rank and ordering system of the company. Rarely will a subordinate utter public disagreement with a superior, as this is a violation of social cohesiveness and rank. Silence would be the better alternative.

"AMERICAN STYLE DIRECTNESS"

Make no mistake, demolishing a Toshiba radio cassette player with a hammer is embarrassingly childish behavior for any politician. But even this can be interpreted as a somewhat extreme manifestation of American-style directness. I would venture to add that it is probably preferable to allowing one's irritation to seethe within.

(from Saeki Soichi, a professor of American Literature at Chuo University, Japan; from "Rediscovering America's Dynamic Society," in *Japan Echo,* Spring 1988.)

CHAPTER 21

The Listening Culture of Japan

When Americans reach beyond the more obvious differences plaguing U.S.-Japanese business relations, they stumble upon the "deeper structure" of Japanese behavior. In order to break through what linguists call the "surface structure," it is vital to look for the less visible cultural principles underlying and guiding Japanese corporate action. Without a knowledge of indigenous Japanese behaviors, it is hard to understand the roots of conflict or the sources of Japanese styled negotiations, adaptation and compromise.

U.S. Managers Would Rather Talk than Listen

U.S. managers would rather talk than listen.[1] Ours is primarily a "talk culture," and business communication experts report that there is much room for improvement in this area. The recent shift toward "management by walking around" (MBWA) and other more theory Y, participatory management efforts to empower workers—have placed a stress upon listening behavior. Yet, there is reason to believe that the predominant U.S. paradigm for listening is inseparable from the talkative, assertive, argumentative national culture. Oftentimes a "double think" is the U.S. norm: an alleged theory Y manager is still in the process of trying to put empathic listening skills into practice but is most comfortable with vertical downward information flows.

Japanese Listening Style

Even the most empathic of U.S. expatriate managers, emerging from theory Y corporate cultures, will be caught off-guard in the Jap-

anese listening climate. Japanese are more oriented toward a listening style that prioritizes feelings rather than factual listening.[2] In fact, Japanese listening can be directly linked to Japan being an empathic and feeling culture, or an *omoiyari* culture.[3]

What does this mean for U.S. expatriates on the assembly line, in diplomatic relations, or at Osaka negotiating tables? There are numerous ramifications, pointing toward the "living out" of culture in specific business communication behaviors. For example, "trained" to listen for feelings, Japanese associates typically listen in a highly interactive fashion. As another Japanese or American speaks, Japanese frequently offer feedback and reinforcement through numerous nods of the head. Nonverbal listening is joined by a myriad of brief verbal acknowledgements of the speaker, such as "yes," and "I am listening." Especially in interpersonal communication, there is active Japanese listening, with this constant reassurance that your listener is right there with you. Oftentimes, it is unclear whether the Japanese listener is purely empathic, or agrees with you in idea and substance.

The powerful presence of the Japanese listener and their style of caring became an anticipated and welcomed fact during my time spent living and working in corporate Tokyo. Leisurely conversing in English, the Japanese regularly listened by saying: "yes, yes, yes," "of course," "I know what you mean," etc. The empathic listener combined frequent verbal and nonverbal feedback.

U.S. Misunderstanding of Japanese Empathic Listening

For Americans unfamiliar with this actively empathic style of Japanese listening, they may easily misunderstand Japanese intent. With no experience of the reassuring "yes, yes, yes" listener, it is tough to distinguish between Japanese *tatemae* and *honne.* Newly expatriated managers and visiting U.S. negotiators walk away from a conversation believing that their Japanese friends are in complete agreement with American proposals. Only later, through indirect means, reading between the lines, and a sometimes unfortunate confrontation and face-threatening showdown, they figure out the difference between Japanese acknowledgment and agreement. *Empathic listening usually supplies the speaker with an abundance of acknowledgment—not to be confused with substantive agreement.* Lacking insight into Japanese empathic listening, it is quite likely that Americans will read the Japanese listening behavior from a U.S. frame of reference.

Americans must also sort through the strongly spoken Japanese words of acknowledgment ("yes, yes, yes"), continually interjected by avid Japanese listeners. The frequency and vocal dynamics of these active and empathic listening techniques may lead Americans to see Japanese as uncharacteristically argumentative, intrusive and impatient. Typically, nothing could be further from the truth. Based on Western models of managerial and workplace listening, U.S. expatriates feel rushed, anticipate that Japanese are thoroughly briefed on the issues, and quite capable as English speakers. Hindsight reveals that many Japanese were neither well briefed or masterful English conversationalists, only engaged in the act of empathic listening.

Reverse Culture Shock

A curious side note comes to mind. Upon returning to the U.S. after living in Tokyo, I had to make some serious readjustments to the U.S. style of communication. When addressing colleagues I felt a strange sense of insecurity, as if I wanted some kind of feedback that wasn't there. I finally recognized that the source of this was reverse culture shock due to a lack of the "yes, yes, yes," head nodding, variety of empathic listening that I became so accustomed to in Japan. I was going "cold turkey." Searching for confirmation and feedback, I only found a cooler, more aloof American listener. Until I reacclimated, I developed a habit of overly and obsessively interjecting such confirmation seeking phrases as "do you know what I mean?", "are you with me?, and "does this make any sense?"

While first bewildered by Japanese listening practices when a new expatriate in Japan, I later became dependent upon the Japanese style of empathic listening. I grew to expect a nurturing, collaborative listener, impassioned and in tune with my feelings. Back in the U.S., I only found this from close friends when in heated debate or private disclosures. As you immerse yourself in Japanese business and society be on the lookout for some of these differences in listening. Listen and observe closely and you'll hopefully begin to distinguish between U.S. and Japanese style listening.

"ON JAPANESE AND U.S. UNIVERSITY STUDENTS"

At Berkeley I gave a course on Japanese literary theory using works translated into English. The lively, direct response of my American university students puts to shame anything one could expect in Japan. Questions, comments, arguments, and counterarguments flew. In Japanese universities even considerable effort on the teacher's part usually fails to elicit any response or reaction. When the teacher solicits the students' opinions, they sit in stony silence, many of them casting their eyes downward lest they be called on . . .

(from Saeki Soichi, a professor of American Literature at Chuo University, who was a visiting professor at U. of California, Berkeley; from "Rediscovering America's Dynamic Society," in *Japan Echo,* Spring 1988.)

CHAPTER 22

Recognizing Cultural Entrapment: The Shock of Communicating and Receiving Compliments

When Japanese expatriates are relocated to subsidiaries in the U.S., they find that strongly contrasting approaches to compliments can be a source of culture shock. Japanese find it to be contrary to the group to offer compliments to individual U.S. workers—even when their performance is outstanding. Especially in public workplaces, Japanese are accustomed to directing their praise to groups of workers, not individuals.

American managers and workers with Japanese bosses, within the U.S. or in Japan, literally have no social or business precedent for the extreme group emphasis. Motivation, Western style, is to a high degree reliant upon individualized meanings, feelings of self-worth and dignity, personal satisfaction, self-actualization, and reinforcement or reward policies directed toward the solo worker.[1] Although there is also an accompanying (and varying) group-orientation in the workplace, it rarely equals Japanese interdependency (*amae*) and the subsuming of the individual within the objectives of the organization.

American expatriate managers in Japan are understandably startled when learning that their compliments directed to an individual Japanese factory line worker or engineer is ill-received. Bringing to mind the Japanese maxim, "The nail that sticks up gets banged down," the expatriate discovers that it is a great embarrassment to be singled out. Oddly enough, it does not matter, particularly, whether you are singling out a Japanese worker for inefficiency, lack of productivity or motivation, or for excellence. To bring attention to the solo worker is to invite cultural clashes.

The inclination is to personify these cultural clashes, as both Japanese and Americans are prone to believe that the manager in question is "rude" or "abrasive." Other workers, either starved for compliments and reinforcement, or embarrassed by public praise, bask in total condemnations of Japanese or U.S. corporate and social culture. Underlying the emotions of U.S. and Japanese strangers, unfamiliar with the other's business protocol, is the assumption that something as "simple as a compliment" could not possibly be relative, misconstrued or botched. The gut level response is a combination of shock, hurt, disappointment and bewilderment.

Further reflection, however, is in order. U.S. expatriates or managers serving under Japanese superiors in the U.S. can begin by seeing both Japanese and Americans as suffering from a kind of "cultural entrapment."[2] Americans are not only accustomed to a certain style of reinforcing communication, they are initially unable to even conceive of an alternative system of expressing praise. Likewise for Japanese, who in the course of experiencing the roles of the "insultors" and the "insultees," may have to dig down deep to find the source of the conflict.

Viewed as one of a myriad of expressions of "cultural entrapment," the problem of how to understand, respond to, and negotiate taken for granted managerial and worker behaviors is a fundamental dilemma. Being forewarned, briefed, and trained for these predictable confrontations is a first baby step toward the challenge of intercultural communication. Cultural entrapment is barely detectable when a U.S. manager has no clue as to the respective "holds" of both Japanese and U.S. culture. Only through briefings, cross-cultural training, or repeated on-the-job cultural shocks, can it be viscerally and mentally acknowledged that our behaviors and responses are largely "entrapped" within the dictates of culture.

"A TALE OF KOSHINJO"

JOHNSTONE: Now that we have known each other for a few years, there's something that I want to get off my chest . . .

TANAKA: Please . . . I'd like to hear it . . .

JOHNSTONE: Remember when you used *koshinjo* . . . an investigating agency . . . to look into my background . . . after I interviewed for the manager's position?

TANAKA: Of course I do. It is customary to use a *koshinjo*.

JOHNSTONE: I was quite upset over you doing that.

TANAKA: It is strictly company policy.

JOHNSTONE: It's Japanese way, isn't it? It's not unusual to investigate someone you're going to hire?

TANAKA: Certainly.

JOHNSTONE: Why don't you just call up former employers and check out references as carefully as you want . . . ?

TANAKA: I am not sure that would be a smart policy. Former employers may say a worker is very excellent, even if they were very poor . . . they want to get rid of him or just say what they want . . .

JOHNSTONE: But don't you think it intimidates Americans who are going through such scrutinizing?

TANAKA: I think maybe it is sensible and it is somewhat fair. Even fathers check out future sons-in-law through investigators.

JOHNSTONE: I think this needs further thought. It upset me very much. It would upset an American who wanted to marry your daughter, and it will upset future American employees of Tanaka International.

TANAKA: I will give this some thought, but it is the Japanese way.

Analysis: U.S. expatriates and players in U.S.-Japanese joint ventures, subsidiaries, mergers, consortiums and acquisitions are frequently shocked by radically contrasting approaches to the hiring process.

In "A Tale of *Koshinjo*" the Americans feel insulted that they are being investigated by Japanese employees. It is unfortunate that the Americans were not prepared for this inevitability.

While it is important that Japanese corporations consider the adverse effects of *koshinjo* practices on U.S. personnel and business partners, it is paramount that human resource departments, on both sides of the Pacific, address such an explosive issue.

Human resource departments (or personnel departments) and top management must carefully sort through and catalog numerous differences in U.S. and Japanese approaches to employment, interviewing, recruitment, and hiring practices. It is naive to view koshinjo as either "right or wrong;" it is rather a case of identifying this practice, inquiring into its corporate and cultural origins, and adapting to it—if warranted. More in-depth understanding of conflicting human resource practices between U.S. and Japanese companies can lead to the prospect of "negotiating" some of these policies, behind the scenes—rather than leaving these differences unnoticed. Left to "trial-by-error," it is quite possible that major, public, managerial conflicts or incidents will develop, leading to crisis situations between Japanese and U.S. companies. Frequent, intelligent, probing intercultural communication may divert such conflicts.

"JAPAN BASHING II"

Japan's geographical and linguistic isolation makes it fairly easy to convince the great television-watching public that they are constantly threatened by an unfriendly world—idiot American congressmen bashing Japanese cassette recorders with hammers help to confirm this belief. Criticism from the outside, uninformally labelled *"Japan-Bashing,"* is seen as a result of natural Western aggression and misunderstanding of Japanese culture. Toshiba, for example, did not seriously threaten the security of Japan and her allies by selling sensitive technology to the Soviet Union, but is simply the victim of Japan-bashing by jealous, aggressive Americans, or so it would seem from the Japanese popular press.

(from British author, Ian Buruma, in an article for *The Spectator*, August 22, 1987.)

CHAPTER **23**

Keiretsus and Zaibatsus: A Framework for Japanese Organizational Communication

MEDIA BRIEFING

"ABOUT AMERICA: A JAPANESE PERSPECTIVE"

America is the closest place to paradise for people who want to be free, who want to do their very best. It's a great experiment for human beings. There are so many diverse people from different backgrounds.

(from Satohiro Akimoto, a young executive with Mitsubishi Trading Company; appearing in the *Dallas Morning News,* July 6, 1986.)

A working knowledge of the powerful force of Japanese *zaibatsus* and *keiretsus* is vital to U.S. expatriates. Managerial communication with Japanese is oftentimes strongly influenced by *keiretsus,* as the *keiretsus* provide a context or framework for Japanese organizational communication.[1] Interrelationships between organizations guide the communicative behavior of individual Japanese and companies. As the Japanese negotiator is bound to group consensus, the single Japanese corporation must also listen to the group voice of the *keiretsu*. To conceive of face-to-face communication with an individual Japanese negotiator or a single Japanese organization apart from broader affiliations and obligations, is to remain naive to the *contexts* operating.

Zaibatsus: Precursors of Keiretsus

Keiretsus are modern day, post-second war variations and modifications of pre-war Japanese *zaibatsus* or "corporate groupings." Oftentimes challenged by U.S. and other Western free trade interests, as a Japanese version of a monopoly or cartel, the *zaibatsus* were broken up and disbanded under the rulings of the post-World War II occupation of the Americans in Japan. But in the opinion of Che Nakane, "the principle of their organization survived below the surface." The emergence of the *keiretsu* mirrors some of the collectivist policies of the earlier *zaibatsus*. The principles of the *zaibatsu* interorganizational groupings is described by Nakane:

> Besides its links with larger and smaller institutions of its own kind, each institution has constant dealings with an array of differing institutions, for example, those supplying necessary services; together, they form still another functional group. A bank, an insurance company, an industrial plant, an export-import firm, a shipping company and other numerous related operations might form *one group* (my emphasis). These were indeed the component elements of a *Zaibatsu. Zaibatsu* monopoly was not directed to a particular interest, but covered a wide range of interests in industry. . . . Within the group, duties and obligations are so rigorous that there is little opportunity for the entry of others.[2]

The *zaibatsus* were characterized by strong, centralized, authoritative management and decision-making, with the predominant flow of information, vertical-downward. This autocratic, theory X style of management kept a strong hold on intra- and interorganizational communication messages and networks; managers and employees closely followed an organizational chart, with the top management usually located in the *honke* or "main house." According to Tomoko Hamada, the *zaibatsu* can further be described as a

> group of Japanese companies controlled and dominated by a family-owned holding company in Japan before World War

II. Each *zaibatsu* had at its center a holding company, owned by the founder family. The holding company owned a large proportion of each of the dozen or so core companies, including the bank, the trading company, the trust company, and the insurance company. There was a great measure of centralized management.[3]

The problem that current SII representatives from the U.S. are having with the Japanese *keiretsu* is echoed in the depiction of a French designer's problems of doing business within the deeply entrenched network of Japanese *zaibatsus*. For although modern day *keiretsus* are in principle "legally independent companies,"[4] in actuality, they are bound to stay within their corporate grouping network, and utilize materials and services from members only. See how the French designer could not effectively find a way of strategically communicating as an outsider, within the *zaibatsu:*

> . . . there is a story of a famous French designer who was invited to show his collection by one of the largest department stores in Tokyo and required a particular material for some of his designs. Unfortunately, this material was not made by the textile firms supplying this particular department store, so he asked that the store should get the material from another textile company. However, he finally had to give up hope in the face of the strong resistance shown by the department store on the grounds that the firm which made the particular material did not have established dealings with the store.[5]

The frustration felt by the French designer is surely matched by current U.S. business visitors and corporate joint venture candidates' experiences with Japanese associates. Although both Japanese and American organizations are certainly concerned with bottom lining costs, it is perhaps uniquely Japanese to place cost and pragmatics second to long established *keiretsu* relationships. Surely many cultural origins of trade barriers and frictions are derivative of these tendencies.

Understanding Keiretsus

In line with the "we" principle of dominant Japanese national and corporate culture, the *keiretsu* places the individual company within a corporate network. Single Japanese organizations do not have the autonomy and independence of Western companies as the mutual interests of the *keiretsu* subsumes solo agendas.

Unlike the cartel or monopoly, a *keiretsu* does not officially set prices, trade conditions, and engage in other overt competition-limiting strategies. Hamada describes the *keiretsu* as

> a corporate alliance across industrial sectors and markets, often tied through client-supplier business relationships. Competition in each market is fierce among firms with different *keiretsu* connections. *Particularly powerful are six groups—Mitsubishi, Mitsui, Sumitomo, Fuyo, Sanwa, and Dai-Ichi Kangyo (Furukawa)—*that link together batches of firms, banks, and trading houses with small cross-shareholdings.[6]

Important in this description is the fact that there is fierce competition between *keiretsus,* with the *soto* (outside), *uchi* (inside) distinction paramount. Boundaries are drawn, and market share is the driving force. But even among competing *keiretsus* the principles of indigenous Japanese cultural and communicative practices remain true to form. Public discourse (*soto*) remains on a gentlemanly level, while the rough words, the rhetoric of rivalry and debunkings is voiced primarily behind closed doors (*uchi*). External organizational communications functions such as advertising and marketing, do not bombard the consumer with fighting words or negative advertising—so prevalent within the U.S. marketplace. It is with a bit more discern that rival keiretsus battle each other—within the Japanese market. There is no daily, obvious articulation of this information, with harsh words confined to closed doors.

The practice of *on* (reciprocity and a system of interpersonal duty and organizational interrelationships within and between companies) is integral between *keiretsu* members, as there is a community of mutual benefits and obligations binding together all "insiders". Within a given *keiretsu,* member organizations have clearly defined communication channels and interrelationships; management does its best to coordinate all member activities, monitoring continuing and potential links and reciprocities. It should be carefully noted that the ties between *keiretsu* members are not limited to the boundaries of Japan, and clearly transcend national borders. The close communication links and channels with the Japanese parent company (*honsha*) and the overseas child company (*kogaisha*), is usually attended to by means of carefully strategized expatriations. Through *keiretsu* personnel transfer systems, a *shukko* (a system of temporary transfer of Japanese workers and management) keeps open lines of communication with the *honsha* and the entire industrial grouping. Transfers to *kogaisha* within the U.S. are usually for periods of approximately three to seven years.

Viewing Keiretsus from the Vantage Point of U.S. Management

Where exactly do the *keiretsu* position U.S. and Western joint venture partners and expatriates? How do they structure dialogue, management, operations, and overall U.S.-Japanese relations?

Obviously, the framework of the *keiretsu* should be considered. U.S. corporations must meticulously study the interorganizational chart[7] and do their very best to unravel the formal and informal hierarchies, and the corresponding lines and channels of communication. If doing business with a *keiretsu* member within the continental U.S., it may be vital to understand the particular relationship of the *shukko* (expatriate) to his home office (*honsha*). Whether this *shukko* is in good graces with the *honsha* is useful information, as is the approximate duration of his tenure in America. Should lines of communication be directed to the *shukko*? If U.S. management is involved with a *tenzoku* (a person who resigned from the parent to be formally hired by the child/*kogaisha*), this alters the complexion of the relationship, as this breed of expatriate is on a permanent overseas assignment.

It is usually through numerous trial and error confrontations with *shukko* and *honsha* that U.S. local nationals and expatriates begin to comprehend the complexities of the U.S. and Japanese based *keiretsus*. *In the U.S., Japanese setups of local manufacturing plants for the production, partial-production, or finishing of products previously exported from Japan, are still intimately tied to keiretsus within Japan.* Although Japanese firms must comply with local laws, much of the indigenous activities of *keiretsus* continue. Or *when engaged in expatriations within Japan, U.S. managers must similarly view the keiretsus as the overriding corporate culture framing all communication and operations.* It is usually ludicrous and a serious breach to attempt to go around or above the *shukko* or *kogaisha* unless special arrangements have been made. And it is vital to remember that the same kinds of interpersonal and group networks binding the Japanese negotiator are even more deeply and broadly entrenched among *keiretsu* members. Pressuring or giving ultimata to a Japanese or U.S. based *shukko* or *kogaisha* is a sum zero game as there is little latitude for charismatic leadership, individual decision-making or prompt responses to Western pressures.

Moreover, the interpersonal and organizational structuring of *keiretsus* makes for a very careful monitoring of outside influences and alliances.[8] Much as the French designer could not influence the *zaibatsu* to open its doors to textiles not manufactured by a member organization, so do U.S. expatriates and business negotiators find that *keiretsus* do not readily accept outside, *gaijin* suppliers. With long established affiliations, *keiretsu* companies have their hands tied when confronted by U.S. automobile corporations. How can the *keiretsu* organization even fathom the prospect of a non-member supplying what a member already supplies? In essence, gaining Japanese acceptance for the entrance of U.S. automobile parts into the domestic market requires that there be a serious challenge levied against the *keiretsus*. Accordingly, the market share and competitiveness war is but the *tatemae* (surface) of the deeper cultural war.

Cultural Import of Keiretsus: International or Ultra-Nationalist?

The pattern of Japanese enculturation embodied in the *keiretsus* should be readily apparent. Numerous parallels exist within Japanese social and business organizations. Take, for example, the analogies to be drawn with negotiating and decision-making. The individual Japanese negotiator is *bound* to the precise and prescribed consensus building practices of *nemawashi* (informal consensus building), literally translating to the "binding of the roots of the tree") and *ringi* (the continued formal circulation of printed proposals until a complete consensus emerges).[9] In a similar fashion, the independence of the individual organization within a *keiretsu* is constricted, as they too must balance and juggle the interests of multiple member organizations.

Communication between *keiretsu* members is a "special" breed of interaction reserved for "members only." To be within a *keiretsu* network, is to be an insider. The *keiretsu* is a pervasive context for communication between members, as there is a comeraderie and varying degrees of mutual obligations, debts, and interdependencies operating (*on*). U.S. and Western organizations are initially "outsiders" in two ways: they are outside the *keiretsu* and "cultural strangers" or *gaijin*.

From an outsider, U.S. perspective, the Japanese "monster" is the *keiretsu*. These powerful groupings of industries operationalizes and frames a solidarity among organizations that cannot be matched in the West. Anti-monopoly and cartel laws have been widely practiced in the U.S., making North American companies particularly vulnerable in competition for world market share. In a sense, it is quite convenient for Japanese that the *keiretsus* do appear to be an understandable outgrowth of centuries of Japanese collectivism. Although the *keiretsus* may represent for Americans the antithesis of the free enterprise system, the support for same among the Japanese public is overwhelming.[10] So in the process of voicing U.S. confrontational rhetoric against *keiretsus* (e.g., via the Strategic Impediments Initiative—SII), we should be aware that we are arguing on two fronts: (1) against the alleged monopolistic system perpetuated by *keiretsus;* and (2) unwittingly clashing with a collectivist system of organizing that appears indigenous to Japanese society.

As the competitiveness discourse heats up on both sides of the Pacific, it is impossible not to draw connections between *keiretsus* and charges of "dumping practices" brought against Japanese. There is reason to believe that the strongest organizational members of a *keiretsu* can sustain the weaker member's entrance into new markets, especially foreign markets. When the *keiretsu* can offer support for temporary losses, a Japanese member with an innovative product and a potential U.S. market can afford to set prices artificially low, ultimately driving all competitors out. Once competition is eliminated (e.g., American competition), then the price is adjusted and the *keiretsu,* as well as the individual company, has prevailed.

How can U.S. expatriates and trade representatives effectively communicate the Western position when the inter-institutional relations of the *keiretsu* are viewed by Japanese as both fundamental to Japanese national culture and another example of *nihonjinron?* Many Japanese deeply believe that the *keiretsu* is a symbol and instrument of the "we society" and cannot be understood by foreign outsiders or *gaijin* (the *nihonjinron syndrome*). The prospects for dialogue severely break down. Americans are determined to break the "communistic like cartels",[11] while the Japanese believe that the frontier minded Americans are incapable of understanding the subtleties, sophistication and group interrelationships of *keiretsu*. Whereas U.S. organizations engage in competitive discourse in the struggle for marketshare (in the U.S.), Japanese reserve the fervor for *inter-keiretsu* competition.

The *Keiretsu* as an Extended Family (*Ie*)

Regarding *keiretsu* parallels to indigenous, historically grounded cultural practices, U.S. management should finally take note of the "*ie*." Numerous Japanese scholars and practitioners repeatedly address the continuance of an "*ie*-society" in Japan, as the *ie* is the basic family institution. Che Nakane eloquently provides the analogy between familiar and corporate *ie*:

> A company is conceived as an *ie*, all its employees qualifying as members of the household, with the employer at its head . . . This "family" envelops the employee's personal family; it 'engages' him 'totally' (*marugakae* in Japanese). The employer readily takes responsibility for his employee's family, for which, in turn, the primary concern for the company, rather than relatives who reside elsewhere . . . The root of the *ie* institution as the distinguished unit in society in pre-modern times is now played by the company.[12]

A bit of reflection upon the nature and structure of *keiretsus* (and *zaibatsus*) can easily conjure up a view of these industrial groupings as "extended families." Additionally, these *ie* are more important than blood families for many Japanese salarymen, as the employee's *ie* is the individual company, and his/her extended family, the *keiretsu*.

Postscript and Implications

It is curious that *keiretsus* do give Japanese a significant "off-the-line" competitive edge that feeds into just-in-time and total quality management systems. A chiseled and packaged inter-organizational structuring of relationships creates closer proxemics, elimination of waste and excess, and breeds reliability and fidelity among workers and *keiretsu* members. The team work required of TQM management, for example, is highly compatible with *ie* and the *keiretsu* system. In the broadest sense, the *keiretsu* offers longterm support and nurturing for the early days of TQM or other organizational restructurings and reinventions.

Regarding U.S.-Japanese management and organizational communication, however, *keiretsus* epitomize an indigenous cultural force in direct conflict with the presuppositions of dominant U.S. national and corporate cultures. Can words, arguments, and organizational communication strategies be found to cross the intercultural abyss? Indeed the farther reaches of the *keiretsus* represents the ultimate challenge for U.S. management and politicians. The intercultural challenge is one of communicating to bring about a reflection upon the very cultural paradigms or frameworks *underlying* our already confrontational, hostile interaction. In other words, can a new breed of interculturally trained organizational communication experts negotiate cultural paradigms? This appears to be what is required in the showdown over *keiretsus*.

MEDIA BRIEFING

"EAST AND WEST"

American people challenge everything. They have the frontier spirit. Europeans are conservative, I think, and Americans are not. I was very impressed because Japanese are very inward looking and pessimistic. Americans are very open and optimistic.

(from the owner of a sushi bar in Tokyo, Akira Baba; appearing in *The Dallas Morning News*, July 6, 1986.)

"UMBRELLA BRIEFING: THE JOYS OF SILENCE"

Umbrellas are a way of life in Japan. A virtual sea of umbrellas . . . as far as the eye can see . . . is an everyday sight on the streets of Osaka or Kyoto. Walking in the rain of Tokyo, in the Ginza, Harajuku or around the factories of Japan Victor Corporation in Chuorinkan or Shinkoyasu, is a fitting test of one's ability to maneuver an umbrella within human traffic. I bobbed and weaved, slipping and sliding, always keeping my sight on the intense job of angling through the maze of tens of thousands of umbrellas. There was no need to make eye contact, observe the reservoir of Japanese bodies, only the immediate mission of weaving through the umbrellas.

Share the Umbrella?

One afternoon I was caught in a Japanese monsoon around Chuorinkan, en route to conducting a training session at the Japan Victor Plant for U.S. bound Japanese executives. A true Japanese gentleman emerged out of the ocean of Japanese, saying "share the umbrella?" I thanked him in English and Japanese, snuggled close to the stranger, and we proceeded to walk for several miles in the rain. Our arms, shoulders and bodies were in constant contact, defying the physical distances that strangers usually observe. It was a struggle to stay dry and on course.

We walked and splashed through the thundering rain, but not a single word was uttered. For approximately thirty minutes I had time to experience the full brunt of this silence. Why were we not speaking? What should I say? Can he understand English, or did he just learn a few stock phrases for *gaijin?*

The half-hour was a cross-cultural eternity. It was a serious challenge to my sometimes glib, talkative nature. Every American bone and vocal chord in this body was stretching, pushing to make speech. But no sounds came out of my mouth. It was high time to dwell on a Japanese silence; a rare juncture where theory and life meet—I now was living the silence.

There was a disturbing magic to the silence. Surely I had no questions as to the purity of "Mr. Chuorinkan's" motives. I realized that his one question, combined with his actions, spoke quite eloquently. But why did I have this dire need to say something? Why was I so obsessed with filling up this alleged void?

I managed to keep my mouth shut. Why tamper with what could be perfection? I began listening to the rain, concentrating on the splatterings against the umbrella, and enjoyed the stranger. He must have gone out of his way, as the Japanese man seemed to follow my footsteps for the last few blocks. I did not have to direct him. He let my steps guide his. We wound up at the front door of JVC. We smiled at each other. No words were spoken.

The Joys of Silence

I've since discovered that Japanese business people, negotiators, and visitors, not only value silence—they are uncomfortable with excessive verbage. The "gift of gab" only makes Japanese distrustful and suspicious. Westerners tend to want to sing in the rain, talk during a monsoon, and endlessly fill the purposeful Japanese silences at the trade and corporate negotiating table. I shared the umbrella and finally contemplated the intercultural challenge of silence. His was a "gift of silence."

While Mr. Chuorinkan may have avoided speaking because he knew little conversational English, or found it cumbersome to speak the language, there is little doubt that silence *is* his friend.

Speak Less

Not only did I escape the Japanese flu on that Tokyo day, I also learned the merits of a prolonged silence. I wonder whether any of the wet politicians and diplomats of the great West have considered the virtues of pregnant pauses? Trying to persuade Japanese representatives to leave their meaningful silences for the chattering of more *tatemae* (surface communication) may not produce great dividends.

While I walked under the umbrella on that rainy day, I also wondered about the U.S. journalists who are suspicious of the sparse replies volunteered by Japanese subjects during interviews. Surely it is ethnocentric folly to interpret these quiet responses as indications that anyone has anything to hide.

The power of silence is within Japanese cultural lineage; it is learned behavior. To search for individual motives is to bypass the stronghold of culture. As a Japanese, he values silence. As Americans, we place a different value on the spoken moments. We are conditioned to speak more, Japanese to speak less. To narrow the gulf I must discover how silence is strategic to a Japanese way of communicating.

Keep in mind that the Japanese who speaks too much is being singular, individualistic, and calling attention to him/herself. This rare species of Japanese may be ostracized in the workplace, in the corporate classroom, at an interview. I struggled to learn how to be just another body under another umbrella, without need of words or recognition. It's what you do not say that goes a long way, in or out of the rain.

"TALKING TURKEY"

TAKESHITA: You insulted the Americans.

WATANABE: You cannot be serious. How?

TAKESHITA: You proceeded too slowly.

WATANABE: Too slowly? I couldn't answer their crazy, fast, demanding and rude questions. They wanted decisions at the meeting. You know I can't make them on-the-spot.

TAKESHITA: Yes, I know.

WATANABE: So, what is the problem?

TAKESHITA: Do they know? Do the Americans understand how difficult they are?

WATANABE: Maybe not. They are inexperienced negotiators with Japanese. They probably only know the American way. According to their narrow minds, I act Japanese and I "insult them."

TAKESHITA: Maybe you should have informally explained that we use *ringi and nemawashi* approaches to decision-making—making it long and tedious . . . for them.

WATANABE: But maybe it's their responsibility to have a sixth grade understanding of Japanese business culture and how we communicate?

TAKESHITA: You are a bit upset. Let's make a solution.

WATANABE: You know that it's so impolite and face-provoking to be bringing these things up in public, but it takes so much effort. And this is only one of many problems . . .

TAKESHITA: Maybe tell me one more obstacle you face. I'd like to know . . .

WATANABE: I have this secret disrespect for that American phrase . . . "talk turkey."

TAKESHITA: "Talk turkey?" I don't understand.

WATANABE: I asked Okabe who just lived in the U.S. for five years. He says it means to "get to the point" and "stop wasting time."

TAKESHITA: You mean that maybe Japanese small talk, politeness, and *ringi* and *nemawashi* are a "waste of time?"

WATANABE: With those impatient Americans, I think anything that is not "talking turkey" is a waste of time. This is really an impossible situation.

TAKESHITA: Yes, it sounds impossible. If you act Japanese you insult them, and if we let them have their way . . . they are oblivious . . . and they insult us.

WATANABE: So much for solutions!

Analysis: Behind the joint venture curtain there are many distressing discussions about intercultural communication conflict. Takeshita and Watanabe are sincerely trying to sort through some of the problems they are having with their American counterparts, and I believe that "listening in" can be of benefit. Essentially, by hearing about Japanese frustration, American expatriates can begin to step into Japanese shoes and see how they appear to their Asian associates.

At the heart of this controversy are two conflicting approaches to stable negotiations and the entire negotiating process. To further complicate matters, there are no neat and tidy solutions to these conflicts, as they are but the tip of a very deep intercultural "iceberg." The adversarial "talk turkey" Westerners are having a very difficult time communicating with the slower paced, consensus building Japanese.

As a starting point, both sides must be extremely well aware of the culturally oriented negotiating styles that they bring to the table. Even though the Japanese style of decision-making is extremely slow, there is no way to waltz into a corporate or political room and "Americanize" the agenda. In an ideal situation, it may be advisable to attempt to "negotiate the negotiation process itself," as Americans speak of their frustrations in an *informal,* relaxed situation. Asking open-ended questions about *ringi* and *nemawashi* should yield some results. By understanding that Japanese must leave the negotiating table and spend time generating complete organizational consensus (between meetings, away from the table), this casts the "talk turkey" syndrome in a slightly different light. Although Japanese negotiators may be gently nudged along a bit, it is very difficult and face-threatening to issue ultimata or attempt to force on-the-spot decisions when the Japanese officials are rarely empowered to speak for an entire company. Even if you view this Japanese "predicament" in a pejorative light, take care to see it more as a consequence of cultural entrapment rather than an individual's non-compliance.

Notes

Chapter 1.

1. For further explanation, see C. Grove and I. Torbiorn, "A New Conceptualization of Intercultural Adjustment and the Goals of Training," *International Journal of Intercultural Relations,* 9, 205–233; E. Hall, *Beyond Culture* (New York: Doubleday, 1976).

2. See J. Condon, *With Respect to the Japanese: A Guide for Americans* (Yarmouth, Maine: The Intercultural Press, 1984).

3. For an explanation of the concept of "cultural strangers," see W. Gudykunst and Y. Kim, *Communicating with Strangers: An Approach to Intercultural Communication* (New York: Random House, 1984), pp. 15, 20–22 and 205–222.

Chapter 2.

1. For an examination of the centrality of intercultural communication in corporate and multinational management between Western and Japanese companies, see A. Goldman, "Strategic Arenas of Interaction with Japanese Multinationals: Organizational, Negotiating, Proxemic and Performance Protocols"; a paper presented at the annual convention of The Speech Communication Association, Chicago, Illinois, November 1993.

2. For further information on bridging cultural differences, see G. Hofstede, *Culture's Consequences* (Beverly Hills: Sage, 1984).

3. For example, see C. Hui and H. Triandis, "Individualism-Collectivism: A Study of Cross-Cultural Researchers," *Journal of Cross Cultural Psychology,* 17, 225–248.

4. See S. Hayashi, *Culture and Management in Japan* (Tokyo: University of Tokyo Press (translated by Frank Baldwin), 1988).

5. See E. Hall and M. Hall, *Hidden Differences: Doing Business with the Japanese* (New York: Anchor Press, 1987).

6. See S. Hayashi, op. cit.

7. For example, see A. Goldman, "Preparing for Negotiations with Japanese Organizations: A Briefing for North American and European Multinationals," *The Multinational Employer,* 7, 16–17.

8. The lack of U.S. corporate investment in predeparture intercultural training for expatriates in Japan is depicted in A. Goldman, "Intercultural Training of Japanese for U.S.-Japanese Interorganizational Communication," *International Journal of Intercultural Relations,* 16, 195–216.

9. See A. Goldman, *Japanese-U.S. Business Communication* (Tokyo: Kirihara Shoten, 1993).

10. Ibid.

11. An excellent, eclectic assortment of cross-cultural training is presented by P. Casse, *Training for the Cross-Cultural Mind* (Washington, D.C.: Sietar, 1981).

12. For a comprehensive examination of Japanese labor, hiring practices, human resource development, and other strategic management issues for U.S. bosses, see T. Nevins, *Labor Pains and the Gaijin Boss: Hiring, Managing and Firing the Japanese* (Tokyo: The Japan Times, 1984).

13. Ibid.

14. For an examination of the concept of "cultural entrapment," see T. Lebra, *Japanese Patterns of Behavior* (Honolulu: Univ. of Hawaii Press, 1976).

15. See T. Nevins, op. cit.

16. For example, see E. Hall and M. Hall, op. cit.

17. For further insight into intercultural and expatriate adaptation, see J. Servaes, "Cultural Identity in East and West," *The Howard Journal of Communication,* 1, 58–71.

Chapter 3.

1. See T. Homada, "Under the Silk Banner: The Japanese Company and its Overseas Managers," in T. Lebra (editor), *Japanese Social Organization* (Honolulu: Univ. of Hawaii Press, 1992), 135–164.

2. I believe that this thesis is shared by many intercultural specialists such as M. Zimmerman, *How to do Business with the Japanese* (New York: Random House, 1985); D. Barnlund, *Communicative Styles of Japanese and Americans: Images and Realities* (Belmont, CA: Wadsworth, 1989); and J. Rauch, *The Outnation: A Search for the Soul of Japan* (Boston: Harvard Business School Press, 1992).

3. This is the view of L. Smeltzer, J. Waltman, and D. Leonard, *Managerial Communication: A Strategic Approach* (MA: Ginn, 1991).

4. See D. Barnlund, *Public and Private Self in Japan and the United States* (Tokyo: Simul Press, 1975).

5. Ibid.

6. A. Roland, *In Search of Self in India and Japan: Toward A Cross-Cultural Psychology* (Princeton, New Jersey: Princeton University Press, 1988).

7. J. Beckwith, "Lawyer Bucks System By Backing Underdogs," *The Japan Times,* November 11, 1991, pp. 1, 6.

8. Ibid.

9. Ibid.

10. Ibid.

Chapter 4.

1. For an analysis of Japanese *ningensei,* see T. Lebra, *Japanese Patterns of Behavior* (Honolulu: Univ. of Hawaii Press, 1976).

2. See Lebra, ibid., for discussion of indigenous Japanese communicative behaviors cited.

3. *Keiretsus* are a modification and outgrowth of disbanded Japanese *zaibatsus.* The *keiretsu* are corporate and industrial groupings of Japanese companies, offering a complex, interrelated support system for organizational members. Although usually thought of by Western competitors as "cartels or monopolies," this description more aptly fit the earlier *zaibatsus,* discontinued under the order of the occupying U.S. forces, during post-World War II. The *keiretsus* appear to embody many of the principles of Japanese collectivism illustrated over the centuries.

4. For a comprehensive investigation of the Japanese negotiating process, see R. March, *The Japanese Negotiator: Subtlety and Strategy Beyond Western Logic* (Tokyo: Kodansha, 1989).

5. Ibid.

6. Ibid.

7. See R. Schonberger, *Japanese Manufacturing Techniques: Nine Hidden Lessons in Simplicity* (N.Y.: The Free Press, 1982).

8. P. Harris, and R. Moran, *Managing Cultural Differences* (Houston Gulf Publishing Co., 1987).

9. For an example of an "intercultural communication training laboratory," see A. Goldman, "Intercultural training of Japanese for U.S.-Japanese Interorganizational Communication," *International Journal of Intercultural Relations,* 16, 195–216.

10. See Schonberger, op. cit.

11. See A. Goldman, *For Japanese Only: Intercultural Communication with Americans* (Tokyo: The Japan Times, 1988).

12. See S. Durlabhji and N. Marks (eds.), *Japanese Business: Cultural Perspectives* (Albany: SUNY Press, 1993).

13. See Schonberger, op. cit.

14. See A. Goldman, "Cultural Abyss at the Negotiating Table: An Examination of Japanese-U.S. Communication Style," *Human Communication Studies,* 18, 101–116.

15. Ibid.

16. See A. Goldman, *International Journal of Intercultural Relations,* op. cit.

17. This led to development of a "cultural drama" approach to intercultural training. I provide trainees with "scripts" representing typical corporate contact situations. Trainees alternately play the roles of Japanese and Americans.

18. Through the reading of their "lines" and direct participation in "cultural dramas," I found that trainees became affectively engaged. Through a "stepping into the shoes" of actual negotiations, contract disputes, and via the "switching of roles," trainees reported experiences of discomfort, anger, confusion and frustration. Effective management of conflict in subsequent dramas led to stress reduction and may be instrumental in actual carryover into the marketplace. This remains to be tested.

19. For example, see E. Hall, and M. Hall, *Hidden Differences: Doing Business with the Japanese* (N.Y.: Anchor, 1987).

20. See R. Hirokawa, and A. Miyahara, "A comparison of influence strategies utilized by managers in American and Japanese organizations," *Communication Quarterly,* 34, 250–265.

21. See M. Matsumoto, *The Unspoken Way, Haragei: Silence in Japanese Business and Society* (Tokyo: Kodansha, 1988).

22. Ibid.; also see A. Goldman, *Japanese-U.S. Business Communication* (Tokyo: Kirihara Shoten, 1993).

Chapter 5.

1. For an examination of waste, excess and unevenness in total quality management in Japan and the U.S., see A. Goldman, "Implications of Japanese Total Quality Control Management for Western Organizations: Dimensions of an Intercultural Hybrid," *Journal of Business Communication,* 30, 29–48.

2. For the most extensive and vital examination available of Japanese *haragei* or "communication of the gut and stomach" through silence, see M. Matsumoto, *The Unspoken Way, Haragei: Silence in Japanese Business and Society* (Tokyo: Kodansha, 1988).

3. For examination of the interrelationships of management systems, organizational theories, proxemics and communication in the workplace, see A. Goldman, "Communication in Japanese Multinational Organizations," *International and Intercultural Communication Annual,* xvii, Beverly Hills: Sage, 1994), 45–74; R. Hirokawa, "Improving intra-organizational communication: A lesson from Japanese management," *Communication Quarterly,* 30, 35–40; R. Hirokawa and A. Miyahara, "A Comparison of Influence Strategies Utilized by Managers in American and Japanese Organizations," *Communication Quarterly,* 34, 250–265; A. Goldman, "The Centrality of *Ningensei* to Japanese Negotiating and Interpersonal Relations: Implications for US–Japanese Communication," *The International Journal of Intercultural Relations,* 18, 29–54.

4. E. Hall, *The Hidden Dimension* (New York: Doubleday, 1966); *Beyond Culture* (New York: Doubleday, 1976); *The Dance of Life* (New York: Doubleday, 1983).

5. It is important to note that "culture shock" is typically viewed as part of a broader intercultural expatriate adjustment cycle that is usually experienced. As a former expatriate I vouch for the following cycle:
a. honeymoon phase marked by excitement, openness and embracement of many new sights, sounds, smells, and experiences of a second culture;
b. culture shock is the phase characterized by many surprises, clashes, conflicts, and confrontations with the second culture;
c. superficial adjustment follows, as the expatriate or sojourner typically believes that s/he is further along in adaptation than they actually are;

d. depression and isolation may be on the heels of recognition of superficial adjustment, as expatriates find that they miss their native culture, have a long way to go toward adaptation, and may feel isolated and overwhelmed by the cultural differences and seemingly insurmountable barriers;

e. reintegration and compensation may be a natural consequence of having survived the depression and isolation, as the expatriate finds a new and stronger will to meet the intercultural challenge; and

f. autonomy and independence is a longer term campaign for expatriates as they immerse themselves in a second culture, gradually accept the differences of the host culture, and learn how to adapt in areas of communication, social and business relations.

6. The power and influence of *manga* or comic books and comic strips should not be overlooked when preparing for business, educational, political or trade relations with Japanese. According to Stanford University Professor Peter Duus, "to think of Japanese comics simply as entertainment for lowbrows is to miss the mark. In Japan, the comics, like television, have become a powerful medium for entertainment, for the transmission of knowledge, and for the diffusion of values." Indeed the term *comics* is a misnomer. Most *manga* . . . are not at all funny. . ." (from an introduction by P. Duus, to a *manga* formatted book on Japanese economics by S. Ishinomori, *Japan Inc.,: An Introduction to Japanese Economics* (Berkeley: Univ. of California Press, 1988), p. i of the introduction.

Chapter 6.

1. For example, see K. Leung and M. Bond, "The Impact of Cultural Collectivism on Reward Allocation," *Journal of Personality and Social Psychology,* 47, 793–804.

2. For the most widely accepted view of Japanese *amae,* see T. Doi, "The Japanese Patterns of Communication and the Concept of *Amae,*" *The Quarterly Journal of Speech,* 59, 180–185; T. Doi, *The Anatomy of Dependence* (Tokyo: Kodansha, 1989).

3. S. Hayashi, *Culture and Management in Japan* (Tokyo: Univ. of Tokyo Press, 1988).

4. Ibid.

5. See C. Nakane, *Japanese Society* (Berkeley, CA: Univ. of California Press, 1972), for an intriguing view of the interrelationships between the historical-cultural roots of Japanese organizing and collectivities and the plight of individuals in contemporary corporate life.

6. See T. Lebra, *Japanese Patterns of Behavior* (Honolulu: Univ. of Hawaii Press, 1976).

7. See I. BenDasan, *Japanese and Jews* (Tokyo: Yamamoto Shoten 1970); A. Goldman, "The Centrality of *Ningensei* to Japanese Negotiating and Interpersonal Relationships: Implications for U.S.-Japanese Communication," a paper presented at the annual convention of The Speech Communication Association, Chicago, Ill., November 1992.

8. See Doi, 1973, 1989; op. cit.

9. E. Hall and M. Hall, *Hidden Differences: Doing Business with Japanese* (New York: Anchor Press, 1987).

10. See A. Goldman, "Implications of Japanese Total Quality Control Management for Western Organizations: Dimensions of an Intercultural Hybrid," *Journal of Business Communication,* 30, 29–48.

11. Ibid.

12. Ibid.

13. See Hall and Hall, 1987, op. cit.

14. See Goldman, 1993, op. cit.

15. Ibid.; and Hall and Hall, 1987, op. cit.

16. See A. Goldman, "Japanese Managerial Psychology: An Analysis of Cultural and Organizational Features of Total Quality Control Management," *Journal of Managerial Psychology,* 8, 17–20.

17. See R. Schonberger, *Japanese Manufacturing Techniques: Nine Hidden Lessons in Simplicity* (New York: The Free Press, 1982); *World Class Manufacturing* (New York: The Free Press, 1986); *World Class Manufacturing Casebook: Implementing JIT and TQC* (New York: The Free Press, 1987).

18. For example, see J. Neustupny, *Communicating with Japanese* (Tokyo: The Japan Times, 1987); D. McCreary and R. Blanchfield, "The Art of Japanese Negotiation," in N. Schweda-Nicholson (editor), *Languages in the International Perspective* (Norwood: Ablex Publishers).

19. W. Ouchi, *Theory Z: How American Business can Meet the Japanese Challenge* (Reading, Mass.: Addison-Wesley, 1981).

20. Schonberger, 1982, op. cit.

21. M. Cusumano, "Manufacturing Innovation: Lessons from the Japanese Auto Industry," *Sloan Management Review,* 1988, 29–39.

22. M. Matsumoto, *The Unspoken Way, Haragei: Silence in Japanese Business and Society* (Tokyo: Kodansha, 1988).

23. For example, see R. Olie, "Culture and Integration Problems in International Mergers and Acquisitions," *European Management Journal,* 8,

206–215; S. Hayashi, *Culture and Management in Japan* (Tokyo: U. of Tokyo Press, 1988).

24. See Goldman, 1993, op. cit.; Hayashi, op. cit.; Ouchi, op. cit.; Schonberger, 1982, op. cit.

25. See Hall and Hall, 1987, op. cit.; Goldman, 1993, op. cit.

26. This policy of "withholding" the names of Japanese journalists is discussed by P. Tasker, in *The Japanese Portrait of a Nation* (New York: New American Library, 1987); specifically see chapter 5, "Directing the Deluge," pp. 110–132.

27. See A. Goldman, "Negotiating Protocol in Japan: A Cross-Cultural Perspective," *International Journal of Management,* 808–813.

28. See Nakane, op. cit.

Chapter 7.

1. See Y. Yum, "The Impact of Confucianism on Interpersonal Relationships and Communication Patterns in East Asia," *Communication Monographs,* 55, 374–388.

2. See T. Doi, "The Japanese patterns of communication and the concept of *Amae,*" *Quarterly Journal of Speech,* 59, 180–185.

3. R. Ramsey, "Double Vision: Nonverbal Behavior East and West," a paper presented at the second *International Conference on Nonverbal Behavior,* Toronto, Canada, 1983.

4. See A. Goldman, *Intercultural Communication Between Japanese and Americans* (Tokyo: Kirihara Shoten, 1989).

5. See A. Goldman, *For Japanese Only: Intercultural Communication with Americans* (Tokyo: The Japan Times, 1988).

Chapter 8.

1. Diana Rowland, *Japanese Business Etiquette: A Practical Guide to Success with Japanese* (New York: Warner, 1985).

2. Alan Goldman, *Japanese-U.S. Business Communication* (Tokyo: Kirihara Shoten, 1993).

3. If you are in doubt, you may want to contact one of the JETRO offices in the United States, as they are a Japanese organization dedicated to helping Westerners do business with Japanese.

4. This recent encounter was with Japanese language translator and consultant, Mr. George Kiyoshi Nakamura, of Phoenix, Arizona.

5. What is at stake here is reverence, respect, and appropriate etiquette and form.

6. Aesthetic messages of form, style, presentation and delivery are of utmost importance. Appropriate *meishi* form is for men *and* women.

7. See C. Nakane, *Japanese Society* (Berkeley: Univ. of California Press, 1972).

Chapter 9.

1. For example, see D. Barnlund, *Public and Private Self in Japan and the United States* (Tokyo: The Simul Press, 1975).

2. See A. Goldman, "An Intercultural Challenge: U.S.-Japanese Communication, *Journal of Communication Studies,* 8, 1–9.

3. R. Okabe, "Cultural Assumptions of East and West: Japan and the United States," in W. Gudykunst (editor), *Communication Theory: Current Perspectives* (Beverly Hills, CA: Sage, 1983), 21–44.

Chapter 10.

1. A. Goldman, *For Japanese Only: Intercultural Communication with Americans* (Tokyo: The Japan Times, 1988).

2. See A. Goldman, "The Centrality of Ningensei to Japanese Negotiating and Interpersonal Relationships: Implications for U.S.-Japanese Communication," a paper presented at the annual convention of *The Speech Communication Association,* Chicago, Illinois, November 1992.

3. See D. Barnlund, *Public and Private Self in Japan and the United States* (Tokyo: The Simul Press, 1975).

4. See A. Goldman, *Japanese-U.S. Business Communication* (Tokyo: Kirihara Shoten, 1993).

5. See J. Condon and M. Saito (editors), *Intercultural Encounters with Japan: Communication—Contact and Conflict* (Tokyo: The Simul Press, 1974); also see, T. Bruneau, "Communicative Silences: Forms and Functions of Silence," ETC, 30 (1973).

6. See R. Oliver, *Culture and Communication: The Problems of Penetrating National and Cultural Boundaries* (Springfield, Ill.: Charles C. Thomas, 1962).

7. See R. Okabe, "Yukichi Fukuzawa: A Promulgator of Western Rhetoric in Japan. *Quarterly Journal of Speech,* 59 (1973), 186–195. An exception is the technical, specialized language of engineering—a more universal graphic, visual and data based language. The fluid communication possible between Japanese and American engineers was recently expressed during the course of an "intercultural training program for U.S.-Japanese leadership" that I delivered to Nissan Inc., North America.

8. For an eloquent explanation on the cultural origins of nonverbal behavior, see M. Merleau-Ponty, *The Phenomenology of Perception* (translated by C. Smith) (New York: Humanities Press, 1961).

9. I base this on personal cross-cultural training and consulting work conducted in Japan and the United States; the popular press accounts of nonverbal behavior for lay audiences is grossly simplistic, whereas the academic exposes are too rarefied and specialized to find their way into the corporate workplace.

10. For example, see Kazuo Nishiyama, "Interpersonal Persuasion in a Vertical Society—The Case of Japan," *Speech Monographs,* 38 (June 1971), 149.

11. See A. Goldman, 1993, op. cit.

12. See E. Stewart, *American Cultural Patterns: A Cross-Cultural Perspective* (Pittsburgh, PA: Univ. of Pittsburgh Press, 1971); and E. Rischauer, *The Japanese* (Tokyo: Charles E. Tuttle, 1977).

13. M. Matsumoto, *The Unspoken Way, Haragei: Silence in Japanese Business and Society* (Tokyo: Kodansha, 1988), p. 51.

14. Ibid.

15. See T. Lebra, *Japanese Patterns of Behavior* (Honolulu: Univ. of Hawaii Press, 1976).

16. Japanese appear to be quite masterful in very subtly articulating displeasure; there is much attention paid to form, aesthetics and details, as the slightest, off-centered imprint of the *hanko* clearly communicates to Japanese organizational players. As is pointed out throughout this book, minute deviations in a flower arrangement or other fixed objects may indirectly communicate displeasure and upset. For the most part, these "insider" cues are sure to be missed by expatriates, as it takes much exposure to Japanese patterns of behavior to detect the nuances of communication.

17. The minor deviation in a flower arrangement can be viewed as analogous to the slightly off-center tilt (2 or 3%) of the *hanko* during a *ringisho.*

18. T. Lebra, op. cit.

19. See E. Hall, *The Silent Language* (New York: Doubleday, 1959); *The Hidden Dimension* (New York: Doubleday, 1966).

20. See A. Goldman, "Intercultural Abyss at the Negotiating Table: An Examination of Japanese-U.S. Communicative Styles," *Human Communication Studies,* 18 (June 1990), 101–116.

Chapter 11.

1. For example, see Alan Goldman, "Cultural Abyss at the Negotiating Table: An Examination of Japanese-U.S. Communication Style," *Human Communication Studies,* 18, 101–116.

2. See Robert Harris and Robert Moran, *Managing Cultural Differences* (Houston: Gulf Publishing Company, 1986).

3. See Goldman, op. cit.

4. See J. Neustupny, *Communicating with the Japanese* (Tokyo: The Japan Times, 1987).

5. See Alan Goldman, *For Japanese Only: Intercultural Communication with Americans* (Tokyo: The Japan Times, 1988).

6. See Robert March, *The Japanese Negotiator: Subtlety and Strategy Beyond Western Logic* (Tokyo: Kodansha, 1990).

7. See John C. Condon, *With Respect to the Japanese: A Guide for Americans* (Yarmouth, Maine: Intercultural Press, 1984).

8. See Goldman, *Human Communication Studies,* op. cit.

9. See Goldman, *For Japanese Only,* op. cit.

10. See Alan Goldman, *Intercultural Communication Between Japanese and Americans* (Tokyo: Kirihara Shoten, 1989).

11. Ibid.

12. Ibid.

13. Roichi Okabe, "Cultural Assumptions of East and West: Japan and the United States," in William Gudykunst (editor), *Intercultural Communication Theory: Current Perspectives* (Beverly Hills: Sage, 1983), 21–44.

14. See Richard Brislin, *Cross-Cultural Encounters: Face-to-Face Interaction* (New York: Pergamon, 1981).

15. Alan Goldman, "U.S.-Japanese Negotiating: An Intercultural Briefing," *International Business Communication,* 2, 3–7.

16. Ibid.

17. Ibid.

18. See Takie Lebra, *Japanese Patterns of Behavior* (Honolulu: Univ. of Hawaii Press, 1976).

19. Ibid.

20. See Goldman, *Human Communication Studies,* op. cit.

21. See Alan Goldman, "Intercultural Training of Japanese for U.S.-Japanese Interorganizational Communication," *International Journal of Intercultural Relations,* 16, 195–216.

22. Ibid.

23. Ibid.

24. Ibid.

25. Ibid.

26. Ibid.

27. Alan Goldman, "A Bicultural Approach to Public Speaking: Facilitating Japanese-U.S. Communication, *Human Communication Studies,* 20, 67–81.

28. Okabe, op. cit.

29. See Goldman, *International Journal of Intercultural Relations,* op. cit.

30. Ibid.

31. Okabe, op. cit.

Chapter 12.

1. One of the most formidable studies of Japanese silences is by Michihiro Matsumoto, *The Unspoken Way, Haragei: Silence in Japanese Business and Society* (Tokyo: Kodansha, 1988).

2. Ibid.

3. The *nihonjinron* syndrome is a fundamentally ethnocentric posture held by many Japanese; it is a belief that Japan and Japanese behavior and ways can only be understood by Japanese—and not by outsiders or *gaijin.* Oftentimes, the *nihonjinron* view of Japanese business and management is

not overtly or directly expressed and is rather communicated behind-the-scenes, with other "insiders," or in private, informal, social situations. The *nihonjinron* syndrome aptly serves the ultra-nationalists and protectionists of Japan—those wanting to minimize foreign influence and cultural "impurities."

4. For example, see D. Hymes, "Sociolinguistics and the Ethnography of Speaking," in E. Ardener (editor), *Social Anthropology and Language* (New York: Tavistock Pubs., 1971).

5. Ibid.; also see: A. Goldman, *For Japanese Only: Intercultural Communication with Americans* (Tokyo: The Japan Times, 1988); J. Neustupny, *Communicating with the Japanese* (Tokyo: The Japan Times, 1987); J. Condon and M. Saito, *Communicating Across Cultures for What?* (Tokyo: Simul Press, 1976); J. Condon and K. Kurata, *In Search of What's Japanese about Japan* (Tokyo: Simul Press, 1973).

6. J. Neustupny, op. cit.

7. There is strict delineation of rank and hierarchy in Japanese language.

8. For an explanation of the difference between the U.S. verbal style of "breaking the ice," and the slower Japanese decorum of "melting the ice," see A. Goldman, *Japanese-U.S. Business Communication* (Tokyo: Kirihara Shoten, 1993).

9. For an investigation of some of these strategic issues central to Japanese-U.S. verbal communication, see, A. Goldman, "Intercultural Training of Japanese for U.S.-Japanese Interorganizational Communication," *International Journal of Intercultural Relations*, 16, 195–216.

10. See A. Goldman, op. cit., 1993.

11. See A. Goldman, 1988, op. cit.

12. See R. Okabe, "Cultural Assumptions East and West: Japan and the United States," in W. Gudykunst (editor), *Intercultural Theory: Current Perspectives* (Beverly Hills, CA: Sage, 1983), 21–44.

13. See Y. Fukuzawa, *Fukuzawa Yukichi Zenshu* (Collected Works of Yukichi Fukuzawa) (Tokyo: Iwanami Shoten, 1969); *The Autobiography of Yukichi Fukuzawa* (translated by Eiichi Kiyooka), (New York: Columbia University Press, 1966).

14. See A. Goldman, "Intercultural Sophistry: Implications of Yukichi Fukuzawa's Struggle to Introduce Western Rhetoric into Meiji Period Japan," a paper presented at the annual convention of The Speech Communication Association, Atlanta, Georgia, November 1991.

15. I. BenDasan, *Japanese and Jews* (Tokyo: Yamamoto Shoten, 1970).

16. See R. Okabe, "Yukichi Fukuzawa: A Promulgator of Western Rhetoric in Japan," *Quarterly Journal of Speech,* 59 (1973), 186–195.

Chapter 15.

1. For a "managerial communication" perspective on fear of public speaking and communication apprehension, see L. Smeltzer, J. Waltman, and D. Leonard, *Managerial Communication: A Strategic Approach* (MA: Ginn Press, 1991).

2. There is a notable absence of studies on *intercultural* communication apprehension, specifically concerning public speaking.

3. This argument is eloquently advanced in K. Jamieson, *Eloquence in an Electronic Age: The Transformation of Political Speechmaking* (N.Y.: Oxford University Press, 1988).

4. For an explanation of the Japanese term *rikutsuppoi,* see D. Rowland, *Japanese Business Etiquette* (N.Y.: Warner, 1985).

5. For example, see A. Goldman, "A Bicultural Approach to Public Speaking: Facilitating Japanese-U.S. Communication," *Human Communication Studies,* 20, 67–81.

6. See E. Hall and M. Hall, *Hidden Differences: Doing Business with the Japanese* (N.Y.: Anchor, 1987).

7. Ibid.

8. See A. Goldman, *For Japanese Only: Intercultural Communication with Americans* (Tokyo: The Japan Times, 1988).

9. For example, see A. Goldman, *Intercultural Communication Between Japanese and Americans* (Tokyo: Kirihara Shoten, 1989).

10. Ibid.

11. See A. Goldman, *Human Communication Studies,* op. cit.

12. Ibid.

13. See J. Neustupny, *Communicating with the Japanese* (Tokyo: The Japan Times, 1987).

14. Ibid.

15. Ibid.

16. See R. Okabe, "Yukichi Fukuzawa: A Promulgator of Western Rhetoric in Japan," *Quarterly Journal of Speech*, 59, 186–195.

17. See M. Matsumoto, *The Unspoken Way, Haragei: Silence in Japanese Business and Society* (Tokyo: Kodansha, 1988).

18. See L. Samovar and M. Porter, *Communication Between Cultures* (Belmont, CA: Wadsworth Publishing Company, 1991), 199.

19. Ibid.

20. The concept of the "stranger" is widely utilized in the intercultural literature. It literally refers to first meetings or early meetings between "cultural strangers."

21. For example, see R. Okabe, "Cultural Assumptions of East and West: Japan and the United States," in W. Gudykunst (editor), *Intercultural Communication Theory: Current Perspectives* (Beverly Hills: Sage Publishers, 1983), 21–44.

22. Ibid.

23. S. Dei, "The Rhetoric of Yasuhiro Nakasone;" a paper presented at the annual convention of The Speech Communication Association, San Francisco, 1989.

24. On both sides of the Pacific, it is common domain that Sony Chairman Morita, is far more moderate than the ultra-nationalist and conservative politician, Ishihara. There has been much inconclusive speculation regarding Morita's motives in "keeping the company" of Ishihara, as a co-author of this widely controversial, U.S. bashing book.

25. For example, see A. Goldman, *Japanese-U.S. Business Communication* (Tokyo: Kirihara Shoten, 1993).

26. See R. Okabe, *Quarterly Journal of Speech*, op. cit.

27. Ibid.

28. Ibid.

29. Ibid.

30. For example, see A. Goldman, *Intercultural Communication Between Japanese and Americans*, op. cit.

31. The "code violations" are primarily "cultural" and "communicative." The highly restricted Japanese communicative codes governing adversarial and confrontational rhetoric in public venues are more at stake than the issues.

32. See D. Barnlund, *Communicative Styles of Japanese and Americans: Images and Realities* (Belmont, CA: Wadsworth, 1989).

33. T. Doi, "The Japanese Patterns of communication and the concept of *Amae*," *Quarterly Journal of Speech,* 59, 180–185.

34. C. Nakane, *Japanese Society* (Berkeley: Univ. of California Press, 1972).

35. See A. Goldman, "U.S.-Japanese Negotiating: An Intercultural Briefing," *International Business Communication,* 2, 3–7; "Reconceptualizing an Adversarial Model of Public Communication: U.S. Speakers Addressing Japanese Audiences." A paper presented at the Eighth Annual Intercultural and International Communication Conference, Miami, Florida, February 1991.

36. See R. Okabe, "Cultural Assumptions of East and West: Japan and the United States," op. cit.

37. See Barnlund, 1989, op. cit.

Chapter 16.

1. M. Zimmerman, *How to do Business with the Japanese* (New York: Random House, 1985), 58.

2. See W. Ouchi, *Theory Z: How American Business Can Meet the Japanese Challenge* (Reading, Mass.: Addison-Wesley, 1981).

3. M. Zimmerman, op. cit., 58.

4. Ibid.

Chapter 17.

1. Alan Goldman, "The Centrality of Ningensei to Japanese Negotiating and Interpersonal Relationships: Implications for U.S.-Japanese Communication." A paper presented at the annual convention of The Speech Communication Association, Chicago, Illinois, November 1992. Winner of the Ralph Cooley Award for The Top Paper, 1992, SCA, International and Intercultural Communication Division. Also see, Alan Goldman, "The Centrality of *Ningensei* to Japanese Negotiating and Interpersonal Relations: Implications for U.S.-Japanese Communication. *The International Journal of Intercultural Relations,* 18, 29–54.

2. Ibid.

Chapter 18.

1. D. Barnlund, *Communicative Styles of Japanese and Americans* (Belmont, CA: Wadsworth, 1989).

2. T. Lebra, *Japanese Patterns of Behavior* (Honolulu: Univ. of Hawaii Press, 1976).

3. See A. Goldman, *Japanese-U.S. Business Communication* (Tokyo: Kirihara Shoten, 1993).

Chapter 19.

1. Ezra F. Vogel, *Japan's New Middle Class: The Salary Man and his Family in a Tokyo Suburb* (Berkeley, CA: Univ. of California Press, 1963, 235.)

2. Takie Sugiyama Lebra, *Japanese Patterns of Behavior* (Honolulu: Univ. of Hawaii Press, 1976), 40.

3. Ibid., 40.

4. Ibid., 41.

5. Ibid.

6. Ibid.

7. See Michihiro Matsumoto, *The Unspoken Way, Haragei: Silence in Japanese Business and Society* (Tokyo: Kodansha, 1988.)

Chapter 21.

1. See L. Smeltzer, J. Waltman, and D. Leonard, *Managerial Communication: A Strategic Approach* (MA: Ginn Press, 1991).

2. See A. Goldman, *Japanese-U.S. Business Communication* (Tokyo: Kirihara Shoten, 1993).

3. See T. Lebra, *Japanese Patterns of Behavior* (Honolulu: Univ. of Hawaii Press, 1976).

Chapter 22.

1. This is particularly true within "theory Y," "participatory management" styled organizations.

2. The concept of "cultural entrapment" is developed by T. Lebra, *Japanese Patterns of Behavior* (Honolulu: Univ. of Hawaii Press, 1976).

Chapter 23.

1. For a Japanese perspective on *keiretsus,* see T. Homada, "Under the Silk Banner: The Japanese Company and its Overseas Managers," in T. Lebra (editor), *Japanese Social Organization* (Honolulu: Univ. of Hawaii Press, 1992), 135–164.

2. C. Nakane, *Japanese Society* (Berkeley, CA: Univ. of California Press, 1972), 98.

3. T. Homada, op. cit., 163.

4. Ibid.

5. Nakane, op. cit., 98.

6. T. Homada, op. cit., 140.

7. As an expatriate in Tokyo, where I served as an intercultural communication trainer and consultant for Japanese corporations, I was one of many *gaijin* who was perplexed by Japanese "organizational charts." Either there was no organizational chart to be found, or the chart was hopelessly complex, due to the positioning of an individual organization within the larger interorganizational network of a *keiretsu.* The absence of a clear organizational chart appeared to be due to the Japanese preference for ambiguity, extreme flexibility, and organizational change.

8. For further analysis of "insider/outsider" boundaries and communicative behaviors of *keiretsu* organizational members see: R. Clark, *The Japanese Company* (New Haven, Connecticut: Yale University Press, 1979); T. Hamada, "Winds of Change: Economic Realism and Japanese Labor Management," *Asian Survey,* 20, 397–406; K. Koike, *Japanese Workers' Skill* (Tokyo: Bunshin-do, 1989); P. Noguchi, *Delayed Departures, Overdue Arrivals: Industrial Familialism and the Japanese National Railways* (Honolulu: Univ. of Hawaii Press, 1990); M. Yoshino, *Japan's Multinational Enterprise* (Cambridge, Mass: Harvard University Press, 1976); and S. Hayashi, *Culture and Management in Japan* (Tokyo: Univ. of Tokyo Press, 1988).

9. For an analysis of the decision-making process of *nemawashi* and *ringi,* see A. Goldman, "Intercultural Training of Japanese for U.S.-Japanese Interorganizational Communication," *International Journal of Intercultural Relations,* 16, 195–216.

10. For a Japanese insider's views on the public support for *keiretsus,* see J. Beckwith, "Lawyer Bucks System By Backing Underdogs," *The Japan Times,* November 11, 1991, 1 and 6.

11. Ibid. Japanese maverick and rebel attorney Kanji Ishizumi repeatedly expresses his fight against the large corporations and the "communistic" cartels. He believes that the *keiretsus* are being underestimated by the U.S. and the Western corporate, diplomatic and political world and represent the single most formidable threat to free trade.

12. C. Nakane, op. cit.; 7–8.

Glossary

akachochin. A. 'red lantern' pub with the lantern hanging at the front door; an afterhours gathering place or 'watering hole.'

amae. Interdependency.

anago. Eel.

arigato gozaimasu. "Thank you very much."

Asahi Shimbun. Widely circulated Japanese morning edition newspaper.

asameshi-mae no shigoto. An expression meaning an easy, "before-breakfast" job.

ba. Place or situation; context or framework for interaction.

bento (box). A box housing a mobile lunch; bento box lunches are a Japanese stable.

bonasu. Twice a year bonuses given to salary workers, in June or July and December; usually from one to three months salary.

bonen-dai. The December office party; summons in the near year; a prescribed time to drink, deal freely with frustrations, failures, dreams, visions, disappointments.

bucho. Department head or general manager.

bucho dairi. Deputy Department head.

bunke. Branch, subordinate and satellite houses under a honke.

bunmei Kaika. "Being civilized."

busu. Ugly, unattractive woman.

charan-poran. An unreliable, dishonest person, does not finish tasks, finds excuses.

chorei. A morning pep talk in companies and offices.

chotto. An opening line for a gaijin who wants to get assistance; for example, "chotto matte" is "one minute please . . ." this may be a phrase used to get a stranger's attention, to summon a waiter, etc.

chukaisha. Mediator.

dorubako. The most profitable produce or business line in a company.

dososei. Alumni networks of Japanese businessmen.

dozo. "Please;" "please enter."

dozoku. A group of "ie," composed of honke or soke and their bunke.

Edo. Old name for present-day Tokyo.

Edo Period. 1600–1868; a period of Japanese isolation prior to the opening to the West during the Meiji Period.

eigo-ya-san. "Mr. English;" refers to workers with "international paths or careers" within Japanese companies, who usually are depended upon for their English language skills; until recently, a "Mr. English" usually had lower status and was most closely aligned with the position of a "clerk." The impact of globalization, however, has elevated the prospects for this kind of appointment, as English language ability is increasingly viewed as vital to expatriations.

Fuku Shacho. Vice President.

futokoro-gatana. A right hand person or confidant of a person in a high position; privy to secret plans of high ranking officials.

gaijin. A foreigner, outsider.

gaijin kasha. A foreign, outsider firm operating in Japan.

gaijin no yona. A caucasian or foreigner.

gakureki. School or university background.

geta. Wooden clogs.

Ginza. An international area of Tokyo.

giri. Dependency.

gomen kudasa. "Pardon me, hello."

gomen kuddasai. "Excuse me;" "may I come in, please?"

gomen nasai. "Excuse me;" "I'm sorry."

hai. "Yes."

hajimemashite. "It's a pleasure to meet you for the first time . . ."

hana pecha. A flat nose.

hanasuji no tota. With a well shaped nose.

hanko. A personal seal affixed in lieu of a signature.

haragei. Belly or gut communication.

harakiri. Ritual suicide.

harikara. A state of being successfully Westernized.

hashigo. The "promotion ladder" in corporate life.

honke. Main, original house of an "ie."

honne. True communication; true intention.

honsha. Japanese main office or parent company.

ie. A household or grouping; as in a corporate entity to be "perpetuated independently of its human composition." (Lebra, 1992, p. 16).

Jinja. A shinto shrine.

Jomu torishimariyaku. Executive Managing Director.

ka. A group or section.

kacho. Section leader, head.

kacho dairi. Deputy Section Chief.

kaicho. Chairman.

kaigai-bu. Overseas division of a Japanese company.

kaigai-jihyo-bu. Overseas operations of a Japanese company.

ka-in. Staff.

kaki-ire-doki. Gift giving seasons in summer and December.

kao. Face; crucial "human" component in social and business relationships; Japanese strive to "give face" and "save face" and avoid "face threatening," "face provoking" conflicts; loss of face is avoided and circumvented for self or others; "face management" is readily practiced.

karaoke. A bar for customer 'singing' to well known songs played in instrumental form.

katakana. One of the two Japanese writing systems.

kata-tataki. "Time to retire" tap on the shoulder for older workers.

keiretsu. A corporate alliance across industrial and corporate sectors and markets, characterized by client-supplier relationships.

kenbei. Referring to "anti-U.S." sentiments and "Japan bashing;" it is an intercultural objective to "get beyond *kenbei*," in the words of Yasuhiro Nakasone.

kenrikin (or 'reikin'). Nonrefundable 'key money' required when renting an apartment in Japan.

kichiku beiei. The "devil beasts" of Britain and America.

kimono. The traditional, wide sleeved Japanese robe.

Kinokuniya. A chain of bookstores in the U.S. and Japan specializing in Japanese-Western literature.

kissaten. A coffee bar or shop.

kogai-no buka. Subordinates personally raised and groomed by a Japanese manager or mentor.

kogaisha. As in "overseas kogaisha" or child company.

kohai. A junior person.

kokoro. The "inner self;" a core, private self, not readily communicable through words.

konketsu no. Foreign ancestry and mixed blood.

koshinjo. Investigative agencies utilized to scrutinize the backgrounds of corporate applicants.

kotatsu. An electric heating unit situated below floor level, under a table; the feet are submerged into this heated area while seated at a low table.

kuro. Hardships (e.g., of overseas assignments; expatriations).

kyu ichi. Japanese slang for a "Jew."

li. Hierarchical form of address.

ma. Japanese term for "silence."

manga. Comic books; widely read by all ages; a significant form of print communication in Japan.

manshon. An apartment of prestige and expense.

manzai. Two comedians who work as a pair on stage.

marugakae. A company family that engages a salaryman/woman—totally.

Meiji Period. The period of 1868–1912, index the rule of Emperor Meiji; a period of Japanese 'westernization' and openness to foreign culture, ideas, and trade.

Meiji Restoration. The transfer of ruling power from the shogunate to the Emperor Meiji, 1868.

meishi. Business card exchange; an interpersonal, group and organizational 'ritual,' including elements of business card exchange, introductions, and greetings.

Me no pacchiri shita. Round and large eyes.

mizu. Water.

mobo. A Westernized man.

moga. A Westernized woman.

nemawashi. "Rootbinding," informal approach to arriving at complete consensus for decision-making within a Japanese company.

newazashi. A 'player' ordained by Japanese management to 'swing deals' behind and beyond the boundaries of negotiating tables—away from the public eye.

nigiri tsubushi. A "crushing in the hand" by a superior of a 'paper proposal' or idea.

nihonjin banare no shita. Unfamiliar or un-Japanese like in appearance and features; Western.

nihonjinron syndrome. Japan and Japanese culture can only be understood by Japanese.

nihon shuji. A form of ethnocentric and chauvinistic nationalism.

Nikkan Gendai. A sexually explicit, sensationalistic, evening newspaper in Japan, widely read by salarymen.

ningensei. "Human beingingness;" the human, personal relationship is of paramount importance; business relationships thrive on the ties of ningensei.

ochoko. A sake cup.

ochugen. Seasonal gifts.

Odaku (Line). A train line in Tokyo, Japan.

omoiyari. Empathy, empathic hospitality.

omote. Front.

on. Social obligations and debts.

on-za-roku. "On the rocks;" in reference to ordering a cocktail.

oseibo. Seasonal gifts.

osekkai. Meddlesomeness.

osenbetsu. Farewell gifts.

oshibori. A hot, wet towel provided before meals.

oyabun. A mentor or master.

oyake. Concerned for the good of the entire group or company.

pachinko. A Japanese cross between 'pinball' and a 'slot machine.'

pecha pai. A flat chest.

rabu hoteru. A "love hotel."

rikutsuppoi. Too logical; too rational.

ringi. A formal approach to reaching complete consensus for decision-making; a printed proposal is circulated between organizational players, with the option of applying a personal seal "upright" for approval, "upside down" for disapproval, or sideways for a "maybe," or points in between for more subtle disagreements or reservations. The proposal is modified in accordance with individual input and continuously recirculated until all seals are recorded "upright."

Rokumeikan. A social club in Tokyo formed to promote westernization.

ryokan. A traditional Japanese inn.

sacho. President.

sakazuki. A sake cup.

sake. A rice based, fermented alcoholic drink.

san. A respectful appendage or suffix attached onto the 'end' of a person's name.

"sate." A transition phrase signalling a change from social pleasantries to business; "and concerning business;" "by the way."

sempai. A senior person.

sengo. Postwar.

senmu torishimariyaku. Senior Executive Managing Director.

senryogun. Occupation forces in Japan.

senzen. Prewar.

seppuku. Ritual suicide.

shacho. President.

shataku. Company housing.

Shinjuku. A centrally located train station and section of downtown Tokyo; a hub.

shinkansen. Bullet train.

shinshu. Concept of a 'divine' Japanese land.

shishin. Private goals; selfishness.

shoji. Sliding door of wood and paper materials.

shokaisha. Someone who introduces.

shukko. An expatriate; sometimes referred to in Japanese companies as "dispatchies."

shunin/kakaricho. Chief.

soba. Buckwheat noodles.

soke. Main, original house of an "ie."

somen. Noodles of fine quality.

soto. Outside.

summimasen. Excuse me, pardon me . . .

sushi. Vinegar flavored rice, usually topped with horseradish and either raw fish and/or vegetables.

tamago. Egg.

tanage. The 'putting on the shelf' of a proposal.

tanshin funin. An expatriated employee, alone, unaccompanied by his family.

tansoku. Short legs and long torso.

tarai-mawashi. A type of Japanese manager who is passed along between numerous overseas assignments, trapped within foreign subsidiaries; he may have fallen out of favor with the parent company, does not have strong connections with the head office, or has lost political battles, sentencing him to corporate exile.

tatami. A straw mat; oftentimes Japanese homes and apartments are described in terms of how many (standard sized) tatami mats cover the floors.

tatemae. Surface communication; outward appearances.

tenzoku. A person who resigned from the parent company to be formally hired by the child (kogaisha).

"tokoro de." A transitional phrase in letter writing, signaling a "by the way" turn from 'pleasantries' to 'business.'

Tokugawa Shogunate. The government of the Tokugawa family, (1603–1867), preceeding Emperor Meiji (1868–1912).

torishimariyaku. Director or Supervisor.

uchi. Inside.

unagei. Eel.

ura. Rear.

wa. Group or team spirit.

wakon kansai. Pertaining to Chinese skill and Japanese spirit.

wakon yosai. Pertaining to western skill and Japanese spirit.

wareware nihonjin. "We Japanese are all alike," and willingness to act as if this were true.

wasabi. Green horseradish.

washoku. Japanese food.

watakusi. Private goals; selfishness.

yakitori. Grilled chicken; many 'yakitori restaurants' and pubs are frequented by salarymen.

yakuza. Japanese criminal groups; the 'mob' or 'Japanese mafia.'

yokogaeri. A Japanese upon return from visiting the west.

Yomiuri Shimbun. The largest circulation newspaper in the free world.

yoshoku. Western, gaijin food.

yukata. A cotton robe.

zaibatsu. An earlier version of keiretsu, disbanded in the aftermath of World War II, during the Allied occupation, a family controlled monopoly or cartel.

Index

309

barriers, 199–200
and business communication, 52
and contracts, 52–53
and deep, surface structure, 255
and ethnocentrism, 48–49
and idioms, 130
and Japanese logic, 52, 184–185
and Japanese tentativeness, 6
and Western logic, 52–53, 184–185
as unreliable and inaccurate, 170
choosing an interpreter, 48–49
English as international tongue, 49
Japanese delayed use of verb and
    ambiguity, 170
Japanese distrust of, xix, 170–171
Japanese pronouns and hierarchy,
    252–253
Japanese study of American En-
    glish, 197
haragei, 52
limits of, 145, 177, 230, 236
problems in U.S.-Japanese relations, 6
slang, 129–130
strict delineation of rank and hierar-
    chy in Japanese language, 293
violence and, 227
Leadership
adapting to Japanese style, 175
and Japanese maxims, 108
and post World War II management
    innovations, 48
charismatic leaders, Japan and
    U.S., 108
General Motors President, Eric Mit-
    tlestadt, 49
Japanese style, 52, 235–236
transporting Japanese style to U.S.,
    14–15, 48, 249–250
U.S. style, 50
U.S. TQM leadership, 249–250
Lebra, Takie Sugiyama, xxvi, 142,
    145, 236, 282, 283, 286, 290, 292
    297, 298
and Japanese hospitality, 246–247
and *kokoro*, 145
Japanese as empathic, delicate com-
    municators, 142
truth as inexpressible, 145
Left Hemisphere (of the human brain)
and American analytical orienta-
    tion, 106

Letter Writing, U.S.-Japanese
Business, 185–187
Personal, 185–187
Leung, K. and Bond, M., 286
Listening, 130, 192, 214, 246
active Japanese listening, 256
and overcoming intercultural differ-
    ences, 44
and corporate persuasion with Japa-
    nese, 192
and management-by-walking-around
    (MBWA), 255
active, Japanese, 256
collaborative, 256
corporate listening, 46
empathic, 256
Japanese designated roles as listen-
    ers, 253
listening culture, 255–257
nonverbal, 256
nurturing, 256
U.S. misunderstanding of Japanese
    listening, 256–7
Los Angeles Times, The, xxvii
Low Context Culture, 81
Love Hotels, 63–65, 89
Loyalty, 99

Management
and decentralization, 14–15
and ethnocentrism, 118
and group space, 100–101
and inefficiency, 259
and joint ventures, 14–15
and motivation, 259
and "office ladies (OLs)," 75
and productivity, 259
and proxemics, 80–81
and right and left hemisphere (brain)
    dominance, 106
and women, 14, 75, 146
discouraging career specialization,
    101–102
gaijin kaisha, 20–30
grooming for expatriations, 19–30,
holistic Japanese managerial prac-
    tices, 107
inner-directedness of U.S. mana-
    gers, 239